Design Thinking

Design Thinking is a set of strategic and creative processes and principles used in the planning and creation of products and solutions to human-centered design problems.

With design and innovation being two key driving principles, this series focuses on, but is not limited to, the following areas and topics:

- User Interface (UI) and User Experience (UX) Design
- Psychology of Design
- Human-Computer Interaction (HCI)
- Ergonomic Design
- Product Development and Management
- Virtual and Mixed Reality (VR/XR)
- User-Centered Built Environments and Smart Homes
- Accessibility, Sustainability and Environmental Design
- Learning and Instructional Design
- Strategy and best practices

This series publishes books aimed at designers, developers, storytellers and problem-solvers in industry to help them understand current developments and best practices at the cutting edge of creativity, to invent new paradigms and solutions, and challenge Creatives to push boundaries to design bigger and better than before.

More information about this series at https://link.springer.com/bookseries/15933.

UX Design with Figma

User-Centered Interface Design
and Prototyping with Figma

Tom Green
Kevin Brandon

Apress®

UX Design with Figma: User-Centered Interface Design and Prototyping with Figma

Tom Green
Etobicoke, ON, Canada

Kevin Brandon
Georgetown, ON, Canada

ISBN-13 (pbk): 979-8-8688-0323-9
https://doi.org/10.1007/979-8-8688-0324-6

ISBN-13 (electronic): 979-8-8688-0324-6

Managing Director, Apress Media LLC: Welmoed Spahr
Acquisitions Editor: James Robinson-Prior
Development Editor: James Markham
Editorial Assistant: Gryffin Winkler

Cover designed by eStudioCalamar

Distributed to the book trade worldwide by Springer Science+Business Media New York, 1 New York Plaza, Suite 4600, New York, NY 10004-1562, USA. Phone 1-800-SPRINGER, fax (201) 348-4505, e-mail orders-ny@springer-sbm.com, or visit www.springeronline.com. Apress Media, LLC is a California LLC and the sole member (owner) is Springer Science + Business Media Finance Inc (SSBM Finance Inc). SSBM Finance Inc is a **Delaware** corporation.

For information on translations, please e-mail booktranslations@springernature.com; for reprint, paperback, or audio rights, please e-mail bookpermissions@springernature.com.

Apress titles may be purchased in bulk for academic, corporate, or promotional use. eBook versions and licenses are also available for most titles. For more information, reference our Print and eBook Bulk Sales web page at http://www.apress.com/bulk-sales.

Any source code or other supplementary material referenced by the author in this book is available to readers on GitHub. For more detailed information, please visit https://www.apress.com/gp/services/source-code.

If disposing of this product, please recycle the paper

To Jim Babbage
—Tom Green

I would like to dedicate this book with my deep appreciation to family, friends, and students who have encouraged, challenged, and inspired me and laughed at my jokes.
—Kevin Brandon

Table of Contents

About the Authors

**Tom Green** is an Emeritus Professor of Interactive Multimedia through the School of Media Studies and IT at the Humber College Institute of Technology & Advanced Learning in Toronto, Canada. He has created over a dozen UX-based courses for LinkedIn Learning. One course – UX Design for Non-Designers released two years ago – has been completed by over 35,000 learners throughout the world. Tom has written numerous books on UX Design for Apress, Que, Pearson Education, and New Riders. Along with his work with LinkedIn Learning, Tom has developed video-based training courses for Infinite Skills, Envato, Video2Brain, and others. He was the Graphics Software expert with About.com and has written hundreds of articles and tutorials for a variety of magazines and websites over the past 20 years.

Tom has spoken and lectured at conferences around the world and universities throughout China and the United States including the University of Wisconsin, the Central Academy of Fine Arts in Beijing, the Wuhan Institute of Technology, and Shenzhen Polytechnic. In his spare time, you can catch him hiking a local trail or paddling across a lake in Northern Ontario.

ABOUT THE AUTHORS

Kevin Brandon started his career in the print industry and then transitioned into web design and user experience design. After completing a Master of Arts in Professional Communication, he entered higher education as a full-time professor at Humber College Institute of Technology & Advanced Learning in Toronto, Canada. Kevin has taught in various programs such as Graphic Design, Advertising, Multimedia, and Film and Television. He is an active Adobe Education Leader, collaborating with fellow educators around the world and learning about upcoming technologies. As a consultant Kevin has provided professional development sessions for teachers through Edge Gain Ltd. Kevin is married and has three sons. When not at work, you can find him enjoying walks with his family and his dog.

About the Technical Reviewer

 **Judy Wood** is an experienced Graphic and Multimedia Design Specialist, with more than three decades of helping clients and students creatively develop user experiences. She has extensive experience in higher education and instructional design and holds a master's in Learning and Technology. A staunch proponent of lifelong learning, Judy embraces cutting-edge technology to ignite her students.

Acknowledgments

Tom, thank you for inviting me to write this book with you. It wouldn't have happened without your experience and hard work, and I am grateful.

—Kevin

Working with a co-author can be a tricky business. It is a lot like a marriage. Everything is wonderful when things are going well, but you really never discover the strength of a relationship until you get deep into it. Working with Kevin over the past several months has been an absolute joy.

Kevin and I first crossed paths 20 years ago when we first met each other as faculty members of Humber College's Faculty of Media and Creative Arts. As we moved through our careers, we were constantly leaning on each other to try new ways of preparing our students to enter into a Digital Media industry that was constantly undergoing fundamental change. I also discovered he has some serious design chops and took full advantage of his knowledge and skills over the years. It was only natural that I bring him in as co-author.

Sowmya Thodur, our Apress production editor, is also due a huge acknowledgment. It is her job to babysit the authors and ensure the manuscript is delivered on time. I don't use the term "babysitting" in the pejorative sense. Sowmya kept us on track and, when things got tough, was a shoulder to cry on.

Finally, writing a book of this size and complexity means I hole up in my home office and generally become moody and difficult to live with as I mull over an exercise or order of a chapter. How my wife and life partner, Keltie, puts up with it I'll never know, but it does work out in the end.

—Tom

Introduction

When we are asked to define the term "UX," our normal response is: "What do you want it to mean?" This is not us being facetious. Ask ten people involved in the industry that same question, and the odds are pretty good you will get 15 different answers. Ask these same ten people what tool they use, and the answer is always Figma.

Having been involved in Digital Design since the mid-1980s, we have seen new tools appear, and after a few years, the profession settles around a tool. That tool – think Photoshop – then becomes a standard in the industry, and its competitors fight over a small slice of the market.

Figma has become the UX Design standard application. The fascinating aspect of that is the proposed acquisition of Figma by Adobe was scuttled due to worries that it would reduce competition. When Adobe and Figma agreed to stop the acquisition, Figma came out on top. Adobe killed its UX Design tool – Adobe XD – which meant Figma's major competitor had left the market. As a result Figma shrugged and moved on.

Figma's strength has never really been its tool. Figma's strength is its rabidly loyal community of designers and developers. The reason for that loyalty is Figma is equally as rabid in listening to its users. When it rolls out a new feature such as the new Dev Mode, it doesn't just drop it into the app with a cheery "Here you go." Dev Mode was a beta feature of Figma for a while, and not only did Figma pay close attention to how it was being used but the Figma Community provided feedback on the strengths and weaknesses of Dev Mode. When it was finally released, it was in the context of "Thanks for the feedback. Hope this is what you were looking for."

This book's genesis started with a simple question that Figma also asks: "What's missing?" For us, the answer was "Something that explains where Figma fits in the UX process."

A common misconception is that Figma is a UX Design tool that churns out the interactive apps which land in our browsers, devices, and tablets. This simply is not the case. Figma is a collaborative tool whose features span the entire UX process from concept to upload. The UX process has been considered a "team sport" where multiple skills are involved to create a project. This explains why this book is not your typical "Here's how to create cool stuff in Figma" book. We follow the process, pointing out where the various features of Figma fit or can be used at each stage of the process and where the team fits.

One other aspect of this book is that we had a huge amount of fun developing the exercises and examples in this book. The word "fun" is important because if learning is fun, what you learn will stay with you.

Book Structure and Flow

This is not a typical software book. There is no common project that runs throughout the book. Instead, each chapter contains a number of exercises and examples designed to give you experience with the core concepts and features of Figma. Then, in several chapters, we turn you loose with a "Your Turn" exercise. To take full advantage of the exercises, you will need to have, at a minimum, a Professional Figma account.

The first two chapters walk you through the Figma interface and how content is added to your Figma projects. For example, we spend a lot of time in Chapter 1 explaining how teams are created and how to invite collaborators to join the team before we dig into the Figma interface. UX is a team sport and you never start work without a team. In the second chapter, we not only explain the various types of content that can be added to Figma but also how to prepare that content in other applications for use in Figma.

Chapter 3 is an in-depth look at the UX process with an emphasis on where Figma fits and what features of Figma are designed to support each step of the process. The key takeaway from this chapter is UX Design is a messy process requiring the team to constantly test and iterate the hypothesis. We also get into User Testing, Accessibility, and Inclusion as a project moves through multiple iterations.

Having been exposed to the fundamentals of Figma's role in the UX process, the rest of the book focuses on specific aspects of the process. Chapter 4 is an in-depth look at where Figma fits into the Documentation process. Chapter 5 deals with low-fidelity prototypes such as wireframes and ends with you being asked to wireframe a login sequence using FigJam. Chapter 6 is an in-depth look at how the boxes and arrows of a wireframe become a medium-fidelity prototype as the content is added and the project starts coming to life.

The next three chapters – 7, 8, and 9 – explore the most popular features of Figma: Interactivity, Motion, and Design Systems. We show how interactivity and motion are added using Prototype mode. These are demonstrated using practical examples and how to share your ideas and subject them to User Testing.

Chapter 9 deals with a topic that is all the rage these days: Design Systems. We don't explain how to create one because they are, quite frankly, complicated. Instead, we focus on the features of a Design System such as Design Patterns, Components, Typography, and Color. We also dig deeply into Figma Variables and the creation of design tokens. Hopefully you will come out of this chapter understanding the creation of a Design System is a methodical and time-consuming process that, when implemented, turbocharges the design process and makes life easier for the developers as they incorporate the tokens and assets into their work.

Chapter 10 is named Building Stuff. The reason behind the word "Stuff" is less intimidating than Practical Projects for Figma. In this chapter, the intention is to give you the opportunity to put everything you have learned to this point to practical use and to further expand your knowledge. This will become evident as you learn how to create a shopping cart using local variables, expressions, and conditionals to move values from one component to the next. We also show how to create a custom video controller, a video progress bar for a video destined to Instagram, how to swap components with each other, and where Boolean operations fit.

The final chapter covers off what you need to know when the prototype is handed off to the development team.

Finally, we are no different than you in that we are constantly learning more about what you can and cannot do with Figma. The constant stream of updates and feature additions to Figma makes this a pretty exciting time for all of us as we discover where Figma fits into the app and web design fields.

Our final bit of advice for you is

"The amount of fun you can have with Figma should be illegal. We'll see you in jail."

CHAPTER 1

Learning the Figma Interface

What is UX?

Let's consider this scenario. You push the glass door to enter a store and almost crash into it because it should be pulled to open it. It is not a good start to your shopping expedition. You have just had a bad user experience. Whether you know it or not, you have also formed a negative impression of the store before entering it.

Here's another we have all had. You are purchasing an item from a company's website or app. You reach the end of the process, but the process fails as you finish entering the required credit card information. You enter it again. Same failure. You give it one more try. Same failure. At this point, you give up and leave your full shopping cart sitting there and move to another site or app. You have just had a bad user experience, and the company lost a customer and a sale.

How about entering an elevator in your hotel (Figure 1-1) and figuring out how to get to your floor?

Each of those bad experiences has a simple solution that turns it into a good experience. The door could have a small, noticeable sign above the handle that reads, "Pull." The website's shopping cart could indicate it requires dashes between the credit card numbers and the expiration date in the form of "m/y."

Those three examples are common UX issues.

© Tom Green and Kevin Brandon 2024
T. Green and K. Brandon, *UX Design with Figma*, Design Thinking,
https://doi.org/10.1007/979-8-8688-0324-6_1

Figure 1-1. *Which floor, please?*

UX is user experience, and those not in the UX field instinctively understand its meaning. Many of those in the business of UX tend to dilute the term to the point where whenever asked, "What is UX?", our response is, "What do you want it to mean?" The reason behind this facetious response is the term has become confused with job titles for everyone involved, ranging from Researchers to Graphic Artists and Developers. So "What is UX?"

There are two aspects to user experience. As Louie Morais of Wayfair explains, "User experience is composed of two parts: the Mission and the Process." The Mission focuses on the User who will use the product. The whole purpose of the Mission is to make life easier for that individual to have that user continue to take advantage of the product, service, website, or app.

The Process answers the next obvious question: "How do we do that?" The answer is the workflow from initial research to upload to the Apple App Store, the Google Play Store, or a web server. This process requires a lot of planning, brainstorming, software tools, user testing, and so on, with all of that moving straight to the final product with multiple changes and iterations. This explains why we regard the UX Process as a Team Sport.

The space where the Mission and the Process intersect is where collaboration happens, and this is where prototyping software like Figma enters the discussion.

Figma and the UX Process

Figma is not a design tool. Figma fits squarely into that space where the Mission and the Process intersect. It is a prototyping and collaboration tool, and that will become glaringly obvious throughout the balance of this book. Collaboration is the heart and soul of Figma, and collaboration does not infer "design by committee." In a collaborative environment, Figma encourages a constant flow of communication between all members of the team and the stakeholders.

The UX process brings together a team of researchers, designers, and developers who apply their knowledge to creating an app or website. They each use their unique skill set to provide users with a positive experience by meeting the needs identified during the Research phase of the project, designing an interface that is both intuitive and easy to use and developed to make interactions both speedy and smooth.

To accomplish this, everyone involved needs to be on the same page and have access to the same material. Figma contains many features that do just that. FigJam, which we get into in Chapter 4, is designed to be a collaborative whiteboard where any team member can participate in the ideation phase of the project. Any page or project can be shared with any team member, and those team members can provide feedback on any aspect of what they are looking at. Dev Mode provides developers and designers a common area to reduce the friction between these two disciplines. Thanks to this feature in Dev Mode, developers can quickly identify which sections of a project are ready for development.

When it comes to documentation, many templates, plug-ins, and features make creating such items as Flowcharts, Journey Maps, Personas, and other documents produced during the Research phase a simple process. This documentation can be posted to FigJam, included in the Team Folder or both.

Figma is also available in both desktop and browser versions, so you are not locked into a browser. You can work on your Figma file on a Mac or PC, and any changes made will instantly appear in the file located in the Figma Dashboard – no upload required. Let's take a look at the Figma Dashboard.

The Figma Dashboard

Whether you are working on the desktop version or in the browser, you first need to log into Figma. When you do, the first screen you see (Figure 1-2) is the Figma Dashboard.

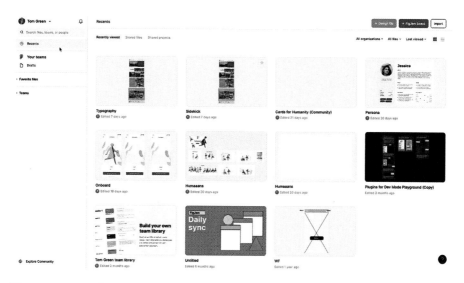

Figure 1-2. *The Figma Dashboard*

The Figma Dashboard shows you all the files you are working on or have worked on. There are three ways of viewing these files:

- Recently Viewed: All the files you have worked on or looked at are shown. To open one, double-click the file.

- Shared Files: This view only shows the individual files shared with the entire team or individual team members.

- Shared Projects: All files in a project that have been shared with the team are shown.

Moving to the right on the menu bar, there are three other ways of viewing the Dashboard:

- All Organizations: This feature is only available to Enterprise subscriptions where workspaces are assigned. Workspaces are where teams, people, and resources are collected and set. For example, XYZCorp

5

could create organizational workspaces for Teams, departments such as Marketing, Cost Centers, or other administrative units. Once that is defined, admins are appointed to create the workspace and assign team members or others to that workspace.

- All Files: This pop-down allows you to filter what you see on the Dashboard. All files are the default, but you can also select Design files, FigJam files, or Prototypes, and only those files will be shown.

- Last Viewed: This is another way of filtering your view options. The pop-down lets you view the files either alphabetically, by Creation Date, or by using default, Last Viewed. There are two other options for bringing order to the Dashboard. You can rearrange them by Oldest or Newest first.

The two buttons on the far right change the view from grid view (shown) or list view.

If you right-click on the file, a drop-down menu (Figure 1-3) opens and offers you several ways to manage the selected file. They are all self-explanatory, but one you will most likely use is Delete. Select this, and the file is permanently deleted from the Dashboard. This feature is handy for creating Figma files to work out no longer-needed ideas.

Figure 1-3. *There are several ways to manage individual files in the Figma Dashboard*

Let's now turn our attention to the panel on the left, commonly called the Left Sidebar. This panel is where the magic happens. Your avatar at the top is where you can manage your Figma account, and that little bell will sport a red dot when a notification regarding a file has been sent to you. This could be something like a comment attached to a particular file.

The file area of the Dashboard can become a pretty crowded place, and scrolling through all of them to find just the one you need can be time-consuming. This explains why there is a Search area right at the top of the panel. You can quickly locate files, teams, and even members of a team by entering the name of the file, team, or individual.

The next item is Your Teams. Before we get into that, it is important for you to understand there are two types of teams when it comes to Figma that depends upon your Figma subscription. If you are trying out the free plan, you have no access to the Teams feature. The best you can do is to invite collaborators. The Professional, Organization, and Enterprise plans let you share projects with your collaborators and create a Team Library. Just be aware the Professional plan limits you to a single team whereas the Organization and Enterprise plans offer a multiple teams feature.

If you have an Organization or Enterprise plan, you are able to create multiple Teams to help organize projects. The Enterprise plan also allows you to set up a collection of teams in Figma Workspaces. In either case, Admins are assigned and will build the teams. If you have a Professional plan, you are limited to a single team and actually don't have access to the formal Teams feature.

Drafts are actually quite interesting. Think of them as your personal Figma folder where you can experiment, work out ideas, and so on. Drafts are not the final product. Though they can be shared, they are rough drafts. Maybe, after polishing, they are acceptable enough to move into a project by simply dragging them into a project.

Favorite files are a handy way of giving yourself quick access to a particular file, such as a template. To add a Favorite, simply drag it in from the Dashboard. If you want to remove it, right—click, select Delete, and it is removed from your favorites. It doesn't delete the file from Figma.

Creating a Team in Figma

We have talked about teams quite a bit so far, and this sections the inevitable question: "How do you create a team in Figma?" Actually, it is quite easy, but it is important for you to understand that those invited to the team must have a Figma account.

Here's how to create a team:

1. Click on Create new team in the Teams area of the left sidebar. The Create a team page appears.

2. Give the team a name (Figure 1-4) and click the Create team button.

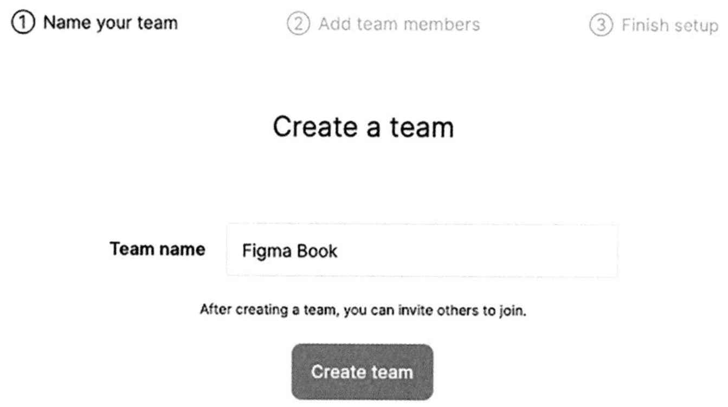

① **Name your team**   ② Add team members   ③ Finish setup

Create a team

Team name   Figma Book

After creating a team, you can invite others to join.

Create team

Figure 1-4. *The first step is to give your team a name*

3. Enter the email addresses of those being invited to join the team. (Figure 1-5). When finished, click Continue.

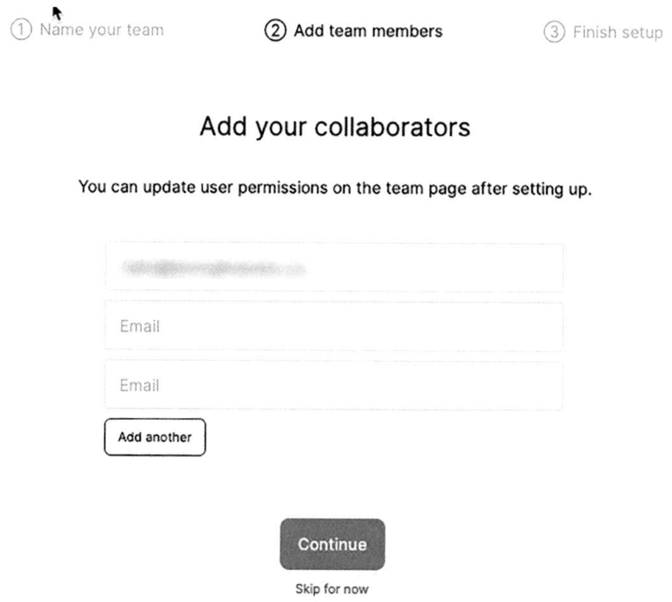

① Name your team   ② **Add team members**   ③ Finish setup

Add your collaborators

You can update user permissions on the team page after setting up.

Email

Email

Add another

Continue

Skip for now

Figure 1-5. *Send an email to the team members inviting them to join the team*

4. You will then be prompted to set up a Paid Team plan. For the purposes of this book, select Choose Starter. The team members will be sent an email invitation.

5. Click on the Team name to open the Admin panel. The team project opens, and three buttons appear on the right side. The first two are self-explanatory, but the one on the far right is where you set the permissions for each team member.

6. Click the button and a dialog box opens. Being the owner, Tom has what we call the "God Mode." He gets to choose who does what.

7. Click the Can edit button and the permissions open as shown in Figure 1-6. For this person, the options are Can edit or Can view. Can view should be assigned to stakeholders and others that only need to see the file. As the owner, Tom can change the permissions at any time or even remove that individual from the team.

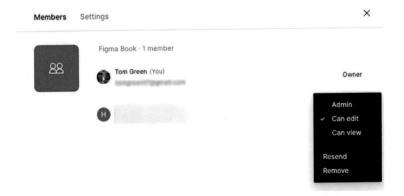

Figure 1-6. *The Administrator or Owner sets the permission for team members*

8. While still in the dialogue box, click Settings. This dialog box (Figure 1-7) allows the owner to add some more information about the team, set the team's library location, and even delete the team. When finished, click the close box to return to the Figma Dashboard.

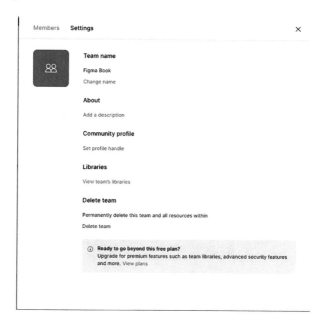

Figure 1-7. *The Team Settings dialog box*

Access the Figma Community

There is a link down at the bottom of the left sidebar that is actually one of the more powerful features of Figma. This is where you can access files, plug-ins, templates, and other material that will not only extend your skills but also extend Figma's functionality. Here's how:

1. Click the Explore Community link. This opens the Figma Community site as shown in Figure 1-8.

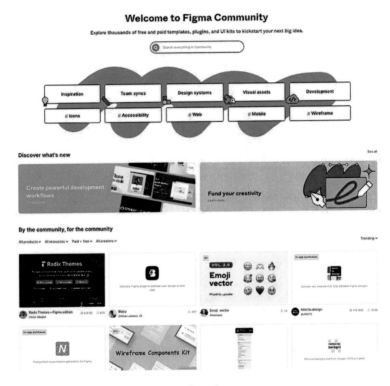

Figure 1-8. *The Figma Community site*

When you first access this site, we admit it can be a bit overwhelming. When you scroll down, hundreds of UI kits, Design files, Figma plug-ins, and so on are presented. This explains why the top of the page is so prominent.

You can explore the paid and free offerings by selecting one of the ten categories or, if you know what you are looking for, you can search for it. For example, let's search for the Stark Accessibility plug-in.

2. Enter "Stark" into the Search bar and, instantly, the Stark Accessibility Tools plug-in is shown (Figure 1-9). Click on the search result and you add this plug-in to your list of Figma plug-ins. In fact, as you will discover later on, this is exactly where you will come to add a Figma plug-in from within your Figma project.

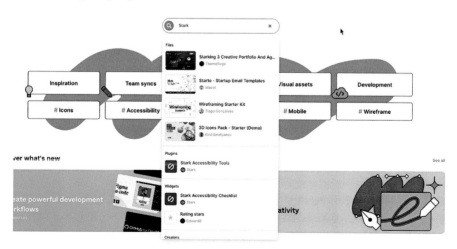

Figure 1-9. *Using Search is a quick way to locate files and plug-ins when using the Community site*

Getting Help

In the bottom right corner of the Dashboard, there is a question mark. This is how you can access Help in Figma.

1. Click the question mark and a dozen options (Figure 1-10) pop up.

    - The first grouping allows you to access the Figma Help files. Access the Support forum where you can pose issues to the Figma Community and maybe even get a solution, access a series of YouTube videos, and check out what has changed in your current version of Figma and of course the usual legalese.

    - The next grouping is focused around getting direct help. If you detect a bug in Figma or think there is a feature missing from the application, Submit Feedback is for you. If you want to know more about using Figma, then there is no better place than the Ask the Community forum. If you are having an issue with your account or something isn't working, then Contact Support.

    - The remaining two categories are pretty well self-explanatory.

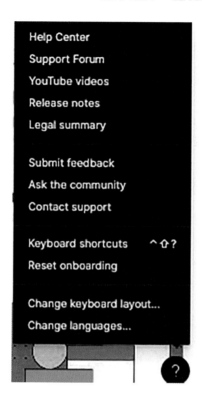

Figure 1-10. *Accessing the Help files*

2. We should also note if you are using the desktop version of Figma, Help is also a menu item as shown in Figure 1-11.

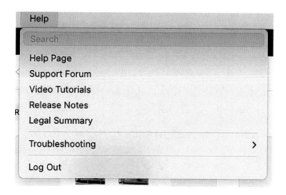

Figure 1-11. *If you use the desktop version of Figma, Help is also a menu item*

15

Having explored all of the features of the Figma Dashboard, now would be a good time to create a Figma file and to explore your workspace. To create a new Design file, click the big blue Design File button in the upper right.

The Figma Workspace

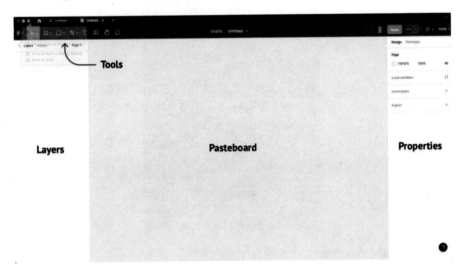

Figure 1-12.   The Figma workspace looks rather basic

When the Figma workspace, also formally known as the Figma IDE or Integrated Development Environment, opens, it looks rather sparse. As shown in Figure 1-12, the interface is composed of four different areas. Along the top is the Tool bar. There is a Layers panel that functions as you would expect. The Pasteboard is where the work gets done, and the Properties panel is where selections can be formatted. Even though we said it looks sparse, it is the exact opposite. It is deep, rich, and indulgent. Let's take a look.

We will be using the desktop version of Figma for the balance of this book. There are no major differences between the browser and desktop versions of the application. The major difference is the menu bar in the desktop version. It contains all of the commands available in the browser version and in fact duplicates the features in the Main Menu drop-down.

Figure 1-13 Expanded Figma tools, drop down menus.

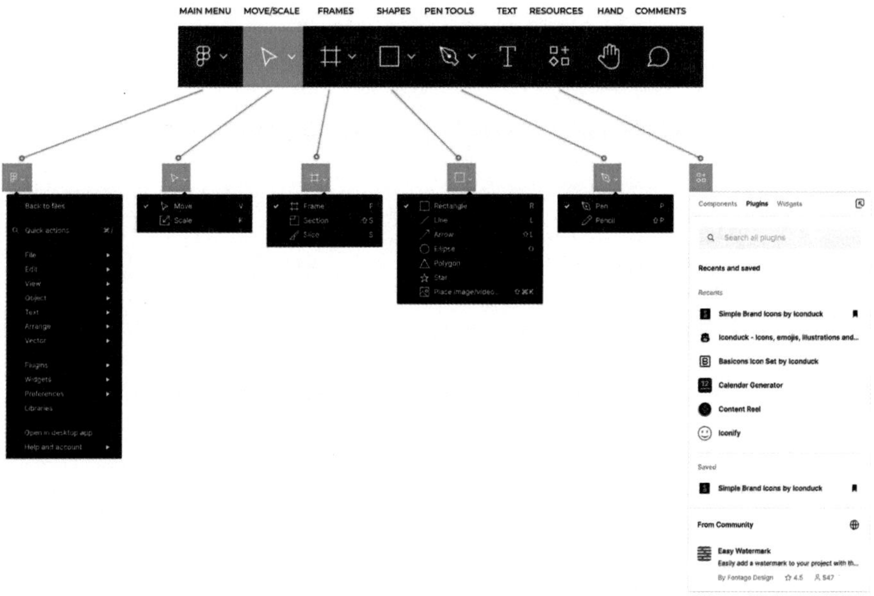

Figure 1-13. *The Figma tools and submenus*

The Home button is how you access your Dashboard; beneath it is a collection of tools you will be using quite a lot. They are as follows, from left to right:

- Main Menu: Click it and a pop-down menu presents you with a number of categories. If you are using the desktop version, each category is contained in the menu bar.

17

- Move Tool: This tool is actually two tools. The Move tool is how you select and move elements around the screen, and the Scale tool is used for scaling elements.

- Frame Tool: Frames are where content is placed, and you will be using this one a lot. The Section tool allows you to group frames on the Canvas – that big gray area you see. The Slice tool does nothing more than slice up the design for Export.

- Rectangle Tool: All of the common shapes can be created by selecting one and drawing it out. These are vector shapes.

- Pen Tool: Use this to create custom vector shapes. The Pencil tool draws bitmaps.

- Text Tool: This tool is used to enter and format text.

- Resources: A quick way of accessing plug-ins or Community Resources added to Figma.

- Hand Tool: Select this to move around the canvas. A quicker method is to hold down the space bar and drag.

- Comments: Select this to add comments to a shared file.

Moving along, all new documents are saved as a Draft. Click the word Draft and you are returned to the Dashboard. Click and hold on the Untitled pop-down and you are presented with a few options. Should you choose to name the file, double-click the word Untitled and you will be prompted to do just that.

That big blue Share button opens a dialog box and prompts you to enter the email addresses of those who can look at the shared file. The next button toggles on the new Dev Mode. The interface will change to a place where the development team can look at the underlying code behind the prototype and, even more important, know if the file is ready for development. We'll get deeper into this later in the chapter.

The next button to the right is the Play button. This one, just like the Frames button, will be one of the most used. You have two options available to you. Present treats the project as a slide deck, and Preview lets you test the file's interactions. In either case, the file is moved to Figma's web servers.

Note   Using the Figma desktop app or using Figma in browser, when you create a new Design file, the files are stored in Figma cloud storage and are accessible in both the web and desktop.

Adding Frames

Before we start, you need to understand Figma works a bit differently than many design applications. They use artboards. Figma uses frames. This is an important distinction. You don't create an artboard; you create a frame, and all content in that frame is placed in other frames. This tells you the frame created for, say, an iPhone is a parent container and all of the contents nested inside that frame are children. Here's how this works:

1.   Select the Frame tool. As you can see, the Properties panel opens up in Design view and you are presented with a plethora of choices ranging from Smartphones to Social Media.

2.   Twirl down the Phone group. A number of devices appear, and the dimensions of each device match that device's viewport.

Figure 1-14 Right-hand Figma Frame tool options.

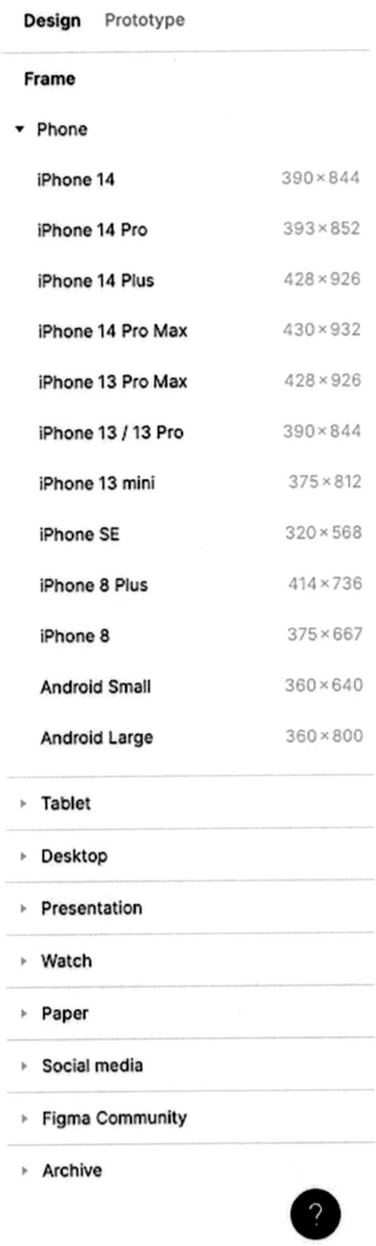

Design	Prototype

Frame

▾ Phone

iPhone 14	390×844
iPhone 14 Pro	393×852
iPhone 14 Plus	428×926
iPhone 14 Pro Max	430×932
iPhone 13 Pro Max	428×926
iPhone 13 / 13 Pro	390×844
iPhone 13 mini	375×812
iPhone SE	320×568
iPhone 8 Plus	414×736
iPhone 8	375×667
Android Small	360×640
Android Large	360×800

▸ Tablet

▸ Desktop

▸ Presentation

▸ Watch

▸ Paper

▸ Social media

▸ Figma Community

▸ Archive

Figure 1-14. *Your first frame is always tied to a device*

3. Select Android Large. The frame appears on the pasteboard, the Layers panel lights up, and the Properties panel changes to show you all of the properties applied to the Frame. There are two things we need you to pay attention to. Notice how the Frame sports a Hash mark in the Layers panel and the name also appears above the frame on the pasteboard.

4. Double-click the name in the Layers panel. Change the name to "Frame" and press the Return/Enter key. Notice how, as shown in Figure 1-15, the name changes on the pasteboard. Double-click the name of the pasteboard and change it to Figma. Once again, the name changes in the Layers panel.

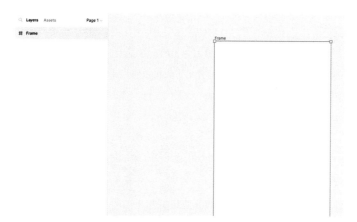

Figure 1-15. *Frames can be renamed either on the pasteboard or in the Layers panel*

5. To delete a frame, either select the frame on the pasteboard or in the Layers panel and press the delete key.

6. To add more frames, you have a number of choices.

- Select the frame in the Layers panel and copy/paste.

- Select the frame and duplicate it by pressing Command-D (Mac) or Control-D (PC)

- With the frame selected on the pasteboard hold down the Option key (Mac) or Alt key (PC) and drag to copy the frame.

7. To nest frames, select the Frame tool and place the cursor inside the first frame; the cursor changes to a plus sign. Drag out a new frame. Notice how the new frame is indented in the Layers panel. This tells you this new frame is inside the Parent. You will also see a Tool Tip showing the frame's Width and Height values. The dotted lines indicate distance from the left and top of the parent frame. You can see these values in the Properties panel as shown in Figure 1-16.

Figure 1-16. *A frame's properties are shown on the parent and in the Properties panel*

From this point on in the book, we will be referring to the parent frame as an artboard. This way we don't wind up confusing you. It is also common for Figma users to refer to these parent frames as artboards.

Changing Frame Properties

Frames are not static objects. They can be moved and manipulated to get them just right. Here's how:

1. Click inside your new frame and drag it to a new location. This tells you frames can be repositioned.

2. Here's another method. Select the frame and place the cursor over the X in the Frame properties. It changes to a split cursor. With the mouse button held down, drag the cursor to the left or right. The value changes, and the frame moves up or down.

The term for the previous technique is called "Scrubby Numbers." Say what? The technique is taken from applications containing a timeline. When you drag the playhead in a YouTube video to the left or the right, you are "scrubbing" the playhead.

3. For even more precision, change the X and Y values to 0. The frame jumps to the upper left corner of the frame.

4. To add a stroke to a frame, open the Stroke
    Properties. As you can see (Figure 1-17), the default
    value is a black stroke inside the frame that is 1 pixel
    thick. We are going to get a lot deeper into working
    with strokes in the next exercise, which is why we
    are staying with the default values.

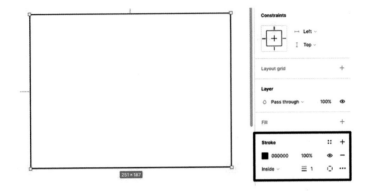

Figure 1-17. *Strokes and fills can be applied to frames*

Using the Properties Panel

The Properties panel is where you will spend a lot of your time. This is
where you finesse objects, commonly referred to as elements, in a Figma
frame or artboard. This is where elements get resized, moved around,
colored, rotated, have strokes applied, and become opaque. This is where
text is formatted and images manipulated. This should also tell you it is a
Contextual Panel. Depending on which element is selected, the Panel will
change to show the Properties that can be manipulated. To get yourself
started, open the Properties.fig file found in your Chapter 1 Exercise folder.

1. When it opens, you will see four shapes created
    using the Shapes tools, a photograph, and a piece
    of text. If you look over to the Layers panel, you will
    see these shapes listed, and the icon beside their

name indicates each one is a shape. The same goes for the House image and the Text. As you may have guessed, the Layers panel tells you what you are looking at. If you look over at the Properties panel, only the Page has color and opacity properties showing. That color is the frame's background color. Here's how to change it.

2. If selected, deselect the Properties frame.

3. Click the color chip in the Page area of the Properties panel to open the Color Picker (Figure 1-18) and choose a different color. When finished, double-click the Hex value and enter #F5F5F5 to return to the original color. What you have discovered is you can change the artboard color without selecting the frame.

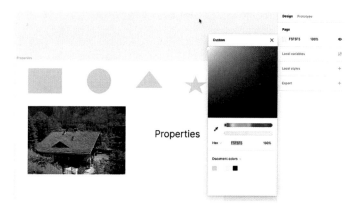

Figure 1-18. *The Figma Color Picker is a powerful tool*

Using the Color Picker

Now that you understand how to change color properties, let's go a bit deeper and take a closer look at the Figma Color Picker. We are going to work with a shape because Figma sees shapes as being composed of a Fill and a Stroke. For those wondering, Figma regards images and text this way as well. Here's how to work with a Fill:

1. Select the Rectangle on the artboard. The Properties panel changes to let you know which properties of the selection can be changed. We will start with the background color which is set in the Fill properties. This panel has a bit more to it than simply picking a color. The four dots let you access a color library that may be attached to the project. The + sign applies presets, which we will get not in a minute. You know about the color chip, and eyeball hides the color and the - sign removes it. Select the color chip to open the Color Picker.

2. When working with the Color Picker, you need to understand the key word is "Fill." The five icons at the top from left to right are as follows:

    *   Solid Color Fill

    *   Gradient Fill: You have four choices: Linear, Radial, Angular, and Diamond.

    *   Image Fill: You are prompted to fill the selection with an image.

- Video Fill: You are prompted to fill the selection with a video.

- Blend Mode: These are the Booleans modes, and we will explore them later on in this book.

3. The slider lets you change color, and the one below it adjusts opacity. The eyedropper lets you sample a color on the artboard and use it.

   The hex pop-down (Figure 1-19) lets you choose one of five color spaces:

   - Hex: The alphanumeric standard used on the Web.

   - RGB: Commonly used for both the web and mobile design, expressed as 217, 217, 217. The 100% is the value from the opacity slider.

   - CSS: This is actually the RGBA color space where the fourth value is Alpha or opacity. The color will be shown as RGBA (2171, 217, 217, 1), which is how it will be expressed if using CSS.

   - HSL: Hue, Saturation, and Lightness.

   - HSB: Hue, Saturation, and Brightness.

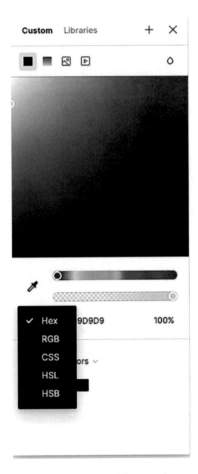

Figure 1-19. *You have your choice of five color spaces when it comes to choosing color in Figma*

Note   You may be wondering what the difference is between HSL and HSB. The "B" includes nothing about the whiteness of the color, only blackness. The "L" concerns itself with both the black and the white.

---

4. Select the red (255,0,0) and that color is applied to
    the rectangle.

5. Select the eyedropper tool and click on a green in
    the image. The rectangle turns green. That circle
    lets you choose a pixel color. If you move the tool
    around the image, the pixel is highlighted.

6. Close the Color Picker.

Gradients

Gradients, when used properly, are a very effective means of pulling a
User's attention to an element, providing a delightful background color
for the artboard or other element, and, when subtly applied, can provide
the necessary contrast for elements on a dark or bright background. Here's
how to apply a gradient:

1. Select the rectangle and open the color picker. When
    it opens, click on the Gradient icon. If you look at
    the rectangle, the gradient has already been applied
    (Figure 1-20), and the colors are shown in the picker.
    The chip on the left is the start color, and the chip on
    the right is the end color.

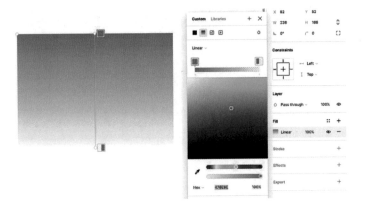

Figure 1-20. *Select a gradient type and it is automatically applied to the selected object*

2. To change the colors, select the End color chip and change it to a Red. And pull the Opacity slider to the right or enter 100 as the opacity value.

3. Move the Start and End color chips. Note how the look of the gradient changes. You can do the same thing by moving the chips up or down on the artboard.

4. Click and hold on the bottom handle of the color chip on the aboard. Drag it up and down. This is how you extend or compress a gradient.

5. Change the gradient types and play with the colors and handles to explore different effects that you can create.

6. Deselect the rectangle.

Strokes

As pointed out earlier, any selected element can have a stroke applied to it. Strokes are an important design element in that they separate design elements such a Cards from each other. Here's how to apply a stroke to an element:

1. Select the Circle and open the Stroke area (Figure 1-21) in the Properties panel.

Figure 1-21. *There is a lot under the hood when it comes to the Stroke panel*

The color chip and opacity value are self-explanatory. The three items at the bottom are where the power resides. The Inside pop-down determines how the stroke is applied to the selection:

- Inside: The stroke is applied inside the selection.

- Center: The stroke is applied equally both inside and outside of the selection. For example, if a 4-pixel stroke is applied, 2 pixels will be outside the shape and 2 pixels will be inside.

- Outside. The stroke is applied to the outside edge of the selection.

2. The next item is the stroke width. You can change the width using the Scrubby Numbers or manually by double-clicking the value and entering it. Go ahead, try it.

3. The ellipsis is where you can get creative. Click this and the Advanced Stroke options dialog box appears as shown in Figure 1-22.

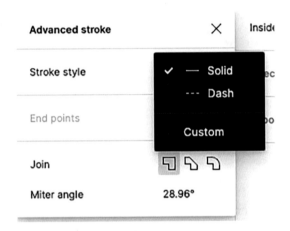

Figure 1-22. *The Advanced Stroke options lets you get creative with stroke styles*

The Style options are Solid, Dash, and Custom. Select Dash and you get to set dash length, the space between the dashes, and the shape of the dashes. Custom is where you unleash your creativity. Here you can set varying dash lengths and shapes.

Using the Polygon Tool

In simple terms, a polygon is a shape with multiple sides. The triangle you see is a three-sided polygon and is the default shape. Here's how to turn the triangle into a pentagon:

1. Select the Triangle.

2. At the top of the Properties panel, the number
    three you see is the number of sides applied to the
    polygon. Change it to 5. As shown in Figure 1-23,
    you have created a pentagon.

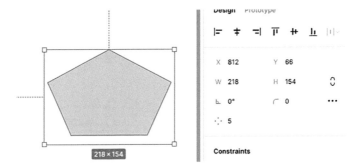

Figure 1-23. *Increasing the side count for a polygon*

> So far the shapes all have sharp corners. Such
> elements as buttons have rounded corners. Here's
> how to round a shape's corners.

3. Select the pentagon.

4. In the Properties panel, right under the H value is a
    curve with the number 0. This is the corner radius
    tool. Select the 0.

5. Change the zero to 5. The corners are rounded off.

6. Change the value to 10. The rounding is more
    prominent.

Cards, which are a common UI element always, have a roundness
value of 12 to 15 pixels applied to their shape.

---

7. Select the star. As you can see, the star's default value is five arms. In fact stars have two shape properties: Count and Ratio as shown in Figure 1-24. Count is the number of arms, and ratio is the distance of the inner points of the star from the center of the star. The value is simply a percentage of the star's diameter.

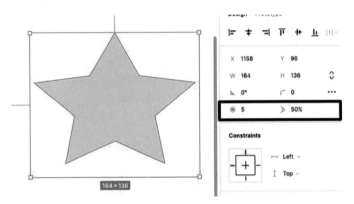

Figure 1-24. *Stars contain two editable shape properties*

8. With the Star selected, change the count value to 15 and the ratio value to 50. You have just created a starburst as shown in Figure 1-25.

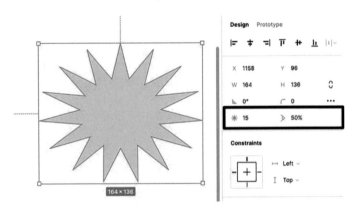

Figure 1-25. *Changing a star's shape properties to create a starburst*

Multipoint stars are ideal for creating such UI elements as Badges or highlights.

Using the Layers Panel

If there is one panel you will use as often as the Properties panel, it has to be the Layers panel. The Layers panel is where everything appearing on an artboard, or the pasteboard, is shown. It is especially invaluable when creating complex screens with groups of objects. You can simply select the element in the Layers panel and go to work. Here's how:

1. Open the Card.fig file found in your chapter download. When it opens, you will see a simple card used in a frame that highlights the city of Bern, Switzerland.

2. Over in the Layers panel (Figure 1-26), you can see all of the elements that make up the card are listed. At the top you can choose to view Layer or Assets. Assets are components, and we will dig deeper into them later in this book. At the top of the list is the current artboard indicated as a Frame and all of the elements located on that artboard.

Figure 1-26. *The Layers panel contains all of the objects contained on the pasteboard and the artboard*

3. In the Layers panel, select the Rectangle layer. The blue square lights up showing it is selected.

4. Drag the Rectangle layer above the Learn More layer. The text is hidden. What you have just done is to reorder layers. In this case, the Rectangle layer is above the text layer.

5. Drag the Bridge layer to the top of the stack. Move the Bern and Founded Text layers under it and then move the line layer up below the Founded text. Finally, move the Rectangle layer below the Learn More layer. What you have done is to reorder the layers from the top to the bottom of the Card.

6. Roll the mouse over the Bridge layer. Two icons – Lock and Visible – appear.

7. Click the Lock. If you try to select the Bridge layer on the artboard, you can't. Locking a layer is a handy way of ensuring an element is not moved or otherwise manipulated.

8. Click the Visibility icon. The Bridge layer disappears, and the eye icon changes to a closed eye. Turning off layer visibility is a handy way of working on a selected layer without the distraction of the rest of the content. Turn the Bridge layer back on by clicking on the closed eye.

9. Right-click on the Learn More layer. The Layer Options menu (Figure 1-27) opens. We are not going to get into them now because we will be using them quite a bit throughout the book.

Figure 1-27. *Right-click on a Layer to open the Layer Options*

10.   With the Shift key held down, select the Learn More and Rectangle layers. Press Command-G (Mac) or Ctrl-G (PC) to group the layers. Group is also available in the menu options. The group appears in the Layers panel. Double-click the name and change it to "button". If you twirl down the group, you will see the Grouped items.

To Ungroup the Button, select it on the artboard and press Command-Delete (Mac) or Ctrl-Backspace (PC).

We have not talked about Pages found at the top of the Layers panel. The Layers panel is where an organization hierarchy is established. Pages are a way of organizing the project into separate themes such as Journey Maps, Wireframes, Personas, Prototypes, Assets, and so on, all in one page.

A frame defines a specific area of the canvas, within a Page, such as the artboard for a device and asset placement. Frames can be contained within other frames. You can have a frame named Home, defining the width and height of the area, and inside that frame is one named Nav; there might be another frame containing a Hero image and another frame named Footer at the bottom. All of these frames are found inside the layer named Home in the Layers panel. Groups as you saw are a great way of combining layers to create a single layer. Thus, we have a Page named Web Site. Inside that Page are the Frames that compose Home page, and inside the Home page, items have been grouped together into a group named button.

To wrap your head around Pages, Frames, and Groups, think of a Page as a workspace for your designs, a Frame as a container for the elements in those designs, and a Group as a collection of layers inside a frame.

Testing Your Work

It is a common practice to test your work to discover issues or to ensure interactivity does what it is supposed to do. This can be done right inside Figma. Here's how:

1. Open the Play.fig file in your chapter download. The file contains a simple interaction. When the user clicks the Learn More button in the Card artboard, the Cathedral artboard opens.

2. Click the Play button to test.

3. The Screen turns black and just the artboard is shown (Figure 1-28). What has happened is Figma has uploaded the file to its server.

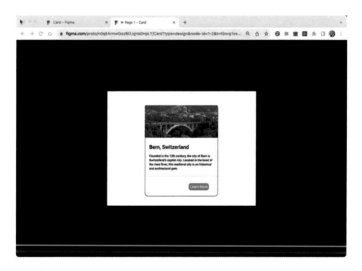

Figure 1-28. *Previewing a file in Figma's browser version*

If you are using the browser version of Figma, you will see a URL for the file. On the desktop version, this URL isn't visible.

---

4. Click the Learn More button. Note how the cursor changes when you roll over the button. This tells you this element is interactive.

5. When the Cathedral artboard opens, click the image. You are returned back to the first screen.

6. To return to Figma, click on the Card tab if you are using the browser version or on the Card tab at the top of the desktop version's view. Alternatively, you can simply close the previews.

Community Resources and Templates

We have all been there. The creative synapses aren't firing; you need something in a hurry or just need some inspiration. You could do a web search, or you could turn to the Figma Community.

As we briefly pointed out earlier, the Figma Community site has become the "Go To" page for anything related to Figma. This is where Figma users go to obtain templates, UI kits, plug-ins, and widgets. You may be unfamiliar with what a widget is or does. Widgets, according to Figma, "are interactive objects that extend the functionality of design files and FigJam boards." Plug-ins, on the other hand, extend Figma's functionality and have a very specific purpose. The great thing about these add-ons is you don't have to leave your project to grab one. Here's how:

1. With a file open, click on the Figma pop-down to open the Main Menu. At the bottom of the pop-down is where you go to obtain plug-ins or widgets.

2. When this side menu opens, you can see which plug-ins are currently installed. Click one, and its interface opens. To add a plug-in, select Manage Plugins (Figure 1-29). This will open the Resources Window that is launched when you select the Resources tool. This should tell you there are two ways of grabbing plug-ins. The problem with both methods is you need to know exactly what you want. If you enter a general term in a plug-in search, it will suggest a list of Community plug-ins.

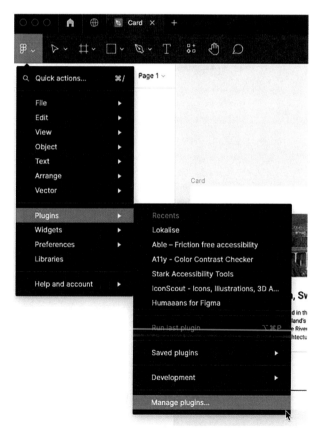

Figure 1-29. *Using the Figma menu to obtain plug-ins and widgets*

3. With the Resources menu open, enter the word
   Photo. As you can see, we already have one plug-in
   installed, and the list of Community Resources with
   ratings is presented as shown in Figure 1-30.

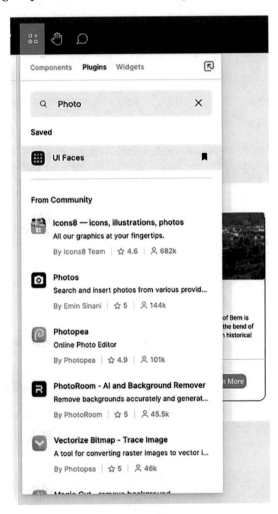

Figure 1-30. *An alternative way to obtain plug-ins and widgets is through the Resources panel*

4. To install a plug-in, click on it, and when the plug-in
    with description appears, click the big blue Run
    button. The plug-in appears in the Resources list.

5. Note: There is a difference between installing a
    plug-in and saving a plug-in. Installing is pretty
    close to a single use. If you want to add the plug-in
    to your lineup, click the bookmark icon beside the
    plug-in in the Resources panel.

6. Another, more general approach to obtaining
    plug-ins, widgets, and templates is to open the
    Community page from the Dashboard. Enter
    Plugin into the search bar, select Plugins and you
    will be presented with all of the plug-ins, including
    price and rating as shown in Figure 1-31. If you are
    looking for free plug-ins, change the Paid + Free
    option to Free. If you click the Try it out button, a
    demo will appear in Figma, and if you like it, use the
    Resources panel to save it to your lineup. This is also
    a great place to find a template or widget that meets
    your needs.

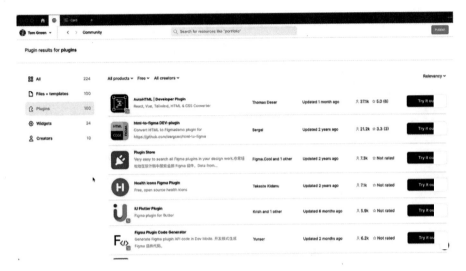

Figure 1-31. *Using the Community Resources to locate plug-ins, widgets, and templates*

Obtaining the iOS and Android UI Kits

When it comes to mobile, there are two operating systems: Android from Google and iOS from Apple. Though there are a number of kits for both found in the Community Resources, we prefer to go right to the source. Here's how:

1. Open your browser and navigate to `http://m3.material.io`. Select Figma design kit for M3 (Figure 1-32). This will take you to the Figma Community, and you can download and install the kit from there.

Figure 1-32. *Accessing the official Material Design UI kit*

2. For iOS, point your browser to developer.apple.com/
design/resources. In the Design templates area,
select Figma as shown in Figure 1-33. Again, you
are taken to the Community page where you can
download and install the templates.

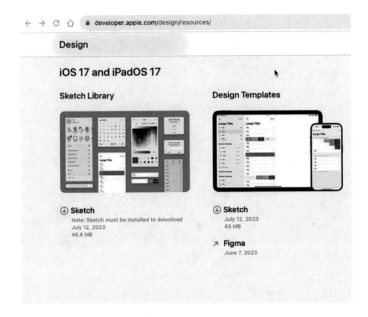

Figure 1-33. *Locating the official iOS UI kit*

Sharing

Figma, as we have said, is a team sport. A lot of very skilled people are also working on the project and collaborating with each other to ensure the project remains faithful to the project's intent. A key to collaboration is sharing your work and receiving feedback. Figma's sharing feature is where this important communication within the team takes place.

That is why there is a great big blue Share button on the toolbar. Here's how to share and communicate with a team member:

1. Open the Share.fig file found in your Exercise folder.

2. Click the Share button and a dialog box opens asking you to enter the recipient's email as shown in Figure 1-34. You also can choose whether the recipient can edit the file or only view the

file. Setting the status to can view is ideal for stakeholders and other team members who only need to see the file but can also comment. You can also copy the link and include it in an email to selected recipients. Once you have added the recipients, click the Invite button.

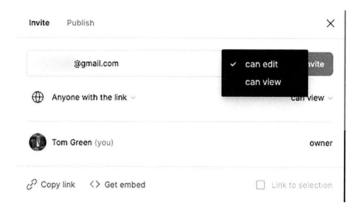

Figure 1-34. *The Share dialog box is where you can invite the team to review the project*

Don't think just anybody can be on the Share list. You may be tempted to share the link with family or friends to show them what you are up to and ask the inevitable, "What do you think." Don't do it. This group will tell you what they think you want to hear, not what you need to hear. We will focus on User Testing in the next chapters.

3. The recipient will receive the following email and tell they can open the file in Figma (Figure 1-35).

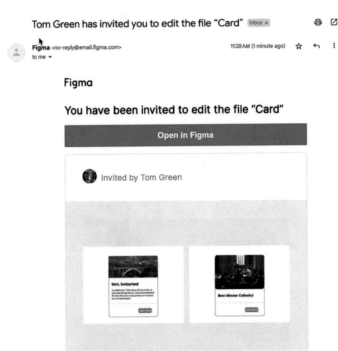

Figure 1-35. *The recipient receives this email and can open the file in Figma*

4. To comment on the file, the recipient clicks on the
    Comment tool in the toolbar, for instance, asking
    if the Keyline in the card is really necessary. When
    finished, click the up arrow in the comment to
    attach it to the file.

5. The comment will appear on the sender's file as
    a pin with the respondent's avatar. As well, the
    Comment tool will spot a red alert circle saying
    there is a comment.

6. To view the comment, click or roll over the comment
    – the shape with avatar is called a "pin." The
    comment will open as shown in Figure 1-36.

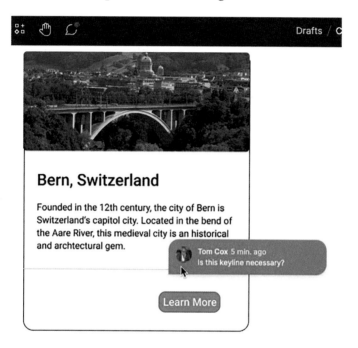

Figure 1-36. *Viewing a comment. Note the Red dot above the
Comment tool telling you a comment has been added*

7. When the Comment dialog box is opened, clicking
    on it, you can reply. Click the ellipsis to open the
    comment actions, click the circle with the check
    mark to resolve it, or click the DockTo Side button to
    open a longer conversation. If you reply, click the up
    arrow, and the recipient will see it on their copy of
    the project (Figure 1-37).

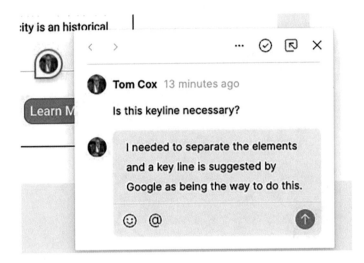

Figure 1-37. *Replying to a comment*

8. When the issue is resolved to everyone's satisfaction, delete it by selecting the resolve button in the dialog box.

Dev Mode

As Figma states, "Dev Mode is a developer-focused interface for inspecting and navigating designs." In many respects, this is where the developer can start ripping apart your prototypes and wiring them up.

Dev Mode is a robust area designed to make your development team's life easier. When the developer clicks the Dev Mode button – right next to the Share button – the Properties and Layers panels change as shown in Figure 1-38. In the Layers panel, the developer can not only see if a file is ready for development but also track the changes made to the file before it was ready for development.

Figure 1-38. *The Figma Dev Mode Interface*

The "magic" is found in the Properties panel. As the developer rolls over the elements, the panel changes to reflect what is selected. The developer can then choose to view the code in a number of ways: CSS, iOS, and Android along with any associated plug-ins that also provide code. The Code pop-down gives the developer the opportunity to introspect the code and properties associated with the selection. The developer can also access code bases located in Storybook, GitHub, and other repositories.

The Layout and Style areas show the code associated with the selection's layout and style. This code, if the developer so chooses, can be copied and pasted right into a code editor.

Conclusion

In this chapter, you have

- Learned of Figma's role in the UX process
- Toured the Figma Dashboard
- Learned how to create a Team

51

- Explored the Figma Interface

- Used the Layers and Properties panels

- Tested and shared a file

- Learned how to access Community Resources and Templates to extend Figma's functionality

- Reviewed the new Dev Mode

There is a lot you have learned in this first chapter that should give you a grasp of the Figma fundamentals. In the next chapter, we dig into the various content types that can be added to Figma such as images, line art, and video. Not only do we review them, but we also explain the underlying technologies behind them. The reason is simple: They will get handed off to development, and if handoff goes smoothly, the assets become a workflow accelerant.

CHAPTER 2

Adding Content to Figma Screens

In the previous chapter, we covered a lot of ground focusing on the various features of the Figma interface. In this chapter, we focus on the content that will be placed into the Figma frames. The content falls roughly into four categories: images such as photographs, line art such as icons and illustrations, video, and text. We'll start with what you need to know about graphics when it comes to working with Figma.

Graphics come in two flavors: vector or bitmap. Vector images are traditionally created in a drawing application such as Adobe Illustrator, and bitmap images are created in such applications as Photoshop.

What you need to understand about Figma is at its heart, Figma is a prototyping application where assets are assembled into layouts and eventually those layouts are chopped up by the development team as they wire up the application. By that, we mean the assets appearing in the layouts are essentially ripped out of Figma and, through the use of code, those layouts, with their assets, are reassembled. This explains why we sometimes refer to Figma as an Assembly application.

In this chapter, we focus on preparing content for handoff to development. For example, images destined for frames in Figma aren't simply imported into the frame and resized and it is off to the next screen. Do that and your developers and users are going to have issues.

The developers will be constantly asking you, for example, to provide

© Tom Green and Kevin Brandon 2024
T. Green and K. Brandon, *UX Design with Figma*, Design Thinking,
https://doi.org/10.1007/979-8-8688-0324-6_2

them with images containing the proper scaling factors for the targeted devices. They might ask you for the .svg code along with the .svg file. You may be told that cool video you added to a layout in a project needs to be optimized for the target devices. As for the users, you will hear loud and clear when the project is sent out for User Testing, those issues development raised are also resulting in a bad experience, or they find the text very difficult to read. Constantly fixing asset issues costs both time and money. Properly prepare the Figma document the first time and those issues boost workflow efficiency.

Vectors and Bitmaps

To differentiate between the placed static images in Figma, we refer to photographic assets as "raster or bitmap images" and logos, line art, and geometric shapes as "vector graphics"; this helps when talking with project collaborators as opposed to saying "images" for every asset within a website or mobile app (Figure 2-1).

What makes vectors so appealing is they require very little computing power to be shown on a phone or tablet. Vectors are nothing more than code. For example, a circular red button is composed of five points – Center, Top, Right, Bottom, and Left – and those points are used in the mathematical calculation that results in the diameter of the circle. It also needs to know the fill color and the color and thickness of the stroke, if there is one. By needing only seven bits of information, you can quickly understand why vector images are so lightweight.

Bitmap images are a whole different beast. To create that red circle, each pixel's location in the circle must be remembered. Not only that but the three bits of color information – red, green, blue – must also be remembered. On top of all of that, the computer also needs to draw and map each pixel on the background. Let's assume that red circle is 100 pixels in diameter and it is sitting in a white box that is 150 pixels square.

This means each white pixel needs to be mapped as well. This means producing a simple red circle in a white box requires thousands of bits of information that need to be used to show the image on a device or table.

What types of graphic objects can Figma use? Figma uses four types of graphic objects:

- Geometric Shapes: These are vector objects created by Figma's Shape Tools: Rectangle, Line, Arrow, Ellipse, Polygon, and Star tools.

- Drawing Objects: These are the shapes created using Figma's Pencil tool.

- Complex Shapes: These are vector graphics imported into Figma or drawn using Figma's Pen tool.

- Bitmaps: These are the pixel-based images imported from Photoshop or some other imaging or drawing application.

Shapes: These are vector images either imported into Figma or drawn using Figma's Pen tool.

Drawing Objects: These are the shapes created using Figma's Pencil tool.

Primitives: These are the vector objects created by Figma's Shape Tools: Rectangle, Line, Arrow, Ellipse, Polygon and Star tools.

Bitmaps: These are the pixel-based images imported from Photoshop or some other imaging or drawing application.

 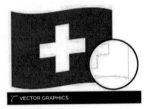 

Figure 2-1. *Examples of common graphic assets that can be placed into Figma*

Bitmaps and Figma

When it comes to bitmap images, these objects are ubiquitous in websites and apps. They support the message of information and, in many respects, are responsible for excessive loading times in a world where, if it doesn't instantly appear, users are not prepared to wait for more than a couple of seconds. After that, impatience sets in with an idea that something is wrong. When it comes to apps and websites, in the case of images, small is beautiful.

There are two main culprits behind this: the physical size of the bitmap and its resolution. Being aware of and accommodating these two factors not only removes a potential loading bottleneck but also will remove any potential friction between you and the developers.

Here's an example.

Figure 2-2 shows an image of a flower box sitting on a windowsill in Bern, Switzerland. It is an Adobe Photoshop (.PSD) image that has the physical dimensions of 3872 × 2592 px, with a resolution of 300 px/in, and weighs in at 28.7 MB. The spec for Figma is it needs to fit into an area of a web page that is 1200 × 800 px.

Figure 2-2. *Great image but file size is a major issue*

Obviously .PSD is not a format that can be used in Figma. We use this to sensitize you to the relationship between file size and resolution.

Simply dropping the image into Figma and resizing it is not a good idea – same file size, 28.7 MB, but in a smaller area. One option would be to scale the image in Photoshop to the correct dimension. The file size will drop, but the main reason for the reduction would be cropping the Photoshop artboard to fit the dimensions of the scaled image. On the surface, this may appear to be acceptable, but there is a better way.

1. Open the WindowBox.psd image in Photoshop.

2. Select Image ➤ Image Size in the menu bar. The Image Size dialog box shown in Figure 2-3 opens. The Width, Height, and Resolution along with the File Size values are shown.

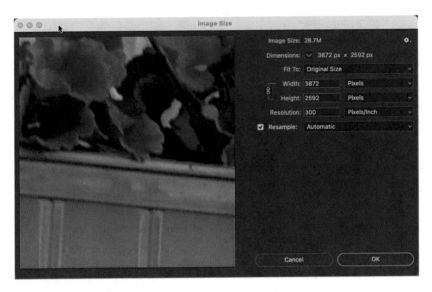

Figure 2-3. *Photoshop's Image Size dialog box*

3. Making sure the width and height values are linked,
    change the width value to 1200. The height value
    will automatically change as does the file size.

4. Change the Resolution value to 100 (Screen
    Resolution) and make sure the width value is still
    1200, and the File Size value plummets (Figure 2-4)
    because you have reduced the image's information
    by quite a bit without affecting image quality.

Screen resolution to be precise is 72 pixels/inch, which harkens back
to the early days of computing when monitors really did have 72
pixels per inch. We use 100 because it is an easier number to grasp
and has little or no effect upon the image or its file size.

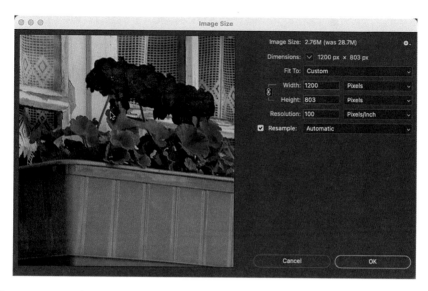

Figure 2-4. *Physical size, resolution, and format are important factors in optimizing images for a Figma project*

5. Click OK to close the dialog box.

6. Select File ➤ Save As... and select JPEG from the Format drop-down menu.

7. Click Save. If you check the original .PSD file size, it weighs in at 28.2 MB but, saved as a slimmed-down .JPG file, is now only 731 KB as shown in Figure 2-5.

Figure 2-5. *Not only do size and resolution play a role, so does file type*

As you see, outputting a .PSD file to the .JPG format resulted in a massive reduction in file size. To understand why this happened, you need to understand how the .JPG format works.

The JPG (Joint Photographic Experts Group) file format is almost ubiquitous when it comes to images for websites and mobile apps. As you saw, it creates for you and the developer an image that will be quick to download and render on a smartphone, tablet, or web page. JPG is a method of compressing an image using contiguous color. By that, we mean the compressor looks at all of the color areas in the image and replaces blocks of pixels with a more uniform color. As you may have guessed, color information is thrown out, which results in the small file size. This is why JPG is known as a lossy compressor. Keep recompressing a JPG image and eventually the image develops serious quality issues.

The other format that Figma accepts is the .PNG (Portable Network Graphics) format. This format was developed as a free lossless alternative to the GIF format for the simple reason that GIF was owned by Unisys and royalties had to be paid. What makes the .PNG format so appealing is it contains a transparency channel. The upshot is .PNG is ideal for situations where an image overlays content. The trade-off, of course, is .PNG files, due to their lossless nature, are larger than their .JPG cousins. That same .PSD image when converted to .PNG results in a file size of 1.4 MB compared to the .JPG size of 430 KB.

Again, decisions around when to use .PNG and .JPG images should be made prior to the Design phase (Figure 2-6).

Figure 2-6. *Comparison of image quality and file size between .PNG and .JPG images*

Scaling Factors

There is one task that must be decided before you start a UX project: What are the target platforms? Though this may be more of a general decision, it has a profound effect on the images you will add to Figma and send to the development team during Developer handoff. The reason is that device manufacturers compete around their screens. What it comes down to is pixel density or the number of pixels they can jam into one linear inch on a screen. For example, an iPhone 15 has 300 pixels per inch and there are Android devices that jam 460 pixels per inch into their screens. By jamming so many pixels into a linear inch, the image has an extremely high resolution, which is why Apple, for example, refers to its screen as "Retina."

Where it can get really confusing is there are now two types of pixels: screen pixels and device pixels. Without getting all technical, your computer screen has roughly 100 pixels per inch. Let's assume you are developing a screen for an iPhone 12. That screen has a resolution of 300 device pixels per inch. Your computer has around 100 device pixels and screen pixels per inch. So what's the difference? Screen pixels are an abstract measurement that is independent of the screen's size or resolution. Device pixels are the real thing, pixels on a device's screen.

This is where scaling factors come into play. iPhone devices have scaling factors ranging from 1x to 3x. Android, due to its open source nature, has factors ranging from .75 or over 4x. If target devices are not determined at the outset of the project, the users are in for a bad experience.

Figure 2-7. *Scaling factors must be considered before the Design phase gets underway*

In Figure 2-7, the device is an iPhone 12. The image on the left has the proper scaling factor of 3x applied to the image. The one on the right has a scaling factor of 1x. Both images are 375 x 375 PX. This is where things can get ugly. In Figma, the image on the left will look great in a frame because it is displaying on a computer screen. Hand it off to development and the user, looking at the image on an iPhone 12, will see the image on the right. This is why it is so important that both the design and development teams determine the scaling factors before the Design and Development phases of a project.

Here's how to apply scaling factors in Photoshop:

1. With your WindowBox image open in Photoshop, select File ➤ Export ➤ Export As... to open the Export As... dialog box shown in Figure 2-8. The magic happens on the left side of the screen.

2. That first image strip you see is the 1x version of the file. Above it are two pop-downs Size and Suffix. This is where you make both your developers and your users happy.

3. To add a 2x version of the file, click the plus sign, and when the strip appears, select 2x from the Size pop-down. And you will notice the suffix, @2x, appears. This will become part of the file's name.

4. Click the plus sign again and another image strip appears. Select 3x from the pop-down. Now that you have indicated the proper scaling factors, select JPG from the Format pop-down and move the Quality slider all the way to the right to set High Quality (Figure 2-8). Doing this maintains the integrity of the information in the file. Click Export and save the resulting files to your Chapter 2 Exercise file.

These are the files that will be handed off when the Figma file is sent off to the developers.

Figure 2-8. *Images with the appropriate scaling factors applied can be created in Photoshop*

When it comes to designing in Figma, every image is shown in a frame with a 1x scaling factor. Though you can apply the scaling factors in Photoshop using the Image Size menu by increasing the Resolution value, our advice is not to do that. In this case, our adage "Let the software do the work" is where you get a productivity boost. If you prefer to do your design work in Sketch, scaling factors can also be applied to the images.

SVG Images and Figma

Before we dig into vector graphics and the .SVG format, let's spend some time examining what a vector graphic is.

You can think of vector graphic as connecting dots, where the dots are placed anchor points connected by vector paths. Vector paths can create straight or curved lines, as open paths. If the vector path connects again to the starting anchor point, it is considered a closed path – often a shape, like a rectangle, ellipse, or polygon, or a unique vector shape.

Vector corners are either angled, such as in a rectangle shape, or rounded using a Bezier curved from an anchor point. When you are using the Shape Tools in Figma, you are creating vector shapes. These are easily modified to create wireframe layouts, or graphic elements such as buttons. Vector shapes can continue to be modified after they have been created.

Vector shapes also differ from raster images as they are not created within a resolution pixel grid, meaning that resolution is not an attribute of a vector graphic – dimensions: width and height, fill and stroke. Which makes vector file formats indispensable for logos and icons, as they can be scaled with no issues of poor resolution.

Using the Pen tool or Pencil tool in Figma allows you to create unique vector paths to create icons, symbols, or even vector illustrations. The vector shapes can be filled with solid colors, gradients, images, or videos; an alpha transparency can also be applied to these shapes.

Complicated vector graphics such as logos and icons have traditionally been created in desktop applications that focus on vector graphic creation such as Adobe Illustrator or Affinity Designer. Once created, the files are then saved as SVG files for placement into Figma.

You may think about vector graphics as a connect-the-dots exercise (Figure 2-9) but with much more precision. The anchor points are all connected with vector paths. Control of anchor points can create straight paths, or angled corners, rounded corners (called Bezier curves) with handles that help determine the height, length and angle of the rounded corners.

Figure 2-9. *Vectors can be regarded as a connect-the-dots format with the dots being anchor points*

Scalable Vector Graphics or .SVG images are traditionally used for line art such as icons or illustrations and are created in such applications as Adobe Illustrator, Affinity Designer, or Bohemian Coding's Sketch. You can also use Figma's Pen tool to create .SVG images. There is also a Figma plug-in- LottieFiles - which are, essentially, animated .SVG files.

What makes the .SVG format so efficient is that it is code driven and device independent. By that, we mean they are independent of device resolution and can be scaled up or down without any quality issues. The other advantage to .SVG files is they are code driven, meaning your development team can directly add the .SVG code, shown in Figure 2-10, to their code base or "tweak" the code with the approval of the UI design team.

Though Illustrator's .ai native format can't be imported into Figma, you can still select the object on the Illustrator artboard and copy and paste it directly into Figma.

Figure 2-10. Adobe Illustrator lets you save line art as both a .SVG graphic and code

Figma and Video

We have all had the experience of watching a video on a smartphone and it stops and starts throughout playback. This is not your fault or that of your provider's 4G or 5G network. The video has not been optimized for streaming playback. In very simple terms, a video's information streams into a cache. When the cache has enough information to play the video, the video starts playing. Why a video starts and stops is due to the cache emptying and the video starting when the cache refills and this stop and start frustration continues until the end. Before we get to optimizing a video for playback, it is important for you to know how Figma handles video.

The video formats that Figma accepts are as follows:

- Mp4: This format has become the standard for web video. It, like the other two, is a container format. By that, we mean the container is composed of a video track and an audio track. Each track requires a specific compressor. The video track is compressed using the H.264 standard, and the audio track is compressed using the AAC (Advanced Audio Coding) standard.

- Webm: This is Google's "royalty-free" version of the .mp4 format.

- Ogg: This format is another "royalty-free" file type primarily for the Opera web browser.

Royalty-free does not mean you have to pay to use .mp4. The H.264 video compression codec patent is owned by MPEG LA. The royalty is paid by the browsers, hardware manufacturers, and OS vendors, among others.

From the knowledge above you will understant that Apple's QuickTime .mov and m4v video formats can't be used. In very simple terms, the main reason QuickTime files can't be used is that QuickTime is a lossless compressor and results in rather large files.

M4V is another beast altogether. If you are a Mac user, the odds are pretty good you have encountered this format when playing videos through iTunes. This format was developed by Apple and is a version of mp4, but with a difference. M4V files are protected with Digital Rights Management (DRM) to prevent piracy and can only be played on a computer that has a valid Apple ID to play the video through iTunes.

There is a common misconception that all one has to do is change the m4v file extension of an unprotected video to mp4. Don't do it. This may or may not work. To do it correctly, use a video conversion utility such as the Miro Video Converter.

Preparing Video for Figma

This will inevitably happen to you. The video is not only the wrong size but also the wrong format. You can send it back to the video crew and wait a few hours or days for the correct version to arrive or spend ten minutes to fix it yourself.

In this exercise, we will be using the Adobe Media Converter to convert a .mov file that is 1920 × 1080 and weighs in at 88.9 MB to a .mp4 file optimized for playback on every device out there. Let's get started.

1. Open the Media Encoder and drag the LAX.mov file found in your chapter download into the queue area. All the Queue does is tell you it is a QuickTime video using a preset and the location of the video.

2. To actually encode the video, click QuickTime to open the Encoder's Export Settings window (Figure 2-11). This is where the magic happens.

Figure 2-11. *Video is optimized in the Export Settings window of the Media Encoder*

3. As you can see, this window is broken into two areas. On the left is where you can trim the video. The In Point and Out Point sliders are under the timeline, and the playhead is at the top. Drag the bottom right slider, the Out Point, to the 20-second mark. This reduces the duration of the video, and trimming off a couple of seconds has a minimal effect on the file size.

4. Over on the right is where all of the work is done. This is where you choose file format, codec, and so on to optimize the video.

5. In the Format pop-down, choose H.264, not MPEG 4. H.264 is the mp4 video compressor. The Export side tells you the Estimated File Size is now 29 MB.

6. Ensure both the Export Video and Export Audio boxes are checked.

The Video settings are where you compress the video track to reduce the file size and to ensure smooth mobile and browser playback.

1. You will notice the dimensions are now 720 × 480. That is the standard 16:9 Aspect Ratio. If you feel those dimensions are too small, use width values that are divisible by 16 and height values divisible by 9 when creating the Figma frame for the video.

2. Uncheck the Frame Rate and select 30 from the pop-down. This is the standard Digital Video frame rate.

3. Uncheck Aspect and choose Square Pixels from the pop-down. Computer screens use square pixels, not the rectangular pixels on a TV.

4. Scroll down to the Bitrate Settings and select VBR, 2-pass. The compressor will mark areas that need more compression on the first pass and do the compression on the second pass.

5. Set the Target Bitrate to 5 and the Maximum Bitrate to 10. This is how you avoid a video starting and stopping. You are controlling how fast information arrives in the buffer. If you take a look at the file size, you have just shaved off another 14 MB.

6. Select Use Maximum Render Quality. You have dealt with the video track (Figure 2-12). It is time to deal with the audio track. Here's how.

Figure 2-12. *The video compression settings using the Adobe Media Encoder*

7. Select the Audio tab.

The Audio settings compress the audio track contained in a video. Even if there is no audio track, you still need to compress the audio track because one has been added and is inevitably in the wrong format and size.

---

8. In the Basic Audio Settings, change the Sample Rate to 16,000 Hz. If there is an audio track, the standard setting is 24000 Hz.

9. Change the Channels to Mono. 48000 Hz, Stereo is CD quality. Devices only have one speaker so Mono is a logical choice.

10. Reduce the Bitrate to 16 kbps. If there is an audio track, use 24. If you check the File Size (Figure 2-13), you will see you have reduced the Estimated File Size to 13 MB from the 88.1 MB you started with.

Figure 2-13. *Compressing audio also reduces file size*

11. Click OK to Return to the Media Encoder Workspace.

12. To create the mp4, click the Green Start Queue button or press the Return key. You will see the video being compressed twice in the Encoding area (Figure 2-14).

Figure 2-14. *Encoding a video in the Media Encoder queue*

Typography and Figma

Typography is a critical content subject because your choice of font will affect the readability of the text. For example, if you are building a mobile app or website for a senior audience, it would look a lot different from one aimed at children. The reason why font choice is so important is because the text on a page is how users access information. Everything else, images, videos, and icons support the information presented in the text. Choose a font that is difficult to read, and you have prevented that access to information. The other thing to keep in mind around font choices is fonts do have a personality. For example, let's assume you have been invited to a wedding: How you would dress for the event if the invitation was set in a handwritten font or a formal script? (Figure 2-15). While the letters are in the same order and the words are the same, a meaning and personality can be derived from the selection of typeface.

Wedding

Wedding

TYPEFACE SCHOOLBELL   TYPEFACE LAVISHLY YOURS

Figure 2-15. *Example of how a typeface selection can influence meaning or add a personality*

Typeface meanings are influenced by their culture, use, and time period. Typefaces convey feelings or communicate confidence or a personality. You may see typefaces selected that contrast the meaning to add curiosity or rebel against a specific understood meaning.

Typefaces are commonly organized based on characteristics. This helps when you are looking to choose a specific kind of typeface; in most large-type websites, you will see an option to filter fonts by categories. There are arguments on how many categories typefaces should be organized into, but here is a short list of eight major categories:

- San serif typefaces can give a modern feeling to text by offering a clean, simple appearance. These typefaces are created to have low stroke contrast by using a common weight to each letter stroke. Examples of san serif typefaces are Helvetica, Arial, Roboto, SF Pro, Open Sans, etc.

- Serif typefaces can give a classical feeling to text as the letters reflect the letter forms from the Greek and Roman lettering. These typefaces tend to have more contrast in letter strokes as well as apply a serif to the end of the main letter for me. Examples of serif typefaces are Times New Roman, Georgia, Garamond, Merriweather, etc.

- Slab serif typefaces generally have the appearance of a serif typeface but with a heavier serif applied. These fonts became popular in 19th-century advertising. Examples of slab serif typefaces are Roboto Slab, Museo Slab, Josefin Slab, Rockwell, etc.

- Decorative/display typefaces offer the greatest number of unique typefaces. They are rarely used for large amounts of text and generally applied to headings to make strong visual statements or to evoke a feeling or emotion. They can represent a specific time period – think about the 1960s psychedelics or grunge from the mid-1980s. Examples of decorative/display typefaces include Droog, Fit, Black Ops One, etc.

- Script typefaces can fall into two categories: formal scripts or calligraphic scripts. Formal scripts reflect 17th-century writing styles where many letters connect in a flowing pattern – think about typefaces used on traditional wedding invitations. Calligraphic scripts often appear to have been written with a flat tipped calligraphic pen; these fonts may or may not have connecting letters – think about the lettering at the end of old black and white movies. Examples are Kuenstler Script, Stonington, Storefront Pro, etc.

- Handwriting typefaces convey a more personal feeling as they try to mimic casual handwriting as opposed to a formal script. Similar to the calligraphic typefaces, some typefaces are designed to have letters connect, while others are more like children's handwriting and convey a child-like reference. Examples are Comic Sans, Marydale, Skippy Sharp, Kollegan, etc.

- Blackletter typefaces reflect manuscript lettering from the Middle Ages. These letters have elaborate swatches and swirls, often with contrasting thin line weights. Examples of blackletter typefaces are Fraktur, UnifrakturCook, Pirata One, etc.

- Monospace typefaces can convey the idea of typewriters where most characters are designed to have the same letter width. Examples of monospace typefaces are Courier, Source Code Pro, Roboto Mono, etc.

Figure 2-16 Examples of eigth common typeface classifications.

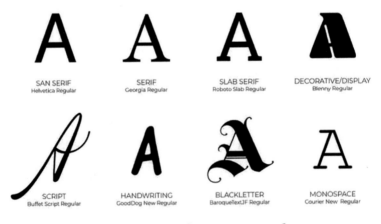

Figure 2-16. *Eight typeface classification examples*

Every application from Google Docs to Adobe InDesign has a default font when you use the type tool. The Figma design team created their own default font titled "Inter" (Figure 2-17). It was created by Rasmus Andersson with the goal of making text easier to read on screen. The Inter open source, san serif typeface, has been used by GitHub and Mozilla for their platforms too.

TYPEFACE / FONT

Inter / Thin, Extra Light, Light, Regular, **Medium, Semi Bold Bold, Extra Bold, Black**

Figure 2-17. *Default Figma typeface Inter*

Changing from the default Inter typeface in Figma works much like most other applications; click the font family name "Inter" from the Properties ➤ Font section and choose or search for the typeface you want.

Figma has easy access to all the Google fonts, without needing to have them installed on your desktop computer. Figma also organizes fonts into categories (Figure 2-18) to choose from: All Fonts, In this file, Popular fonts, Google fonts, Variable fonts, and Installed by you. Figma also allows you to search for a specific font from the font menu.

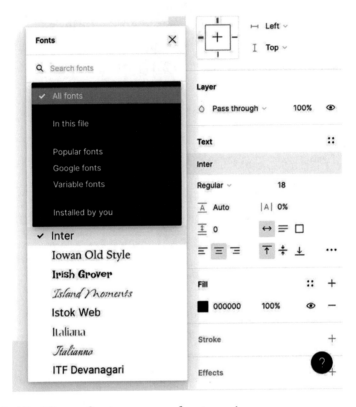

Figure 2-18. Figma font menu and categories

Text Properties

Figma offers all the basic features of type control:

- Select a typeface, Font weight, Font size, Line height, Letter spacing, Paragraph spacing

- Auto width, Auto height, Fixed size

- Horizontal text alignment: Text align left, Text align center, Text align right

- Vertical text alignment: Align top, Align middle, Align bottom

In the Text properties, clicking the triple ellipse icon … will open the Type settings panel displaying more options: Basic, Details, and Variable font options.

Figure 2-19 Figma text properties and type Settings panels.

Figure 2-19. *Figma Text Properties and Type Settings*

Font Pairing

Website or mobile app projects commonly have more than one typeface used in the project, but as a guideline, no more than three typefaces. Using more than three will remove the feeling of professionalism, make the text harder to read, and, in the worst cases, may resemble a ransom note.

Figure 2-20 Example of too many typefaces used in one project.

Figure 2-20. *A typographic ransom note*

Choosing multiple typefaces can be confusing – why are there so many different and similar typefaces? The goal for font selection is to pair two fonts in a way that creates contrast and interest for the reader. Selecting the pairings can be difficult. To help, here are three guidelines to avoid when choosing pairs and three to follow when choosing different fonts for a project.

- Avoid choosing a handwritten and a script typeface. These two compete for attention; instead, pair a script with a typeface that has less contrast like a sans serif. In fact, a rule of thumb is not to use handwritten or script fonts in your work.

- Avoid choosing two different display typefaces as they will compete for the reader's attention. Instead, pair a display typeface with a simple serif or sans serif typeface instead.

- Avoid choosing two typefaces where the letters are similar, for example, Helvetica and Arial; choose fonts that are different.

  Figure 2-21 Examples of poor font pairing.

Figure 2-21. *Examples of poor font pairing*

Now that you know what not to do, here are some suggestions for effective font pairings:

- Choose typefaces with multiple font weights as a simple way to create good typographic contrast. Consider using different font sizes to create contrast and visual hierarchy. You will be exploring this one in the "Your Turn" section of this chapter.

- Choose a sans serif typeface to pair with a serif typeface or vice versa to create a strong contrast.

- Choose a display font to draw attention and pair it with a sans serif typeface to create a balanced contrast between headings and paragraph text.

Figure 2-22 Examples of strong font pairing.

Figure 2-22. *Examples of strong font pairing*

Using two fonts is not a "hard and fast" rule. In fact, both Apple and Google have their own standard fonts that they recommend for their OS. Google suggests Roboto for Android devices, and Apple suggests San Francisco Pro (SF Pro) for iOS devices. Even though they are both quite different fonts, they are both sans serif fonts. The reason has more to do with readability than anything else. Serifs on smartphones can sometimes disappear.

Adding and Formatting Text in Figma

Text in Figma can either be directly entered into a text box or copied and pasted into a text box from a word processor such as Microsoft Word. In either situation, it all starts with a text box. Here's how:

1. Open a New Figma file and add an iPhone 14 15 Pro frame. With the frame created, select the Text tool and click once in the artboard. The cursor will blink where you click, indicating where the text will start. Type your name. If you select the text, you will see it is in a text box.

2.   Select the Text tool and draw out a Text box.

3.   Open the Loremipsum.doc file in the chapter download. When it opens, copy the text, return to Figma, and paste the text into the text box.

4.   In the text properties, use these settings:

- Font: Inter

- Size: 16

- Line Height: 24

- Alignment: Left

- Paragraph Spacing: 20

As you can see in Figure 2-23, the text isn't as crowded in the text box, and there is more space between the paragraphs.

It isn't only the text that you can manipulate. There are three icons beside the Paragraph Spacing area that work only with a selected text box. As shown in Figure 2-23, they are as follows:

- Auto Width: Select this and a block of text is converted into a single line of text.

- Auto Height: Select this and the text box contracts to the bottom of the last line of text.

- Fixed size. Select this and you can enter custom height and width values in the Properties panel or you can draw a side or a handle in the text box to manually adjust the size.

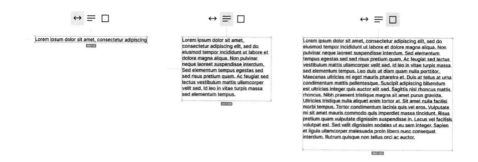

Figure 2-23. *Examples Figma type resizing property controls: Auto Width, Auto Height, and Fixed Size text boxes*

We used 16 for the size and 24 for the Line Height values. You may be wondering: "24 what?" When it comes to typography, type is measured in points. In Figma, all values are measured in pixels. Just to clear up the confusion, when it comes to working with type on a computer, points and pixels are interchangeable. One pixel = one point.

Your Turn

Figure 2-24. *Let's visit Switzerland*

The time has arrived to put everything we have presented in this chapter and the previous one into practice. In this exercise, you are going to create a web page promoting tourism in Switzerland (Figure 2-24). You will start with a blank frame, add a grid, and start adding images, logos, text, and other effects. Let's get started.

1. To start, open a new Design file from your Figma Dashboard.

2. Select the Frame tool, click once on the pasteboard, and change the Width value to 1440 and the Height value to 2550. The frame expands to those dimensions, and your workspace is created. Next double-click Frame 1 in the Layers panel and name it Swiss.

Throughout this exercise, we are going to be rigorous with our use of the Properties panel for placement, alignment, resizing, and so on. This is a best practice for a couple of reasons. The first is if images are simply moved around with the mouse (we call it "Mark One Eyeball"), the odds are very good a value could be 241.3. There is no such thing as one-third of a pixel. Using whole numbers makes the development process a breeze. You won't have the developers constantly questioning these values after handoff. We also should note there is a move toward "Pixel-Perfect" design, which, again, precludes the use of Properties containing a decimal value.

Adding a Grid

Grids are fundamental to UX Design in that they bring order to chaos. Think of a grid as the skeleton upon which the project is placed because it provides a method of controlling the placement of a screen's elements. A grid is also an invaluable development aid in that it provides accurate information regarding column spacing, margins, and alignment of all of the elements on the page. Here's how to create the grid for this web page:

1. Select View ➤ Layout Grids from the Figma menu bar.

2. With the Swiss frame selected, click the + sign in the Layout grid area of the Properties panel. Your grid looks like a sheet of Graph Paper. Let's change it.

3. Click the Grid icon, and when the Grid Properties dialog box appears, select Columns from the Grid pop-down menu (Figure 2-25).

Figure 2-25. *Changing a grid to Column in Figma's Layout Grid pop-down*

4. In the Columns dialog box, enter these values:

   - Count: 12

   - Margin: 50

   - Gutter: 12

The grid will change (Figure 2-26), and your developer now has what is needed when the file is handed off to development. Finally, for the balance of this exercise, we will keep the grid open.

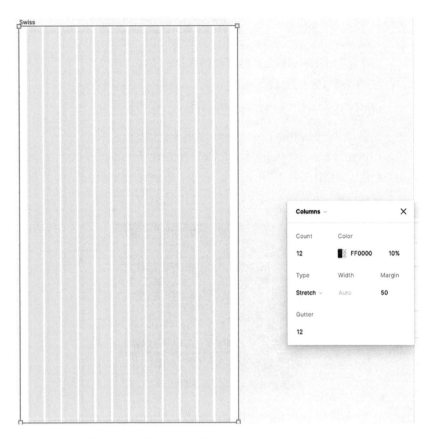

Figure 2-26. *The 12-column grid is created*

Adding the Header

It is a standard practice to add a header that allows navigating to sections of the website. In this exercise, you won't be creating the header. Instead, you will be adding it as a graphic. We are doing this to let you discover there are two ways to add graphic content to a screen. Let's start:

1. With the Figma file open, navigate to your Chapter 2 Exercise file and drag the Header.jpg file onto the page. The Header lands on the screen. As you have learned, Drag and Drop is one way of adding content. Delete the Header.

2. Select the Shapes pop-down and select Place image/video or press Shift-Command-K (Mac) or CTRL-Shift-K (PC) to open your Exercise folder (Figure 2-27).

Figure 2-27. *Using the Shapes pop-down to place images in a Figma screen*

3. Navigate to your Chapter 2 Exercise folder and select the Header.jpg file. Click Upload.

4. At first glance, nothing happens, but if you look up on the toolbar, there is a Place all button. Click it and the Header appears on the screen.

5. If you look over in the Layers panel, the image is sitting above the Swiss frame. Drag it on top of the Swiss frame. The image layer will indent, telling you it is now a part of the Swiss frame.

6. With the Header selected, you have two choices: drag it into place or do it by the numbers. Doing it by the numbers is far more precise than dragging. In the Properties panel, set the X and Y Values to 0.

Create the Hero Image

In this part of the exercise, we are going to add a rather large image to the top of the page along with some text that will serve as the site's headline. These images are typically called "Hero" images. Their purpose is to create a positive impression, and due to their simple design, they support your brand. Here's how to add the Hero image:

1. Using either technique in the previous exercise, add the Hero.jpg image to the Swiss frame. Set its X and Y values to 0. If the image covers the Header, drag the layer under the Header (Figure 2-28).

Figure 2-28. *The Hero image is added and located under the Header layer*

2. To add the headline, select the Text tool and
    draw out a text box. With the text box created,
    press the Caps Lock key on your keyboard
    and enter SWITZERLAND INSPIRED &
    INSPIRATIONAL. Finally, press the Return key
    between Switzerland and Inspired to create two
    lines of text.

Before we start formatting this text block, be sure you have the
Raleway font installed.

---

3. Obviously, the view is far too small. Set the Zoom
    value to 100% and bring the text into view.

Note   There are a couple of ways to zoom in and out of a Figma
project. You can use the Zoom menu in the upper right corner and
choose an option. You can also select the value and enter your own.
The Zoom pop-down also contains keyboard shortcuts. The most
common are Command/Ctrl-1 to fit all of the frames in the screen or
Command/Ctrl-0 to zoom to 100%.

---

4. Select Switzerland and use these values in the Text
    Properties area:

    • Font: Raleway

    • Weight: Regular

    • Size: 70

    • Line Height: 90

5. Select Inspired and Inspiration and use these values:

- Font: Raleway

- Weight: Extra Bold

- Size: 96

- Line Height: 90

If your text box is too big, drag the sides to make it more compact (Figure 2-29).

Figure 2-29. *The Text is formatted and the Text Box resized*

6. Select all of the Text, and in the Text properties, change the color to white (#FFFFFF). A strong contrast makes the text stand out and makes it accessible. If you can't see the text, move it above the Hero Layer.

7. Drag the Text Box into place over the image and drag the text layer under the Hero image. Feel free to select View ➤ Layout Grids to turn off the grid. Alternatively, you can select the Swiss frame and turn of the grid in the Properties panel.

8. Finally, with your Shift key held down, select both
    the Hero and the text layer. Right-click the selection
    and select Group Selection from the pop-down or
    press the Command/Ctrl-G key to create the group.
    Rename the Group to Hero.

Proper naming of your layers is critical. First off, your development
team will thank you because they know exactly what is where. If
you are sharing the work with your team, setting a policy for Layer
Naming before you start designing will boost productivity.

Creating the Explore Section of the Site

In this section, we are going to add five images promoting various
exploration ideas, an SVG image, and a headline for the section.
Here's how:

1. Bring a copy of the Logo.svg file to the page.
    Obviously, it is rather overpowering. Let's fix that.

2. First the logo arrived in its own frame. This can
    complicate things. Twirl down the frame and
    move the two vector layers under the Hero Layer.
    Group them and name the layer Logo. Delete the
    Logo1 frame.

When you add content such as SVG graphics, they will actually be
placed in their own frame. When you move a placed SVG vector
graphic into another layer the frame the contained them will remain.
Always delete the frame to avoid the developers asking what is
supposed to be in that empty frame.

---

3. With the Logo group selected, use these values in
    the Properties panel:

    - Width and Height: 24

    - X: 708

    - Y: 712

4. Add a text box and press the Caps Lock key. Enter
    EXPLORE SWITZERLAND ADVENTURE AWAITS
    FOR TOURISTS AND EXPLORERS.

The text you just added will be quite large. In Figma, the last Text
properties used will be applied to the subsequent text you may add.

---

5. Select Explore Switzerland and add these Text
    properties:

    - Font: Raleway

    - Weight: Bold

    - Size: 32

    - Line Height Auto

    - Click Autowidth

    - Alignment: Centered

    - Click Top Alignment

6. Select the next line of the text block and add these
    Text properties:

    - Font: Raleway

    - Size: 20

- Weight: Regular

- Line Height Auto

- Click Autowidth

- Alignment: Centered

- Click Top Alignment

7. Drag the left and right sides of the Text in to reduce its width. Drag it under the Logo layer.

8. With the Text Box selected, click the Horizontal Centre icon to move the center of the Swiss frame and change the Y value to 750 to move it closer to the Logo.

9. Finally, let's make this text box and Logo responsive. In the Layers panel, select both layers and select Center from the Constraints pop-down in the Properties panel. This ensures they keep their placement should they be viewed with different screen sizes or different devices.

Adding Cards to the Design

When Google included the Card component in its Material Design specification for Android, Cards quickly migrated to iOS devices and web pages. What makes them so effective is they display the contents and action regarding a single subject. Cards contain a single image, some brief descriptive text, and a button that enables a user to examine a specific, focused topic.

To this point in the exercise, you have been placing individual images. Let's look at how easy it is to add five cards with a single click to the Swiss Artboard. Here's how:

1. To start, zoom out to 50%, then select Place image/ video or press Command/Ctrl-Shift-K to open the Exercise folder. You also might want to Grid, Shift-G.

2. With the Command (macOS) or Control key (Windows) held down, select each of the Card images from the exercise folder and click Upload. Your cursor will display a thumbnail image with a red dot and the number of images to place, in this case 5.

3. Click anywhere on the Swiss frame to place each of the Card images. With that out of the way, let's use the grid to create a rather interesting grouping of the cards.

4. Select the Markets card and move it to the left edge of column 3 and change its Y property to 835. The first card is in position.

5. Move the History card to the left edge of column 3 and the Cathedrals card to the right edge of column 5.

6. Select the History and Cathedral cards and set their Y property to 1374. Notice how both cards are evenly spaced from each other and the Markets card.

7. Select the Alps card and move it to the left edge of column 7. When you see a red guide appear at the top of the image, it is aligned with the top of the Markets image. Even so, let's add a bit of distraction and change the Alps Y property to 905. By breaking up the alignment, the user will notice the entire group.

8. Move the Chocolate card to align with the left edge of the Alps card and set its Y property to 1444. The cards are in place (Figure 2-30), and the Explore section is complete.

Zoom in to 100 or higher to ensure elements are aligned to the grid. Use your arrow keys to move them in 1-pixel increments.

---

9. Finally, move the cards under the Text layer and group them. Name the Group Cards. Next select the Logo, text, and Cards layers and group them. Name the group Explore.

Figure 2-30. *The cards are aligned to the grid and evenly spaced*

Adding a Text File in Figma

There will be occasions where you will be handed the copy for your document. Unfortunately, there is no text import feature in Figma. Here's how to get around that:

1. Add a text box to your Figma screen.

2. Navigate to your Chapter 2 Exercise folder and open the Social text file.

3. Select all the text and copy it to your clipboard.

4. Return to Figma, click once inside your text block, and paste the text. It appears in the text box and adopts the last Text setting used in the document.

5. Move the text block to the left edge of column 5.

6. Select the sharing text and change the font setting to Raleway Regular, 20 pixels.

7. With the text block selected, click the Align Horizontal Center icon. The text aligns to the center of the screen.

8. Finally, drag the text layer below the Explore group.

Creating the Social Media Section

With the headline in place, the decision is to add a variety of photos visitors to Switzerland have taken and posted on Social Media. This area needs something to separate it from being perceived as a continuation of the Explore area. The headline somewhat works, but that Swiss flag does exactly this to separate the Explore area from the Hero image. Here's how:

1. Scroll up to the Swiss flag logo and select it.

2. With the logo selected, press and hold the Option/
    Alt-Shift key and drag a copy of the icon to just
    above the text. The Option/Alt key coupled with a
    drag will create a copy. Add in the Shift key and the
    drag is constrained to either a vertical or horizontal
    direction.

3. With the logo still selected, set its Y value to 1770
    and the text block's Y value to 1800. Name this new
    layer Flag.

4. To further draw the User's attention to the photos, it
    is decided to place them on a color background and
    to include an Instagram logo to reinforce the source
    of the photos.

5. Select the Rectangle tool and draw out a rectangle
    that starts on the left edge of column 2 and ends on
    the right edge of column 11.

6. With the Rectangle selected, set its fill color to
    #740C14 (Maroon) with an Alpha value of 70% to
    tone it down. Finally, change the Height value to 560
    and the rectangle's Y value to 1850 (Figure 2-31) and
    name it Background in the Layers panel. Move this
    Layer under the new Logo layer.

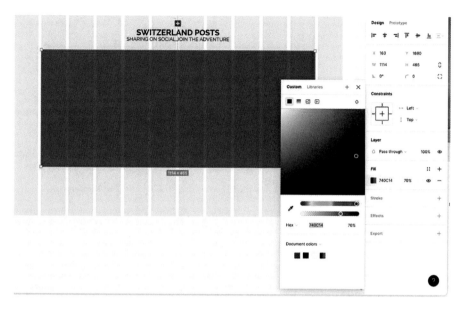

Figure 2-31. *The Fill color and location of the Social Media background are set*

Adding the Images

In this section, we import the "Social" images and deal with one image that is "not like the others." Let's get started:

1. Select all of the images in the SocialImages folder in your Chapter 2 Exercise folder and drag them on top of the background. Move them into position to match Figure 2-32. These images are going to bump up against column edges, and they are somewhat obstructed by the Background's opacity. In the Layers panel, turn off the visibility of the background layer.

Figure 2-32. _The Instagram images are placed over the background_

To ensure the images all align with each other, select each row and click the Top Align icon and then the Horizontal Spacing icon. Do the same thing with the bottom row.

2. To set the Y value for the top three images, select the images and change their Y value to 1900. Select the bottom row of the images and change their Y value to 2130. Not only have we made room for an Instagram logo, but we have also provided a bit of visual interest.

3. You may have noticed the Horn image doesn't have a white stroke. That is easy to add.

4. Select the image, and over in the Stroke Properties, click the + sign to open the Stroke properties panel (Figure 2-33).

5. With the image selected, use these values:

    - Color: White (#FFFFFF)

    - Stroke: Inside

    - Thickness: 3 pixels

Figure 2-33. *Applying a stroke to an element*

Strokes in Figma come in three styles: Centre, Inside, and Outside. They do affect design and development. Let's assume we add a 6-pixel Outside stroke to the image. In this case, 6 pixels will run around the outside of the image and add 6 pixels to its width and height values. If Centre is chosen, there will be three pixels outside the image and three inside. Again, the width and height values increase by 3 pixels. When it comes to hand off to development, the stroke width and type are needed by the development team.

---

6. Finally, turn on the opacity of the Background layer.

7. The final piece to add to this section is the Instagram logo. Drag the Instagram.svg file onto the background. Two issues are immediately evident. It is too large and the wrong color.

8. Open the Instagram frame in the Layers panel and drag the vector to the layer above the Background layer. Rename it "InstagramVector" and delete its frame at the top on the Layers panel.

9. The great thing about .SVG images is they are editable. Double-click the icon and you will see the black fill color in the properties. Change it to white (#FFFFFF).

10. With the color changed, use the Properties panel to reduce its size to 24 × 24 and to set its X value to 708 and its Y value to 1889 (Figure 2-34).

Figure 2-34. *SVG graphics are editable, meaning you can change their color*

11. Select the images, Background, text, and Flag layers in the Instagram section and group them. Name the group Instagram.

Finishing the Web Page

1. To start, twirl down the Instagram group and select the Logo layer. We are going to use this layer in the Footer.

2. With the layer selected, press Command/Ctrl-D to duplicate the layer.

3. With the duplicate selected, set its X value in the Properties panel to 52 and the Y value to 2512. Move the Logo out of the group and change its color to gray (#525252). Change the name to FlagGrey.

4. Add a text box and enter TOUR SWITZERLAND. Use these settings:

   - Font: Raleway Medium

   - Size: 10

   - Autowidth

   - Aligment: Left, Top

   - X Value: 85

   - Y Value: 2518

5. Select both the Logo and the text and add them to a group named Footer.

6. Drag the SVG logos from the exercise files into the bottom of the frame: logo facebook blk.svg, logo instagram blk.svg, logo instagram white.svg, logo X blk.svg and Logo.svg. Open each of the frames and move the vector files into the Footer group. Facebook contains two vectors. Rename them Facebook and FacebookBkgrnd and group them. This will make it easier to resize.

7. Select each of the logos and set their W and H values to 30.

8. Select the Facebook logo group in the Layers panel and move it to the right edge of column 12.

9. Move the X and Instagram logos to somewhat align with the Facebook logo.

10. With the three logos selected, align their tops and select Tidy up for the Horizontal distribution.

11. Close the Footer group and deselect Layout Grids in the View menu to turn off the grid.

12. Zoom out to Zoom to Fit and you have created a page that not only has an interesting design but is ready for handoff to development.

13. Before you hand it over to development, rename the page ExploreSwitzerland.

You Have Learned

- How to create a Figma frame for a web page

- Add a grid to a Figma frame and how to use a grid

- Place properly prepared elements on a grid in a Figma frame

- Select and place multiple items with one click

- Apply scaling factors to images

- Prepare video for mobile streaming

- Use the 1x versions of images and leave the other versions for use by the development team

- Edit SVG images

- Add and format text

- Import a block of text into a Figma Text frame

- How to properly name layers and create layer groups as an aid to development

- How to add strokes around selected elements

We admit this was a rather complicated chapter. Even so, by applying what you have learned in these first two chapters, you have learned how your layout of the UI in Figma will make the inevitable handoff to the front-end and/or back-end development teams go a lot smoother. In many instances, the developers are working ahead of you, handing it off for testing and then asking you to address the issues raised in testing. Do this, and the frustration level between design and development will be reduced.

For the balance of this book, we will be digging deeper into where Figma's many features fit into the entire user experience process from research to development.

CHAPTER 3

Figma and the UX Process

Fall in love with the user, not the technology.

One of the authors was recently asked at a Local Meetup, "What exactly is UX?" His standard response to this question was: "Whatever you want it to mean. I can put 20 UX pros in a room and ask them that question and get 23 different definitions." This confusion is rooted in regarding UX as being confused with such jobs as graphic design, front-end development, UX design, and any other position you can think of.

UX, User Experience, is both a mission and a process, and they are fundamentally different from each other. The UX process is where Figma fits in because the UX workflow is a complex process that starts with initial research and moves into conceptualization, design and development, and off to a web server: Apple's App Store or Google's Play Store. As you may gather, a lot of very specialized skills are brought to bear on the project. These skills may require UX researchers, UX designers, writers, motion designers, interaction designers, user testers, and highly skilled developers. This process involves a lot of software tools such as Figma, brainstorming using, for example, FigJam, and careful planning and budgeting with everything moving through multiple iterations until the prototype is buffed, polished, shiny, and ready to land on devices or web pages.

© Tom Green and Kevin Brandon 2024
T. Green and K. Brandon, *UX Design with Figma*, Design Thinking,
https://doi.org/10.1007/979-8-8688-0324-6_3

The UX mission is, essentially, to fall in love with the user. It focuses on the person who will load the product or service onto their device and makes life easier for that individual in such a way they will continue to use the product or the web page.

The mission drives the process. The process is not the mission. Figma is a crucial tool in the process and ensures the process remains focused on the mission where the prototype can be tested, expanded, refined, and modified to meet the needs of the user.

What Exactly Is a Prototype

Figma's primary role in the UX process is to create digital prototypes that reflect the UX designer's intent. The word "digital" is important because the UX process starts as a hypothesis and then moves to paper, not a computer. As well, there are a variety of prototypes that will be circulated to the stakeholders and team as well as, on occasion, sent out for User Testing, this begs the question: What exactly is a prototype?

A prototype is nothing more than a model of the product reflecting the goals of the project that are set in the research and planning phase. The prototype is constantly iterated and subjected to regular User Testing before release. This constant iteration is important because prototypes identify "pain points" resulting from User Testing that need to be resolved before release. Prototypes, especially digital prototypes created in Figma, are where designers can play what we call "What If Games" and experiment with ideas or approaches. For example, "What if this button turns blue when the User rolls over it." That idea can be quickly created in Figma and circulated to the design team for comment.

As you may have guessed, there are several types of prototypes that can be produced. They include the following:

- Paper Prototypes: These are a low-risk and low-cost method of communicating your design intent. As shown in Figure 3-1, you can sketch a variety of screens and even user test them by asking the testers to perform specific tasks and obtain feedback regarding the placement of the elements.

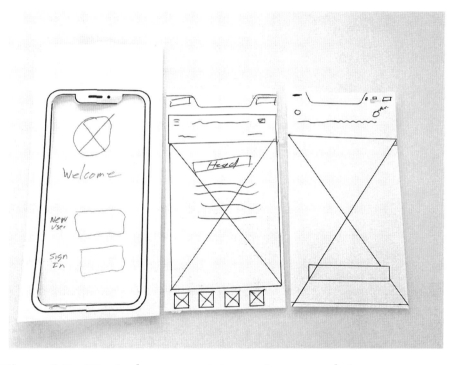

Figure 3-1. *A typical paper prototype using a template*

If you are looking for a template for paper prototypes, the Nielsen Norman Group has a free template for an iPhone or a web page. You can download the template here: Paper_Prototyping_Cutout_Kit_Letter-compressed_1.pdf (http://nngroup.com).

- Low-Fidelity Prototypes: These are essentially digital versions of the wireframes that have been sketched out on paper. LowFi prototypes (sometimes referred to as LoFi mockups) are a step up from the paper prototype because they move into the digital realm. As you can see in Figure 3-2, they are low detail-low functionality artifacts. What they do offer is the ability to add very rudimentary interactivity for User Testing.

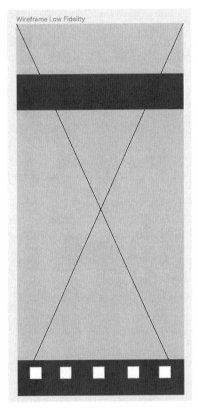

Figure 3-2. *A low-fidelity digital prototype can be created in Figma*

An uncomfortable truth is that many designs start on paper, not in Figma. Why paper? It is cheap and disposable. We are going to get deeper into the use of paper in the UX Design process in Chapter 5 as we examine the process of wireframing.

- Medium-Fidelity Prototypes: This prototype starts the process of bringing the project to life. It presents the designer's intent. It gives the stakeholders their first glimpse at the interface, and if there are a series of screens, the whole series can be presented as a "Click Through" prototype with light interactivity. If this version is based on a low-fidelity prototype created in Figma, it becomes a rather quick process as the images and content simply replace the boxes from the LoFi mockup.

Figure 3-3. *A medium-fidelity prototype can be created in Figma and contains light interactivity*

- High-Fidelity Prototypes: This prototype mimics the final product. It will be subjected to numerous iterations and User Tests to ensure everything does what it is supposed to do. When sign-off is achieved, the files can be marked as ready for development (Figure 3-4) and handed off. When handed off to development, this prototype becomes nothing more than a reference aid and will be sliced, diced, and eventually disposed of by the development team.

Figure 3-4. *High-fidelity prototypes can be marked as ready for development in Figma*

A high-fidelity prototype is not the final project. Once they are sent over to development, they are ripped apart, which is why prototypes should be regarded as disposable artifacts.

Determining the Platform

In many respects, the smartphone and tablet markets are the "Wild West." The device manufacturers compete on screen size, feature set, and resolution. To top it all off, you have no control whatsoever over what device or version of device the User will use to access your app or website. Add two competing operating systems – iOS and Android – and you have no control over which version of the OS is being used to access your content. A great example of this is Apple's addition of the Dynamic Island to the iPhone 14, which isn't available on previous versions that only have the "Notch" because the Dynamic Island increases the height of the Status area. Therefore, it is critical for the team to identify what devices to design for once the Research phase of the project is completed.

Figma gives you a very handy way of accommodating device choices. Here's how:

1. Open a new Design File from your Figma Dashboard. When the document opens, click the Frame tool. The Design area of the Properties panel asks you what size frame to choose based on device.

2. Twirl down the Phone area and select the iPhone 14 Pro. A frame with those dimensions is added.

3. Select the Frame in the Layers panel and press Command-D (Mac) or Ctrl-D (PC) twice to create two duplicate frames. Name the frames Home, Login, and Main (Figure 3-5).

Figure 3-5. *The iPhone screens are in place and ready for content*

At this point, you could add three Android screens under the iPhone screens. As you keep adding screens, though, the workspace will become chaotic. There is a better way. Use Figma's Pages feature to bring order to this potential chaos. Here's how.

4. Over in the Layers panel, click on the Page 1 link to open the Pages area. Double-click Page 1 and change the name to iPhone 14.

5. Click the + sign. A new page – Page 2 – opens. Rename it to Android Large.

6. With the Page selected, add an Android Large frame and, again, duplicate the frame two times and rename them Home, Login, and Main (Figure 3-6).

7. Click the iPhone 14 page and the iPhone frames appear.

Figure 3-6. *Use the Pages feature of Figma to manage designing for various platforms*

Figma's Pages feature does a lot more than simply separating design spaces. For example, a series of Pages could contain all of the documentation for the project, or a place for master components. You could use a page to experiment with various designs or interactions. The best aspect of the Pages feature is they are all contained in one document and anyone with access to the project can open any page to check progress or add to the page. For example, one designer could be tasked with designing for iPhone while another is tasked with designing for Android. Instead of separating Figma documents, both platforms can be worked on, simultaneously in a single Figma document.

Building a Team in Figma

We have always regarded UX Design as a team-based sport. By this, we mean a team of specialists who bring their very specific skill set to bear upon the project at various points between concept and upload. This is

115

why the term UX designer or UI designer can no longer be vaguely defined. Budgets and project scopes have increased, and even though there may not be the resources for a full team ranging from researchers to full stack developers, there is still room for a few "generalists" with a very specific role in the UX process.

The odd thing about UX Design being a team sport is the size of the team can range from just you to a dozen or more people with very specific roles. Even so, the process follows a somewhat common series of steps, and the individuals involved in them have rather defined roles but are involved in the multidisciplinary approach to UX Design.

Each member of the team should be able to:

- Understand the problem and potential solution

- Clearly communicate their thinking to the other members of the team

- Embrace the importance of feedback

- Collaborate with the other members of the team

- Have a broad view and understanding of the role of each member of the team

So who are these people and what do they do? A team could include the following:

- The Client: This may seem out of place, but you need to understand the UX designer is the client's advocate and ensures the client's business objectives are met. This requires the client to be regularly briefed on the project's progress and will be involved in the approval process.

- UX Designer: Contrary to popular belief, the UX designer doesn't design Figma pages. This individual is responsible for managing the UX process and ensuring the business objectives are achieved.

- UI Designer: This role is responsible for developing the User Interface in Figma.

- Interaction Designer: This role is charged with the design of all interactions from button presses to navigation. In many cases, this individual is deeply involved in the creation of the HiFi prototype and even User Testing.

- Motion Designer: This role is responsible for creating the animations and screen transitions that remain faithful to the project's intent without interfering with the user's goal of accessing information.

- UX Writer: Responsible for creating user-friendly content and ensuring the integrity of the branded message.

- Front-End Developer: This individual will be responsible for coding the UI, including HTML, CSS, and JavaScript.

- Back-End Developer: This individual codes the server-side logic for the product including databases, APIs, and server-side scripting.

- Technical Writer: This individual is tasked for writing the product's technical documentation including user manuals and tutorials.

- Usability Specialist: This could be an individual or a team who conducts regular User Testing as the product moves through production. This testing ensures the product meets user needs.

Though you may think each member simply completes their task and moves on, you would be wrong.

Each member of the team will be involved, at all times, in all phases as the project moves from concept to release. UX designers couldn't do their job if they didn't clearly understand the conclusions from the Design Researchers. UI designers couldn't do their job if the Visual Designers, Copywriters, Content Strategists, and so on if feedback is not provided at all stages of the project. Finally, the Developer couldn't wire up if they were not working closely with the UI designer.

As we said at the top of this section, this is a team sport and collaboration is the key to a successful project completion. Just understanding that the UX process is not a straight line from concept to release will help manage project expectations in producing a well-thought-out product. This is why we refer to the UX design process as being "messy."

Creating a Team Project

Figma has firmly tied itself to a collaborative work environment and has built the Teams feature into your Dashboard. Just be aware that there are limits to the features available based upon which plan you or your organization has purchased. For this book, we will be working with a Professional plan, but as you can see in Figure 3-7, the feature set depends upon the Plan type and price.

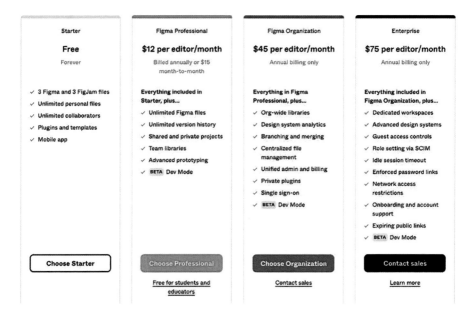

Figure 3-7. *The various plans available*

Setting up a team in Figma is a relatively simple process that is usually done by the UX designer. Here's how it works:

1. In your Dashboard, click the Create new team button (Figure 3-8) and give it a name. In our Dashboard, we have set up a Team Project named Figma Book. At the moment, there is only one member.

Figure 3-8. *A team has been created, and the only member is the person who created the team*

2. If you click the Admin Console button, the team members appear (Figure 3-9). The Admin Console is where you can see who the members of the team are including their Permissions and Roles.

Figure 3-9. *The Admin Console is where you manage the team*

3. To add New members, click on the Team name and click the Invite button. The Invite team members dialogue box opens (Figure 3-10), and this is where you can not only issue the invitations but assign a role. As you can see, there are two possible roles:

    • Can View: This individual, for example, the client, can see the files and comment.

    • Can Edit: This individual, such as the UI designer, has access to the team file and can work on it.

4. Individuals can be invited by sending them the link or invited to participate directly by email.

As you can see in Figure 3-10, one individual has been invited with Can Edit privileges. The client, with Can View privileges, has been sent the link to the Team. In both cases, the recipients have to accept the invitation.

Figure 3-10. *Figma teams are created by Invitation Only*

A major feature of Figma is Collaborative Editing. When this feature is in play, two designers with Editing permissions can, simultaneously, work on a single screen or Page, and each will see what the other is doing. Showing how this works in a book is not possible. Instead, Saasdesign.io has a rather concise explanation of Collaborative Editing in Figma (`www.saasdesign.io/learn/figma-real-time-collaboration/`).

Sharing and Collaboration

Though Figma is an awesome design tool, its ability to share files and collaborate with team members is what sets it apart from the rest of the prototyping applications currently available. Every Figma document available to the team has a big blue Sharing button up in the right corner of the toolbar. Just be aware that shared files can only be viewed in a browser.

Here's how to share a file:

1. Click the Share button.

2. A dialog box (Figure 3-11) opens, and this is where
    you can share the prototype with stakeholders using
    the same methods as inviting team members to the
    project. You will notice there is an extra permission:
    Can view prototypes. Select this and the recipient
    has access to the prototype but not the Figma Pages
    associated with that prototype.

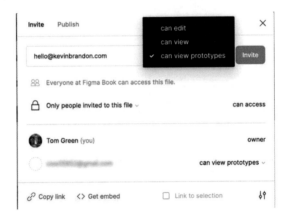

Figure 3-11. *Figma files can be shared with stakeholders and others
but can only be viewed in a browser*

There is also another critical feature built into sharing: Feedback.

If ever there was a minefield located in any UX Design project, it is
feedback. Ego can get involved. Personalities can clash. Stakeholders in
various areas remain silent and uninvolved because they may be afraid of
embarrassing themselves and a host of other pitfalls and faux pas.

When building an app or a website, it is critical to incorporate user
and team feedback focused on the end goal as you move through the UX
Design process. Why? Getting relevant user and team feedback in the

very early stages allows you to maximize your design and development resources by limiting the number of iterations each phase will undergo as the project moves to completion.

There are a number of ways of gathering it. They include the following:

- In Person: This is invaluable because not only do you benefit from the comments but also get to see how the user interacts with the interface. When it comes to the team, this could be in the form of a design or project review. Just keep in mind the comments should not be in the realm of "I don't get it." If you don't get it, say why you don't get it.

- Use Figma: Figma allows you to circulate your concepts and prototypes to users and the team, and they can provide specific, not general, feedback. This is accomplished by letting people pin their comments to a specific element, which we will get into next.

- Email is probably the worst method. Most of the feedback will overwhelm specifics with generalities. For example, "I found it difficult to order an item because it took me a while to figure out how." If you do use this method, you also might want to include a series of questions relating to the specific task to be examined.

Our advice is to determine your feedback policy right at the start so you can develop a protocol for assessing any feedback and how it will be integrated into your UX Design process.

Having said all of that, here's how to add comments that provide feedback:

1. In this screen (Figure 3-12), the file has been shared and is open in the reviewer's browser, and the Comment area in the Properties panel has been selected.

2. The reviewer notes an issue with the Flag icon. He clicks beside it, and a text box opens where he can present his concern. Note the blue text balloon. This indicates where the reviewer is commenting.

3. Once the comment has been added to the Text input box, clicking the Blue arrow attaches the comment to the screen.

Figure 3-12. *Reviewers can attach comments to the screens*

4. When the comment is submitted, it will appear on the project's screen. The reviewer's icon appears where the comment was made, and when the icon is clicked, the comment opens (Figure 3-13).

Figure 3-13. *The reviewer's comments and feedback appear where the comment was added*

There are a couple of ways of dealing with comments:

- A reply to the comment can be sent to the reviewer.

- Click the ellipsis in the Comment properties, and the comment can be marked as unread or the comment and all responses can be deleted. Once the issue has been dealt with, clicking the arrow in the Comment marks it as resolved (Figure 3-14).

Figure 3-14. *Once an issue has been successfully dealt with, the comment or thread can be marked as resolved*

Figma and User Testing

Let's start by being really clear about User Testing: It is not a Nice-to-Have. It is a Must-Have. The reason is welded directly to that first word in UX: User.

We are not huge fans of the word "user" when it comes to testing. It is too impersonal because it forces you to regard the people, with all of their flaws and idiosyncrasies, that will use your application or website as being somewhat homogeneous. This actually runs counter to all of the research and documentation you will have gathered about your users before you start the Design phase. Even more important is that regarding your users as homogenous runs counter to the UX Mission.

Testing is both humbling and exhilarating. Humbling in that we, initially, make informed assumptions about what the users need. We then plunk the projects down, and people unfamiliar with our assumptions have the uncanny ability to either confirm the brilliance of our assumptions or utterly destroy them. Either way, they will illuminate the path through your project and let you know, in no uncertain terms, what makes things easy or difficult for them as they move through your project.

In its purest form, User Testing is no more than watching people interact, unaided, with your project by asking them to do something. For example, during any prototype phase, you might ask, "How would you get to the next screen?" (Figure 3-15). Then you sit back and watch. Then be prepared to be surprised. You are going to discover one of two things: Your design and assumptions were correct, or you discover what doesn't work, which isn't a bad thing because you learn early on in the process what needs to be fixed.

Figure 3-15. *Paper prototypes are ideal where the user is asked:*
"What would you touch to…."

There is one thing you need to know about choosing who will do the test. Don't select friends or family because they will tell you what they think you want to know. The same goes for the team. They are too close to the project and won't give you a dispassionate response. Of course, they know what element to tap because they had a hand in creating it.

The bottom line is this: Test. Test. Test. Test early and test often. Why? It is cheaper to fix a major issue at the various stages of the project than to withdraw the project and start over. This usually happens when it is released into the wild and you start hearing rather nasty things from people who tell you, "This just doesn't work."

Usability Testing vs. User Testing

When it comes to testing your designs or, even more granular, your hypothesis, User Testing is only half of the equation. There are actually two types of testing: Usability Testing and User Testing.

User Testing is a more global approach in that it focuses on all potential users. Usability Testing focuses on a specific segment of the users. For example, a Usability Test may be conducted to learn how families touring Switzerland will use the app, and another may be conducted at the same time to learn how younger tourists would use the app. A User Test could be conducted on both groups to examine how easy it is to use the app. In short, the User Test validates the hypothesis, whereas the Usability Test validates the design.

So what's the difference?

User Testing involves observation and interviews to understand user behaviors, needs, and expectations. These tests are conducted during the early stages of design and development and help to answer such questions as

- Who are the users?

- What are their goals?

- What are their frustrations and pain points?

- What motivates them to use the app?

Usability Testing is more granular in that it evaluates how easy and efficient it is for users to interact with the design. This testing method is regularly employed as the project moves through both the design and development phases of the project. Using the Sharing features of Figma, prototypes can be put in front of users to answer such questions as

- How easy is it for users to learn how to use the product?

- How quickly can users complete certain tasks?

- What are the common errors users make when using the app?

- How satisfied are users with the experience?

As well, Usability Testing doesn't need to be conducted when the screens or pages are being designed. For example, the Sign In/Log In process for the app could be tested to identify any issues with the process and then conduct another test to ensure the issues have indeed been resolved.

Testing early and testing often is far more cost-efficient than doing major tests at various milestones and, literally, starting over based on user feedback. Best of all, you get to watch users stumble through your project, which, as we said earlier, is humbling. By watching your potential users actually use the product, you gain a deep insight into what they do, not what you think they should do.

Usability Testing Requires Context

Being able to subject your designs or project to rigorous Usability Testing through the browser and commenting highlights major issues. Even so, they do nothing more than showing the screens or pages on a black background. In many respects, they have about the same context as viewing an image in Apple's or Google's Photo applications. At some point, your Figma work is going to have to be subjected to testing on an iPhone, an Android phone, and an Apple or Android tablet. It is at this point the testers can see your efforts in context.

Keep in mind, these are the target devices determined during the Research phase of the project and you, and the testers, are about to discover not all is as it seems when viewed in a browser. This is due to the fact that no two devices are the same. For example, you may choose to design for the iPhone 15. Not so fast, as you can see in Figure 3-16, there are three different models with two different screen sizes. Go deeper, and you'll discover the Pro Max version has a higher resolution than the other two models. Android is even worse with the manufacturers creating wildly different devices and screens. Each of these differences could affect the usability of your project.

Figure 3-16. *One iPhone model, two different sets of specifications*

Eventually, you are going to have to move the work onto a device for testing. Here's how.

On your smartphone, navigate to the App Store or Play Store and locate the Figma app.

1. Open the app and log into your Figma account. A list of your recent projects will appear (Figure 3-17).

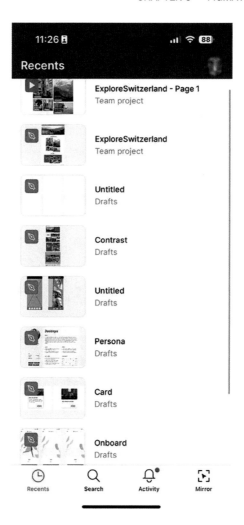

Figure 3-17. *You start by selecting a file in the Figma Smartphone app*

2. Select the file to be viewed. In this case, it is the Explore Switzerland screen shown in Figure 3-18. When it opens, all interactivity and motion will be available. If this is a Usability Test, the person conducting the test will ask the user to perform

specific tasks and carefully note any stumbles or issues. This report will be shared with the team, and the issues can be addressed.

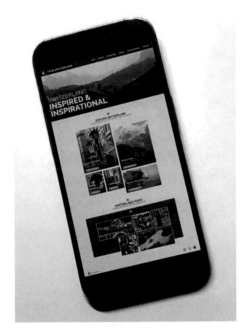

Figure 3-18. *The Figma project opens in the Figma app on your phone*

Iteration and the "Messy" UX Design Process

There is no such thing as a straight line from research to launch. As you have seen, regular Usability Testing is going to identify issues that need to be changed. For example, an important button on a device can't be easily reached with the user's thumb. The Sign In/Log In process is seen as too complex and needs to be made more user-friendly.

It isn't only User Testing that will bring issues to the surface. As the process moves along from ideation to development, it is not uncommon for the team to settle on a design, only to discover it is too complex or the developers notify the design team that a feature takes far too long to load. This brings us to the point that iteration doesn't end when the project is handed off to development. One company, Intercom, has actually formalized this process as shown in Figure 3-19. Any project starts with a discussion between the design and development teams to roughly map out the intent of the project. Intermission is where a one-page document is prepared summarizing those discussions and the Design process gets underway. As the parts of the project are handed off to development, the development team makes suggestions: "It takes too long for the API to grab the approval from the vendor. A spinner might not be appropriate." The design team iterates on the spinner, and once everyone is satisfied with the solution, the project is sent out for Usability Testing and the design/build cycle restarts.

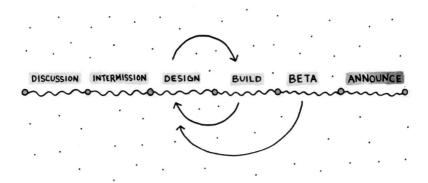

Figure 3-19. *The Intercom process is a collaborative effort between the design and development teams*

In fact, the UX process is a lot like sanding a piece of wood. You start out with a rough plank – your concept – and by repeatedly sanding using finer and finer sandpaper, that rough piece of wood becomes a smooth plank that is added to a table.

Iteration is crucial to the successful completion of a project. It is a cyclical process where projects move through conceptualization, prototype development, testing, and, finally, evaluation. Repeat. Eventually, that rough design is sanded down and results in a more effective user-centric solution than the one the team started with.

Here are other reasons why iteration is so important:

- Enhanced User Experience: By designing and refining based on user feedback, the experience becomes more personalized.

- Reduced Risk: There are two aspects to this. From a Design point of view, usability issues are revealed, and they can be resolved before they become so big; a complete redesign is undertaken. That is expensive. There is also the business risk. Remember that loading issue pointed out by the development team? Users might assume the app has crashed, and if it continues, they will abandon the app.

- Promotes Innovation: This is where what we call "What If Games" become the catalyst for innovation. A simple "What if...?" question such as "What if these three screens were reduced to one screen?". The team will then spend time thinking this through and prototyping a variety of concepts and discovers, after User Testing, the concept they have landed on that users find it remarkably easy to complete that three-screen task in one screen.

As we stated at the beginning, iteration is a messy process. Here are some of the issues that make it messy:

- Time: Iteration takes time, and in Agile, Lean UX, or rapid prototyping environments, this can be a real bump in the road. In this case, the key is to clearly define the problem and the possible solutions. Do this and User Testing will result in focused feedback that guides you to the solution or supports your hypothesis.

- Resources: Iteration requires people, time, and budget. The solution is to ensure the right tools are available and the iteration and workflow methodologies are clearly established and, in some cases, documented.

- Stakeholder Resistance: Stakeholders have a financial risk they are willing to undertake. Stopping or adding resources to iterations affects the budget. In this case, before the project starts, stakeholders need to be aware of the importance of iteration.

As you have discovered, iteration is directly related to and from user feedback. Each test needs a clear goal; if you don't know what information you want to obtain, you risk running a test that is doomed to failure due to a lack of actionable insights. It is much easier to run a series of small, highly focused tests throughout the design and development process than a couple of big ones here and there.

Accessibility and Inclusion in Figma

Accessibility and inclusion are two subjects that have to be addressed during the Planning phase of a project. Treat these two subjects as an afterthought or something to be dealt with when a project is in the Design phase, and you will discover a significant number of your potential users won't be able to use the project and move on. For example:

- Have you considered the kinds of physical disabilities that can impede access to your website or mobile app?

- How many of you include cultural differences in determining the potential worldwide access of your project? It could be something as simple as text that flows from right to left, color choice, or even imaging.

- How many of you have actually seen how an individual with color blindness "sees" your images?

- How many of you are familiar with the various federal Accessibility regulations in the countries where your work will be accessed?

- How many of you are familiar with the WCAG 2.0 Accessibility guidelines found at www.w3.org/TR/WCAG20/?

Accessibility is not just worrying about vision. Accessibility actually splits into two distinct components: perception and inclusion. What you need to know is Figma deals with neither aspect of the topic. That job is left to some pretty powerful plug-ins. Before we move into the plug-ins, let's step back and consider what the term "perception" involves.

The Cambridge Dictionary defines perception as "The faculty of an awareness of things through the physical senses, esp. sight." What it comes down to is how your users will see something and understand what they are seeing. There are two plug-ins – Stark and Adee – that are commonly regarded as dealing with vision issues. Dig deeper and your team will discover they also deal with how people will perceive on-screen elements and how they will move around your interfaces and perceive your color choices, all of which, like the words on the screen, will affect their access to understanding. Bottom line? They force us to change our assumptions regarding how our work is perceived.

For example, not everybody will perceive an image of a Swiss city as you would. As shown in Figure 3-20, the images may look like they have been color graded or blurred.

Figure 3-20. *Perception is how your users perceive images based on their vision impairment*

Are we inferring that you need to accommodate every vision issue into your work? No. These plug-ins ask us to become aware of how segments of our User Base will perceive our work and for us to make informed accessibility decisions before a single pixel is illuminated.

The other half of accessibility is inclusion. As a social issue, inclusion and diversity are intertwined and becoming more prevalent every day. The UX process requires us to empathize with our potential users, and inclusion is a key component of empathy. This is often overlooked in our rush to get a project shipped.

How is it overlooked? One of the authors' ages is north of 50. Rarely, if ever, does he see a recruiting ad or an image of a company's management team on their website that includes his cohort. Another example of this is the distinct lack of females in the admin or the senior management team. This is not to shame anybody but to pause and allow the question "How do others perceive these omissions?" to be answered.

Inclusion also involves federal regulation. Both of this book's authors are Canadian, and our US friends always find it amusing that all of our packaging is in French and English. What they don't understand is Canada has two official languages: French and English. As such, federal law mandates they be used. What our US friends also don't comprehend is there are two versions of the French language: Classic French and Quebec French. The differences between them are subtle and have more to do with history and dialect than anything else. In Canada, if you are working with or for any government, from Federal down to Municipal, there must be French and English versions of the content.

As you have learned, accessibility has two distinct aspects that must be addressed before one pixel is lit up. Once that happens, three plug-ins can help you address accessibility.

Adding Plug-ins in Figma

Though we are going to show how to install three Accessibility plug-ins into Figma, the plug-in installation process is the same for any other plug-in you may require. The great thing about plug-ins is they do one thing spectacularly well. They also extend the functionality of Figma by reducing the dreaded "Feature Bloat" that is common with applications. Here's how to install a Figma plug-in:

1. Figma plug-ins are found in the Figma Community accessed through your Figma Dashboard or located within Figma itself. Open your Dashboard and click the Explore Community link located in the bottom left-hand corner. The Figma Community page (Figure 3-21) opens.

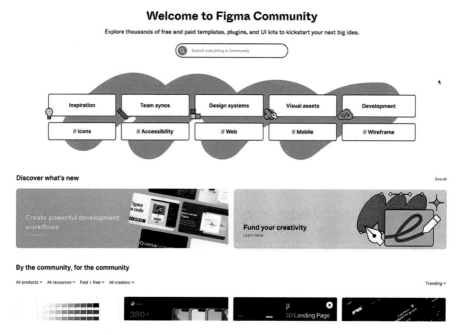

Figure 3-21. *The Figma Community page is one place to access plug-ins (*`www.figma.com/community`*)*

2. Click the Accessibility button. There are a lot of categories to choose from. In Figure 3-22, on the left in the second row, is where you can click on the #Accessibility category to display all the plug-ins focused on Accessibility. You can further reduce the list by selecting Paid or Free from the Paid + Free drop-down menu."

Figure 3-22. *You can select a plug-in or filter the choice to Free or Paid as well as Free + Paid*

3. Click on the Stark Accessibility Tools and a full explanation (Figure 3-23) of what Stark does is presented. To install Stark, click the Try it out button. This opens Figma.

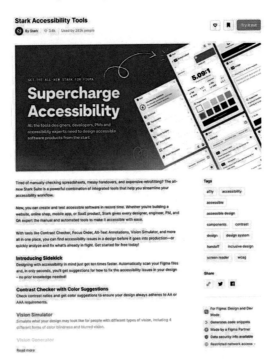

Figure 3-23. *All plug-ins contain an explanation of what they do*

4. Stark will not only open a Tutorial but also open the dialog box shown in Figure 3-24. Click the Run button and Figma will install the Stark plug-in. This is how you install any Figma plug-in.

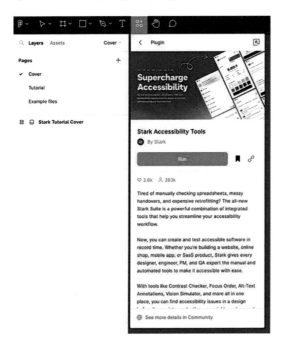

Figure 3-24. *Clicking the Run button installs any plug-in*

Stark does offer a free limited version of the plug-in. To get the full feature set, you will need a paid account and will be prompted to log into your account to run the plug-in.

You can also access the Community Plugins from within Figma. Here's how.

5. Click the Resources icon in the Main Menu, and when it opens, select Plugins ➤ Manage plugins (Figure 3-25). This will take you to the Community page.

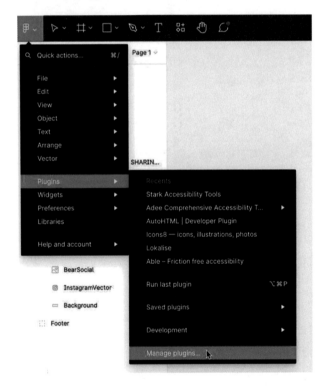

Figure 3-25. *Plug-ins can be added from the Main Menu right in Figma*

6. If you are using the desktop version of Figma, plug-ins can be accessed by selecting the Figma menu and choosing Plugins ➤ Manage plugins.

For the purposes of the following exercise, you will also need to install the Adee and Cards for Humanity Plugins.

Though we will be presenting a single feature of the Stark and Adee plug-ins, we will also be using other features of Adee and Stark throughout the balance of this book.

Using the Accessibility Plug-ins

In this exercise, we are going to be using the Stark Alt Text feature and Adee's Color Contrast feature. We'll start with Stark's Alt-Text Tool.

Writing Alt Text for images is not an afterthought. Take this attitude and you have potentially alienated a rather large group of users. Alt Text is how you communicate images to those using screen readers or when images don't load and leave a blank space on a web page. In today's UX environment, Alt Text is mandatory, and Stark makes the process smoother by identifying common errors. Here's how:

1. Open the Accessibility.fig file and select the image frame. As you can see in Figure 3-26, the image is that of a young woman playing the cello on a street in Berne, Switzerland.

Figure 3-26. *This image needs Alt Text*

2. With the image selected, open the Stark plug-in
    and select Alt Text. When the dialog box opens, the
    pop-down offers you two choices: add Alt Text or
    treat the image as decorative. Choose decorative if
    the image provides no new information or the page
    contains a caption. In fact, Stark will tell you this.

3. To start adding Alt Text, click the Add button and the
    Stark Alt-Text dialog box opens (Figure 3-27).

Figure 3-27. *The Alt-Text dialog box is where you enter the Alt Text*

The first thing you should notice is there is a suggestion handed to you. This is Stark's Sidekick AI coming into play. That 0/200 value you see in the bottom right is the maximum character limit; as you enter the text, Stark will keep track of the characters being entered.

4. We are going to ignore the suggestion. Click once in the text input and enter "A picture of". Stark will immediately tell you the text just entered is redundant and strike it out. When entering Alt Text, you describe the image, not what it is. Instead, enter: "A young woman playing the cello on a street in Bern, Switzerland." When you enter that text, as shown in Figure 3-28, the check mark indicates the text, as written, is acceptable and the character count does not exceed the limit. If you do exceed the limit, Stark will tell you by how much and suggest what needs to be deleted. Click Done.

Figure 3-28. *The correct Alt Text has been written, and Stark tells you it is acceptable and that you haven't exceeded the character limit*

Don't add emojis to Alt Text. Stark regards them as evil. The only acceptable use of an emoji in Alt Text is when the image being described contains one.

---

5. When you click Done, the image is annotated, and a locked layer is added to the Figma Layers panel (Figure 3-29). The combination of annotation

and locked layer serves two purposes. First, your development team will know exactly what text is to be added and it gives the team and stakeholders an idea of what Alt Text is to be added to the image.

Figure 3-29. *Stark annotates the Alt Text and adds it to the layer stack*

The number associated with the Alt-Text annotation tells you it is the first one. If your screen contains a number of images, each one will have a different number and will be added to the Alt-Text layer.

Using the Adee Color Contrast Tool

There was a time when the gray text on a dark gray background was regarded as "too way cool." It was, but for those with vision impairments, it wasn't cool; it was an impediment. The reason is simple: Text is how you communicate the message, and if it isn't readable, the message is lost. This also holds true in any situation where text is over a color background or where the background color changes with a state change. In this exercise, we are going to use Adee's Color Contrast tool to deal with a contrast issue.

1. To start, open the Accessibility.fig file and open the Adee plug-in. When it opens, the default, as shown in Figure 3-30, is selected.

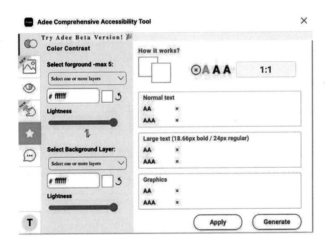

Figure 3-30. *Color Contrast is the default*

Before we start, let's go through the tool:

- On the left you can select the foreground layer in the pop-down. We don't recommend this approach if your screen contains multiple layers. Below is the color selected. The same applies to the background layer.

- The area on the right checks the Contrast Ratio based on the WCAG 2.0 standard. The higher the ratio, the more the contrast moves into compliance. There are two standards: AA and AAA. The AA standard is rather broad and applies to all normal text and visual impairments. The AAA standard is a bit different and really is a judgment call on your part. This score applies to those with severe vision issues that can't be corrected with glasses.

2. Open the Contrast frame and select the Text and Background layers. You will notice (Figure 3-31) the test fails on all levels including those with no visual impairments.

Figure 3-31. *Though you may not think there is a contrast issue, Adee tells you there is*

We'll deal with the text layer first. You have two
choices: use the lightness slider or manually change
the color in the Color Picker. Just be aware that using
either method will change the text color.

3. Slowly move the lightness slider to the right. As
   shown in Figure 3-32, the contrast has moved into
   compliance. The AAA test still fails. If you do want to
   accommodate the AAA test, a minimum ratio of 7:1
   is required.

The lightness slider does not apply opacity. It moves the color value
of the selection to a lighter color.

Figure 3-32. *Using the Lightness slider moves the text color into compliance*

4. Click the Apply Button to change the text color. The
    Generate button creates a report, in its own frame,
    that can be shared with the team and stakeholders.

Explore Inclusion with Cards for Humanity

The Cards for Humanity plug-in neither runs an accessibility test nor
changes anything on the Figma screen. What it does do is challenge your
entire team, from research to development, to confront and solve issues
of inclusion and accessibility. In many respects, this plug-in is a great card
game to play prior to determining the project's Accessibility Policy.

1. With the Accessibility.fig file open, select Cards for
    Humanity in the installed plug-ins. When it opens,
    you will be told that two cards will be dealt, and it is
    up to the team to determine how they would solve
    the issues presented in the cards. We should add
    cards are dealt randomly so you may not see the
    scenario presented in the figures.

2. To start, click the Deal Cards button. Two cards, as
    shown in Figure 3-33, will appear. In this case, we
    have an upbeat 55-year-old woman who is deaf.
    How would the team accommodate that issue?

Figure 3-33. *How would the team accommodate Lucia?*

3. If you click the icon in the upper right corner
    of each card, the team is presented with some
    considerations that apply to each card (Figure 3-34).

Figure 3-34. *Flip the card to see some issues to consider*

If the issues presented are too esoteric, you can change the cards by swapping them with another or dealing a new pair of cards that might be more relevant to your project.

You Have Learned

- Where Figma fits into the UX process and why it is a collaborative tool.

- A prototype is nothing more than a model of the product.

- Prototypes are disposable.

- The various types of prototypes.

- The importance of determining the platform and how to use Figma's Pages to accommodate them.

- How to build a team and use Figma to invite the participants.

- How to share Figma files and add comments to shared files.

- Why Figma is an essential tool for User Testing.

- The importance of iteration.

- How to address inclusion and accessibility in Figma.

- How to locate and install Figma plug-ins.

- How to use the Stark plug-in to add Alt Text.

- How to use the Adee Color Contrast tool.

- How to increase the team's awareness of the importance of inclusion and accessibility by using the Card for Humanity plug-in.

CHAPTER 4

Creating UX Design Documentation

There is a common misconception that Figma is a design tool and comes into play when the UX Process phase begins. Thankfully, the wizards at Figma are dispelling this myth and highlighting Figma's role in every step of the process, from concept to development, using the Dev Mode feature of Figma. This is why the UX process starts with Research because you can't just make it as you go along. The reason is simple: the financial risk of taking that approach is too high.

Simply claiming the reason for building an app or website for visitors to Bern is no reason to build it. Based on the research, a solid business case can be created to initiate the process and reduce the financial risk. The harsh truth is that the claim of no app or website existing is ignored once the Research phase starts. The research team will find one or more apps and websites that do just that and do a competitive analysis of the strengths and weaknesses of the products examined. They might also identify common design patterns and features that may or may not benefit the project. When they finish, the team is presented with a deliverable that can be used to guide their thinking.

While the team thinks about approaching the product, a User Researcher will start using qualitative and quantitative methods to answer a fundamental question: Why and how will they use it? This is where you can begin establishing a clear path for the project. For example, the

© Tom Green and Kevin Brandon 2024
T. Green and K. Brandon, *UX Design with Figma*, Design Thinking,
https://doi.org/10.1007/979-8-8688-0324-6_4

Research discovered a reviewed product has too narrow a focus, such as hostels in Bern. Though the app or website is relatively comprehensive, the researchers uncover a data point from reviews that they feel is essential – the product doesn't answer a fundamental question: What can we do while we are in Bern?

Another complementary approach is downloading and installing competing apps or analyzing competing websites to identify the product's strengths and weaknesses. App stores with user feedback are invaluable resources for discovering what users like and dislike about the experience.

Let's assume the Research, based on interviews and other sources, reveals, among other things, the following data points:

- Potential visitors have heard of Bern but aren't familiar with the city.

- They need to know how to get to Bern from wherever they are located.

- Public transportation information is essential.

- Lodging and price are significant.

- Cultural sites and local history are important.

- Visits to the Alps are imperative.

What the Research has revealed is a potential path for the project. Each data point has uncovered something to be included in the final product. We are willing to bet that when we first mentioned a Bern tourist site, you had already formed a mental picture of the product and that it changed as the team reviewed the research. Do your Research and do your homework before jumping into creating a project. By talking to real people, not users, you quickly realize that you are designing for people, not users.

Using the Figma Presentation Mode

So where does Figma fit in all of this?

Eventually a research document is going to be created summarizing the results. Consider creating a Figma page that could be used as a slideshow for presentation to the stakeholders and even the team. By doing this, the Research is attached to the Project document and is readily available to anyone with access to it. Here's how:

1. Open the Research.fig file found in your chapter download. When you open the .fig file, you will see it is nothing more than two screens.

2. Select the Frame tool and in the Properties panel select Presentation ➤ Slide 16:9 (Figure 4-1). A new slide is added to the Layers panel. One thing to notice is the layer name indicates it is slide 3.

Figure 4-1. *Create a slide deck using the Presentation frames in Figma*

3. Change the name of Page 1 in the Layers panel to Research.

4. Change the name of Slide 1 to Main, and the second slide's name to Summary, and the third slide 3's name to Slide 3.

The slides can be arranged horizontally or vertically.

Once the deck is completed, it can be shared with the team and the stakeholders. Here's how to play the slide show.

5. Click the Play button pop-down and, as shown in Figure 4-2, select Presentation. The presentation will open on the first slide.

Figure 4-2. *Figma is also a presentation tool*

6. If this is being viewed through a browser, you can move forward and backward in the presentation by tapping the left or right arrow keys on your keyboard or clicking the forward or backward icon at the bottom of the screen (Figure 4-3). You should also note you are notified there are three slides in this presentation.

Figure 4-3. *There are two ways to move forward or backward in a presentation. If viewed on a device, tap the left or right edge of the screen*

If the presentation is being viewed on a touch device, tapping on the left or right slide of the screen will move the viewer forward or backward.

With the research summarized and presented to the team, they can start determining how the app or website will work and how a typical user will complete tasks or navigate through the app or website. These deliberations inevitably result in more documentation attached to the project, which the design and development teams will use as reference material. This is where FigJam can play a major role.

Brainstorming with FigJam

When you open your Figma Dashboard, you may notice you are prompted to either create a new design file or a FigJam board.

Introduced in 2021, FigJam is an online collaborative whiteboard for teams to brainstorm and ideate concepts. Rather than drawing concepts on a physical whiteboard or using multiple sticky notes, FigJam can be used to replicate or augment the collaborative brainstorming process. Ideas and digital content can all be added into a shared FigJam file for use with local or distance team members and travel along with the documentation. FigJam is not a design tool. Its purpose is to help the team, including designers and nondesigners, define user problems and explore concepts and ideas. This could include the following:

- Brainstorming and exploring ideas by using the features of FigJam, such as sticky notes, drawing tools, shapes connectors, and other features to express ideas and the team's reaction to those ideas

- Creating decision trees, mindmaps, and diagrams such as flowcharts, user flows, use cases, and sitemaps

- Initiating critiques or feedback sessions on designs without the potential clutter of comments on the Figma design

- Using FigJam templates, widgets, and plug-ins from the Community to create charts or workflows

- Planning meetings or other sessions where the team is involved

- Importing spreadsheet documents in the .csv format

- Creating a Gantt chart

- Kanban boards for agile management and workflows

Figma has built AI into FigJam. It is currently in Beta and, at some point in time, will be fully integrated into FigJam.

Let's start by exploring the FigJam interface.

1. Click the FigJam Board button in your Dashboard. The interface (Figure 4-4) is relatively sparse. Along the top are four tools that allow you to use the AI feature to generate a FigJam board based on a text inquiry, access to the FigJam template collection, and a Comment tool. On the left is the Generate panel, which we will use later on in this exercise, and at the bottom are the tools with the Keyboard Commands in brackets:

   - Select Tool (V): Use this to select objects.

   - Hand Tool (H): Use this to move around the FigJam board.

   - Marker Tool (M): Opens a series of drawing tools and a color picker.

   - Sticky Note (S): Add a sticky note to the Board or an object.

   - Ellipse (O), Square (R), Triangle (Just Click It), and Connector (X): Use these to draw flowcharts and so on.

   - Text (T): Add and format text to a FigJam board.

   - Section (Shift-S): A quick way of creating groups of ideas.

   - Table (Shift-T): Import CSV files or cells into a table.

   - Stamp (E): Use stamps to add stickers on the Board or object to communicate feedback.

   - Access Widgets, Stickers, and Templates. Click the + sign to open the dialog box to search for what you may need.

In the upper left corner is a Timer primarily used by the team to vote for the concept or idea that will add to the project. We won't be discussing this any further.

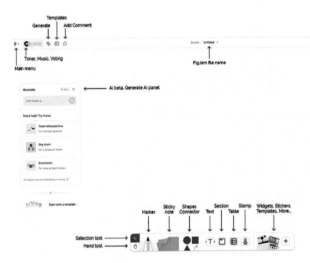

Figure 4-4. *The FigJam interface*

There is an extensive collection of FigJam templates that you can use to get yourself started. To access them, click the Templates icon in the upper toolbar. A dialogue box opens and you can explore the collection. You can scroll through them or explore them by category. You can also search for a specific template. These templates and other elements are accessed by clicking the + sign in the Drawing tools.

How to Use FigJam AI

As mentioned earlier, this feature is currently in Beta. This also explains why a disclaimer – "All outputs can be misleading or wrong" – is at the bottom of the Generate dialog box. Even so, with an emphasis on AI, it is no surprise that Figma rolled out this feature rather quickly.

To use it, you have a couple of choices. Select a suggestion from the dialog box or enter a text prompt. We'll start with a selection from the Generate dialog box.

1. Click "Brainstorm". You will be informed FigJam is looking for possibilities, and as shown in Figure 4-5, a Project Ideas section opens. The little toolbar under the Section lets you change the background color, align objects, or select Items in the suggestion and create new Sections. In the Generate dialog box, you can generate new features. The really neat aspect of everything in the Section is they are all editable. You can add sticky notes, change the text, add stamps, and so on.

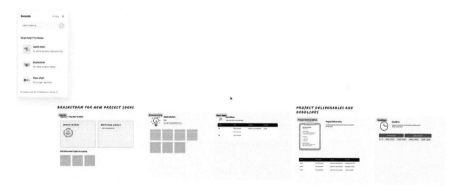

Figure 4-5. *Selecting a Brainstorm FigJam project using the AI*

You can also generate FigJam sections by using text
prompts.

2. Click the Generate button in the toolbar to open the
    Generate dialog box.

3. Enter the following prompt: "A list of project
    deliverables and deadlines". Click the Generate
    button. The Section (Figure 4-6) appears on the
    same FigJam file as the previous one. Again, this is
    fully editable, and you now have a FigJam file that
    contains both a Brainstorm and a Schedule, Gantt
    chart, for deliverables.

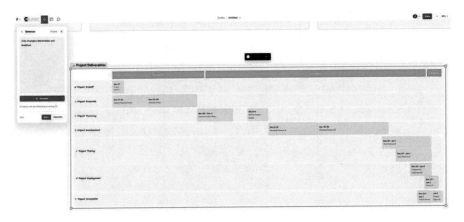

Figure 4-6. *You can enter prompts into the AI dialog box*

You can save FigJam files to your desktop or other location. When
you save a FigJam file to your desktop, the file extension is .JAM, this
differs from a saved Figma file extension, which is .FIG. When using
the Generate feature, display attributes such as typeface, color, and
number of tasks are different with each AI-generated layout. Your
result may not match Figure 4-6.

Using the FigJam Drawing Tools

Though AI is a great timesaver, you can create FigJam files that work for you, not a general team. It is also a communication and collaborative tool. In this exercise, we will create a flowchart showing the logic for a Login Sequence, through a series of pages.

1. Open the FigJam file you have created or open a new FigJam project.

2. Using Figure 4-7 as your guide, draw out a rectangle, a circle, a diamond, and an oval. Don't worry about the colors.

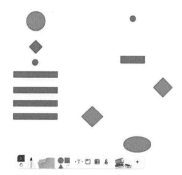

Figure 4-7. *Shapes can be used to create Flow diagrams*

3. Let's now recolor the small circles. Select each of the circle, click on the color chip, and change the color to Gray.

4. Change the color of the two diamonds under the circle to Light Blue.

5. The other two diamonds will indicate an Error. Change their colors to Red.

As you are editing the colors, notice the Shapes in the Drawing Tools change to the selected color.

Using the Connector Tool

1. In the Shapes area, select the Connector tool.

2. Draw a connector that runs from the top green circle to the bottom green circle. Drag it down until it touches the Left anchor point of the bottom circle. Notice how it changes direction when it does. When using connectors, connect to anchor points.

3. With the Connector selected, the dialog box that opens lets you choose to use either a thick or thin line. To thicken the line, click the large dot. The small dot changes the line to a thin one.

4. Obviously, we can't have a line running over the blue boxes. Switch to the Select tool and right-click on the arrow. Select Send to Back.

5. Let's next draw the Connector between the Error diamond and the Blue Box. Select the Connector tool and draw a connector between the two objects.

6. Switch to the Selector tool and select the Connector tool. When the toolbar opens, add a solid arrow to the start and end points of the Connector as shown in Figure 4-8. Change the color of the Connector to red.

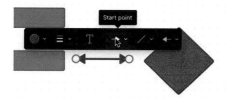

Figure 4-8. *Adding arrows to the Start and End points of a Connector*

7. Draw a connector between the Blue diamond and the Gray circle at the top. You may notice the line isn't exactly straight. Switch to the Selection tool, click once on the Gray circle, and move it down. Notice how the connector follows change in position. If the line is red, change it to black.

8. Select the Connector tool and draw a line from the top Gray circle to the Green circle. If there is a bend in the connector, move the green circle to straighten it out.

9. Draw another connector between two diamonds as shown in Figure 4-9.

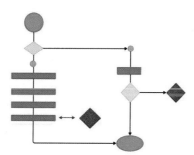

Figure 4-9. *The connections between the objects are established*

Adding Text to FigJam Objects

Each shape you add to a FigJam object also contains the ability to input text. Here's how:

1. Select the Green circle and double-click the text area. The cursor changes to a Text cursor. Enter "Start".

2. To format the text, use the toolbar shown in Figure 4-10. Here are your limited options:

   - Aa: Choose one of four typefaces – Simple, Bookish, Technical, and Scribbled. Select Simple.

   - Large: This pop-down lets you choose the size – Small, Medium, Large, Extra Large, and Huge. You can also enter a value if you don't want to go with the choices. Change the size to Large.

   - B: Changes to the bold version of the font.

   - Strikethrough: This is great for crossing off tasks in a list but wanting to keep a record of the completed tasks.

   - Link: Adds a link to the selected text.

   - Bulleted List: Creates a bulleted list.

   - Alignment: Aligns the text as either Flush Left, Centered, or Flush Right. The default is Flush Left.

Figure 4-10. *The text formatting options in the toolbar*

3. Let's give this chart a name. Select the Text tool and enter "Flow". When the toolbar appears, change the size to 72 and select Bold. If you want to label the remaining objects, use Figure 4-11 as your guide.

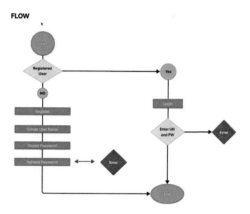

Figure 4-11. *The flowchart has been labeled*

Adding Comments to a FigJam File

When a FigJam file is shared with the team and stakeholders, they can add comments. If the FigJam file is available to team members with "Can Edit" privileges, they can also open the file in FigJam and add comments using sticky notes and stamps. Here's how:

1. Select the Stickynote tool. Notice how a note follows the cursor. Click the mouse where you want the note to appear. To make the note larger, drag out one of the note's sides.

2. If you click the note, you will see four dots. If you roll over the dots icon, it changes to a plus sign. If you click the plus sign, it creates another note with a connector. This is a handy feature for creating threaded conversations.

3. Select the text in the note and enter: "As discussed here is the Loginflow. Please Review and add comments" (Figure 4-12). You will also notice the name of the author is at the bottom. If my coauthor, Kevin, wanted to start the chain, he could add a note to create the thread.

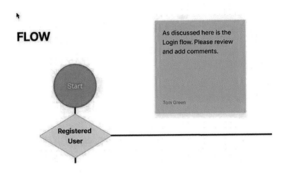

Figure 4-12. *A sticky note is added to the FigJam file*

4. Another way of adding a reaction is to use a stamp. Our advice is to not get carried away with them. When you open the Stamp tool, you get two choices: a happy face that opens a wheel of emojis and the stamp that contains a series of reaction emojis including one that creates an avatar for the current User.

5. Open the happy face, select an emoji, and click on the surface. As you can see, they can rapidly "junk up" the FigJam board.

How to Add a FigJam File to Figma

FigJam files will appear as a file on the Team Dashboard or your personal Dashboard. The issue is how does one add that flowchart into a Figma page. Here's how:

1. Select the whole chart in FigJam and click the Section tool. When the Selection dialog box opens, select the "Wrap in new section" icon (Figure 4-13) and change the background color to white. By doing this, you have essentially created a Group.

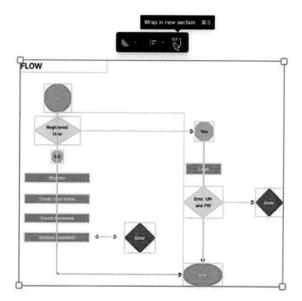

Figure 4-13. *The chart is converted to a Section*

2. Double-click the tooltip and change the name from Section 1 to Flow. Select "Section 1" and copy it to the pasteboard.

3. Open your Documents file and add a new page named "Flow".

4. Select "Paste Here" from the menu.

5. When the chart appears, you will notice all of the elements that make up the chart appear as separate Layers and they are fully editable. Also make sure the connectors are in layers below the objects (Figure 4-14). In the Layers panel, you should also note the chart is not contained in a Frame but in a Section.

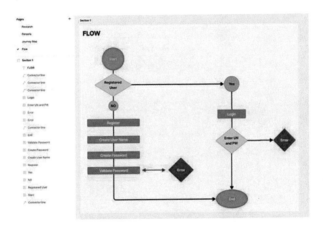

Figure 4-14. *FigJam sections, added to Figma, arrive as editable Layers in Figma*

Creating Personas

Once the research and user data has been handed over to the team, a logical question is what to do with it. The problem with Research is it has analyzed your competition, identified your competitive advantage, and refined the potential market to distinct groupings or categories. This is extremely useful data to have in hand, but groups require descriptions using vague generalities. How does the team deal with this? They don't.

We are storytellers, and stories about individuals in a group bring that group to life in ways that a clump of data simply can't do. This explains the rise of the persona, a document that answers a fundamental question about the group: Who are these people?

A persona's purpose is to get the team to regard your potential users as human beings, not data points. They also bring focus to UX Design decisions by injecting the real world into both your team's decisions and conversations. The most important aspect of a persona is that it is a representation of a particular group or demographic, not an individual.

There may be a tendency to create multiple personas to reflect all the demographics from the Research. This would be overkill. Instead, create three to five personas. That should be a large enough number to cover the majority of your potential users but small enough to be focused.

Don't get carried away with personas. Anywhere from three to five should cover the groups identified and be large enough to encompass the majority of your users but small enough to be rather specific.

When creating personas, you might want to

- Give the person a name and include a picture. Choose any name you want but make it real, so this mythical person feels real.

- Identify the job, role, and company. You have a pretty good idea of what your users do and where they work. Adding this information keeps the team from going off on tangents.

- Tell the User's story. While age, gender, and other information are important, telling the User's story, based on the Research, makes the character's psychology and motivations more compelling than a series of bullet points.

- Keep personas short, no more than two pages, and make sure all the stakeholders have and understand them.

Create a Persona Using a Template

Rather than building one from scratch, we will use a template to create the persona.

1. Open your Figma Dashboard and open the Community link. When the Community page opens, enter "user persona free templates" into the Search area. A number of template suggestions open (Figure 4-15).

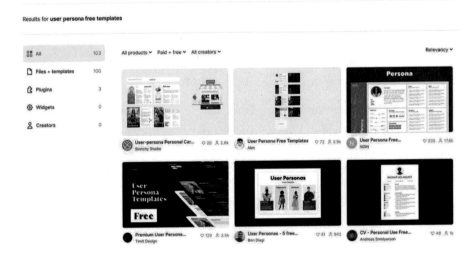

Figure 4-15. *The Figma Community site contains quite a few persona templates*

2. In order to keep this exercise focused, click User Persona Free Templates by Alex. We regard this collection, shown in Figure 4-16, to be an excellent starter collection. Each template contains a Light and a Dark mode, each is fully editable, and the designs are fairly basic. Click the "Open in Figma" button.

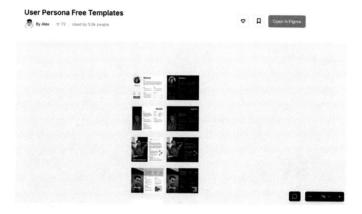

Figure 4-16. *The templates from Alex are a great resource for those who don't have the time, or are new to creating a custom persona document*

3. The template will open in Figma, and you will see it contains four Light Mode versions and Dark Mode complements. The one we are going to use for this exercise is the User Persona #1(Light). Select the layer, right-click, and select copy.

4. Open your documents file and add a new page named Persona.

5. Right-click on the pasteboard and select Paste Here. The template is added to the page.

As you can see in Figure 4-17, the persona contains many of the points outlined earlier, including a name and picture, a story about Jessica, her goals and needs based upon the research data points, pain points around using Travel apps, and a personality profile aggregated from the research data.

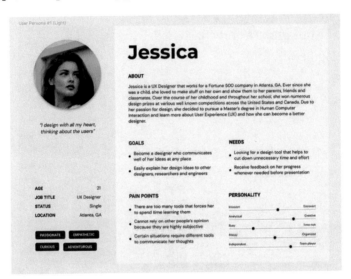

Figure 4-17. *Personas reflect the research data and are concise*

Editing a Persona Template

In the Layers panel, you will see this template contains a number of layers that are editable. What we are going to do in this exercise is to change the image to add some diversity to the persona and change the name. We are also going to make a couple of edits to a couple of text layers. Let's get started:

1. Open the Resources drop-down menu and select Plugins. Enter Photos into the Search area. You will be presented with a couple of choices. UI Faces is one choice, but it really does not permit diversity.

You can choose an AI-generated face, but you can't
be specific. Instead, choose Photos and install the
plug-in.

2. When the plug-in is installed, open the Photos
    plug-in and enter "Chinese Female" into the Search
    area. A number of choices, as shown in Figure 4-18,
    appear. As well you can search specific sites such as
    Pixabay, Pexels, Unsplash, Shutterstock, and Lexica.

Figure 4-18. *The Photos plug-in allows you to include diversity into*
your personas

3. With the plug-in open, double-click on the Jessica image to select it. Click on the image in the Photos plug-in. Jessica's image is replaced (Figure 4-19). Close the Photos plug-in.

Figure 4-19. *Click the image you want and it instantly replaces the selected image*

The images chosen from this plug-in or others are strictly for internal use. It would be prudent for you to clearly understand the Stock Image site's Licensing and Copyright fees and policies.

---

4. As we pointed out earlier, these templates are fully editable. Select Jessica's name and replace it with "Grace".

5. Select the Jessica text in the About text block and change it to Grace. Next, select that entire text block (Figure 4-20) and use these Text settings:

    - Font: Raleway
    - Font Weight: Medium
    - Size: 22
    - Line Height: 28

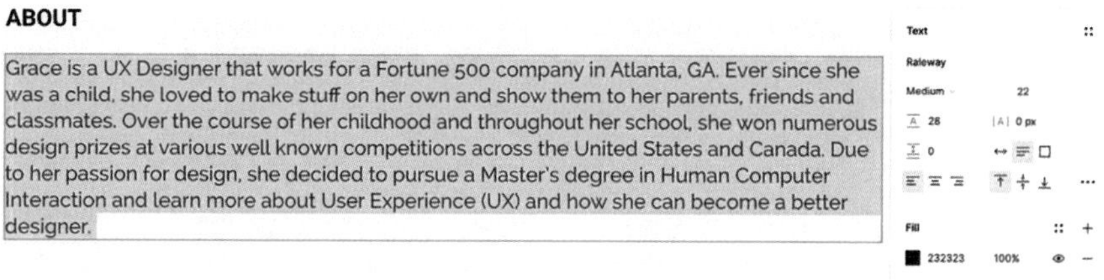
ABOUT
Grace is a UX Designer that works for a Fortune 500 company in Atlanta, GA. Ever since she was a child, she loved to make stuff on her own and show them to her parents, friends and classmates. Over the course of her childhood and throughout her school, she won numerous design prizes at various well known competitions across the United States and Canada. Due to her passion for design, she decided to pursue a Master's degree in Human Computer Interaction and learn more about User Experience (UX) and how she can become a better designer.
Text
Raleway
Medium
22
28
0 px
0
Fill
232323
100%

Figure 4-20. *Changing the font settings is one way of making the template conform to your organization's design standards*

You may notice the word "designer" is sitting all by itself at the bottom of the paragraph. In typographic terms, this is called an "orphan." To fix it, move the right side of the text box inward to force a couple of words to the bottom of the paragraph. Conversely, click in front of the word "she" in the first line and press Return/Enter.

You can also change Grace's personality to indicate she is a bit more independent and willing to explore destinations on her own. Here's how.

6. Double-click the Independent section of the Personality area to select it.

7. Twirl down the selected layer.

8. Select the Oval layer and with the Shift key held down, press the Left arrow key. Using the Shift key will move a selection in 10-pixel increments.

9. With the Oval layer in place and still selected, let's change the Fill color to #2352EC. This isn't really necessary but shows how you can personalize the design of a persona.

Even though we have changed a few things in the text box, you can add your own text either manually or by copying and pasting the text from a word processor into the text box.

Creating a User Journey Map

Having created a persona for Grace, the next step in the process is to answer a rather big question: How will Grace actually use our app? You can't ignore this question because your team needs to understand Grace's experience from Grace's perspective, not yours. This means including emotions, pain points, and even areas where Grace really enjoys using the app. This is where a Journey Map could be created.

A Journey Map is a visualization of the process that Grace will go through to accomplish a goal. This exercise will be about renting a bike. There are a number of ways to visualize this process, but keep in mind this process is based on the Research that yielded Grace's persona, not upon assumptions the team may make. Here are some items to consider when creating a Journey Map:

- Scope: You can approach this in two ways. The first is to create a complex map covering every possible scenario that will affect Grace. The other is to focus upon specific interactions, which is why we will focus on the process of renting a bike.

- Relate It to a Persona: By keeping Grace in mind, you are considering how she will rent a bike and her experience around that process.

- Define a Scenario and User Expectations: In this case, the scenario is Grace decides to rent a bike and is using her smartphone.

- Consider the User's Intentions: This is accomplished by identifying Grace's motivation to rent a bike, where she will interact with the bike rental company, which we will refer to as the Channels where the interactions take place, what Grace will have to do to rent the bike (Actions) and where she may encounter problems, which we refer to as Pain Points, and any personal interactions she may have such as riding the bike and returning the bike.

In this exercise, we will be creating a simple Journey Map. If you are looking for something that is a bit more comprehensive, then open the Community site and do a search for Journey Map. Quite a few templates will be presented. Having said that, let's get started:

1. In your Documents.fig file, create a new page and name it Journey Map.

2. Add a frame that is 3200 × 2500 pixels in size.

3. We start by creating three arrows that will indicate the Channels. Select the Rectangle tool and draw out a rectangle that is 830 pixels wide and 150 pixels high.

4. Select the Polygon tool and draw out a triangle, the default shape, that is 250 × 200. Rotate it to -90 degrees in the Properties panel.

5. Move the triangle over the rectangle to create an arrow. Group them, fill the shapes with #3AB3F1 (Blue), and name the group Blue Arrow.

6. Select the Blue Arrow and press Command/Ctrl-D twice to create two copies of the arrow. Move each copy to the right to space them out, and with the three arrows selected, click the Tidy Up spacing option in the Properties panel.

7. Select the Middle arrow and change its color to #F1B33A (Orange) and change the one on the right to #F13A71.

8. Select the Text tool, click once inside the Frame, and enter Digital Channel. Use these text properties:

   • Font: PT Sans

   • Font Weight: Bold

   • Size: 72

   • Letter Spacing: 4. This adds a bit of space between the letters to make the text more readable.

   • Color: #FFFFFF (White)

9. Duplicate the Text and move the copies over the Orange and Red arrows. Change the Orange arrow's text to Interaction Channel and the Red arrow's text to Personal Channel. Move each text block.

Our channels (Figure 4-21) have been identified.

Figure 4-21. *Journey Maps start by identifying the Channels*

What we need to do next is to identify how Grace will move through the channels to rent a bike. What you need to understand is that the Interaction Channel has nothing to do with the app but more to do with how she will interact with the Bike Rental kiosk. The whole purpose of the Journey Map is to follow Grace as she uses the app to rent a bike, visits the kiosk to pick up the bike, and returns the bike when she is done. What we will identify are those points where Grace will form both positive and negative impressions with an eye to making the process as painless as possible. Here's how:

1. Select the Text tool and enter "Steps:". Set it in PT Sans Bold 72. We are going to outline the steps Grace will take to rent a bike.

2. Select the Rectangle tool and draw a box that is 400 by 300 and filled with #3AB3F1. Make seven copies and move them under the Channels. Change the color of the middle 3 to #F1B33A (Orange) and the last 2 to #F13A71.

3. Select the Text tool and enter Opens app. Set the type to PT Sans Bold 48 and the color to White (#FFFFFF).

4. For the remaining boxes (Figure 4-22), the text will have the same format and color. Create separate text boxes and enter the following:

- Opens Bike Rentals

- Books Rental

- Visits Bike Kiosk

- Confirms Rental

- Inspects Bike

- Rides Bike

- Returns Bike

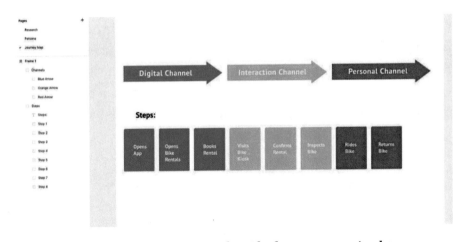

Figure 4-22. *The next step is to identify the steps required to complete a task*

Adding Touchpoints

The final piece of the Journey Map puzzle is identifying the touchpoints involved in Grace's bike rental experience. Touchpoints are the interactions where Grace has a positive or negative experience with a bike rental, and those positive or negative experiences can have financial consequences.

Let's assume Grace is merrily biking through Bern and the chain falls off. She had no idea how to fix this, so she phoned the bike rental company and explained her problem. This experience can go in two ways: Someone from the bike rental company arrives and replaces the bike, or they tell her to chain the bike to a bike stand and return to get a replacement. There are two possible outcomes to Grace's dilemma. The first one is positive, and the second one is negative. When Grace returns to her hotel, her friends ask if she could recommend a bike rental company. We think you can guess her recommendation if she had to walk back to the rental kiosk.

The critical aspect of Grace's dilemma is that it is not limited to a specific transaction, such as renting a bike. It is a process that begins with Grace becoming aware of the bike rental company in the app and includes all of the transactions, interactions, and contacts with the company along the way. This explains why Touchpoint charts have become an integral element in creating a Journey Map. They identify the specific points in time where the User comes in contact with your company, brand, product, or service.

Identifying the relevant touchpoints is a messy process. The process doesn't start in Figma. It begins with everyone having a stake in the project coming together and determining them. They can be written on a whiteboard or on Post-it notes created in FigJam and stuck to a whiteboard. From there, the list is narrowed down to the most important ones, and only then can the touchpoint list be moved to Figma.

Here are some considerations to keep in mind when identifying touchpoints:

- They must be appropriate to meet the User's needs at that point in time.

- They must be relevant in that each one meets a specific need at a specific time.

- They must be meaningful and reflect important interactions with the User, not you.

- They should be endearing. This doesn't mean they are cute. Far from it, an endearing interaction creates a bond between the resource and the User.

Let's look at the possible touchpoints Grace will encounter with her bike rental.

1. Open the Touchpoints.fig file found in your chapter download.

When it opens (Figure 4-23), you will see it is nothing more than a series of dots, a timeline, and some text identifying the particular touchpoint. The dot color relates to a specific channel and potential interaction within that channel. There is one other important aspect to these touchpoints. The Journey becomes much more granular as you go from the Channels down to the touchpoints.

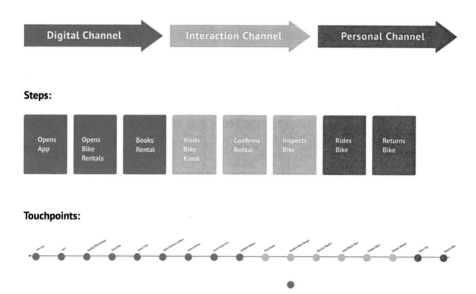

Figure 4-23. *Touchpoints identify specific points when the User comes into contact with a company, product, or service*

You will notice a blue dot under the Interaction touchpoints, which provides an opportunity to understand this Journey Map. Let's assume the kiosk tells Grace they have no record of her rental. Grace finds this somewhat confusing and shows the rental transaction receipt from the kiosk on her smartphone. Grace's interaction could be positive or negative depending on how this interaction is resolved. You may think it is between Grace and the bike rental company. Not exactly. If Grace subsequently posts a negative review of the company on your app, there could be financial consequences for you. If your agreement with the bike rental company includes some sort of revenue sharing, you may have a problem if enough people listen to Grace and avoid the bike rental company.

What we have shown you is a very simplistic Journey Map, including touchpoints. We are not suggesting this is the way to go because no two teams approach Journey Mapping in the same way. If you are looking for a starting point, the Figma Community (`www.figma.com/community`) has several Journey Map and Touchpoint templates that can be opened and edited in Figma.

Creating a User Flow Diagram

Having identified how Grace will rent a bike, use it, and return it, an obvious question is: How did Grace start the process? This is where a User Flow diagram becomes another critical addition to the documentation made available to the team.

User Flows are important because they demonstrate the path a User could take through a website or application to achieve a specific goal. The map also communicates to the stakeholders and teams the screens a User will work through to achieve that goal.

A User Flow diagram is a visualization of a user's steps to log in to a website or an app. It shows the entry points, the actions, the decisions, and the outcomes of the login process. For the development team, a User Flow diagram lays out the logic that will aid the development team. For this exercise, we are going to map how Grace would log into the Bern app. Before we start, there are four important questions to answer:

- Who is the User?

- What is the User's goal?

- What is the business objective?

- What are the steps to achieve that goal?

This is where storytelling can help. Instead of drawing diagrams and so on, a story will present the scenario in a way that is easily understood. It could be something like this:

"When Grace opens the app, she will be asked to log in using her email address and password. If successful, she will be taken to the Home screen. If Grace enters the wrong email or password, she will be asked to try again. Grace will be prompted to reset her password if she still can't remember her password. If Grace is a New User, she will be asked to create a username and password. She will be prompted to enter her new password, and if she fails three times, she will be asked to reset her password."

Keep this story in mind as we create the User Flow Grace will experience when she is asked to log in. Let's get started.

1. Open the UserFlow.fig file found in your chapter download. When it opens (Figure 4-24), there is a rectangle and two circles. If you open the Layers, you will notice they have a different icon than you may expect. We have converted them to components. A component is a "create once, use many" artifact. Rather than drawing out a bunch of boxes and circles then copying and pasting or duplicating, you just drag the component out of the Assets panel to the artboard.

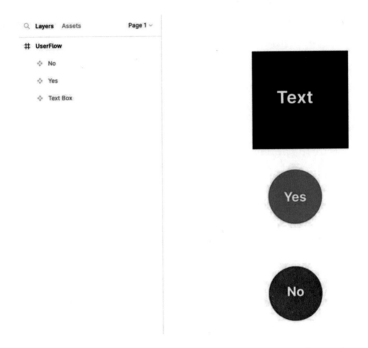

Figure 4-24. *We start the User Flow creation process by using*
components

We'll discuss components in greater detail later in this book. Here, we use them to show how they make a designer's life easier.

---

2. Open the Assets panel and drag a copy of the Text
    Box component to the artboard. Switch back to the
    Layers panel, select the Text tool, and label the first
    Text Box "Welcome" and the second one "Login".

3. Open the Shapes pop-down and select the Arrow
    shape. Draw an arrow between the two boxes. Move
    the Yes component to the right of the Login box
    and move the No component under the Login box.

Draw arrows pointing to the two circles. You have just identified the path (Figure 4-25) Grace will follow from the Welcome screen to the Login screen and shown what happens if the login is accepted, Yes circle, or Grace needs to enter a username and password, No circle.

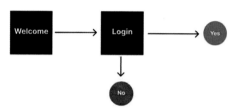

Figure 4-25. *What path does Grace follow if the login is successful or unsuccessful?*

4. Let's deal with what happens if the Login fails. Drag three boxes from the Assets panel under the Red circle. Label them, from top to bottom, "User Name", "Password", and "Confirm PW". Next, draw the arrows and, to keep things tidy, group each of the Boxes and name them (Figure 4-26).

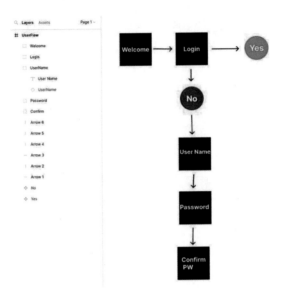

Figure 4-26. *Creating the User Flow for an incorrect login*

If you look over to the Layers panel, you will note the Boxes are hollow diamonds. These are instances of the Text Box component. The key aspect of an instance is, as you discovered, that you can edit the text without affecting the original component.

So what happens if Grace enters the wrong password when asked to confirm it?

5. Drag a No component to the left of the Confirm box and drag a Text Box component to the left of the No component. Label the Box "Reset PW".

6. Draw a line and arrow from the No component to the Password box and do the same thing for the Reset PW box, but connect it to the User Name box (Figure 4-27).

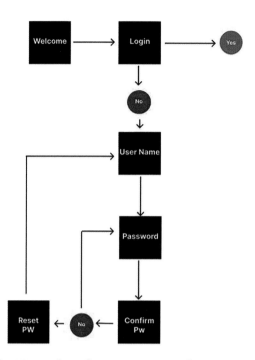

Figure 4-27. *The User Flow for an incorrect login*

This part of the diagram shows that when Grace opens the app's Welcome page, she is asked to log in or become a New User. This part of the diagram shows the Flow Grace will encounter when creating a new account. If she reenters the wrong password, she must enter it again. If she fails three times, she will be asked to reset her password and start the login process one more time.

Let's now deal with Grace logging into her account.

7. Drag two instances of the Text Box component to the right of the Yes component. Label them "User Name" Password and Home.

193

8. Drag an instance of the No component under the User Name Password box, and using Command/ Ctrl-D, duplicate the Reset box and place it under the No component.

9. Drag a Yes component to the right of the Confirm box.

10. Finish up by connecting these new elements with lines and arrows as shown in Figure 4-28.

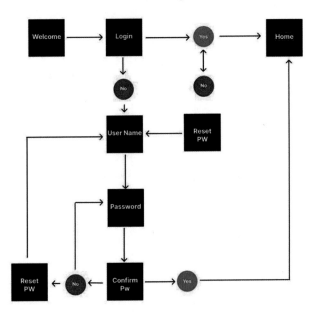

Figure 4-28. *The User Flow for a simple login is not as simple as it may first appear to be*

If Grace has an account and enters the correct User Name and Password information, she heads to the Home screen. If not, she will also be given three opportunities to enter the correct password. If not, she will be asked to reset her password.

This simple User Flow tells the design team they will need to create three screens: Welcome, Login, and Home. They will also have to create modals or screens if a Password reset is needed. The development team can also see the logic required to log in to the Bern app or website.

Feedback and Iteration

We are going to step away from Figma and talk about feedback and iteration. As we have made clear every Figma document created will be subjected to comments and feedback from the team. In many instances, the entire team will often gather to review and critique the project or a screen. This feedback inevitably results in an iteration of the screen to further refine it to the point where it supports the project's intent and makes the User's life easier.

The iterative design process moves through all of the design disciplines that come to bear upon a project to produce an app or website that results in the perception by the user of a product that is a useful, personalized experience. The process is also cost-effective because, through team and user feedback, you are able to identify and fix potential issues before the product is released, not after release.

The most important aspect of this process is to understand ours is a visual medium that starts with a hypothesis and moves into a visual space where the hypothesis moves from the theoretical to the visual. Once it becomes visual, the question becomes: "Does this meet the intent as presented in the research?" If it doesn't, the project is iterated to move it closer to its goals. Human-to-human interactions can only accomplish this as they wrestle to move the project into its final form. This feedback can come through User Testing or between team members.

Feedback can be stressful. If your work is being reviewed, it is only natural to be somewhat defensive as you review the comments or listen to the critiques. If you are the one adding the comments or critiquing, it is only natural to wonder how the recipient will react. Needless to say, commenting can be a minefield of interpersonal relations.

Here are some pointers when commenting or reviewing:

- It Is All About the Work, Not the Reviewer: Don't go granular or deliberately look for mistakes. Pointing out strengths and weaknesses focuses on improving the work.

- Perfection Does Not Exist: This is where the iterative process becomes important. So far, all of the documentation has dealt with generalities. The goal is to get close, not precise, because the design process is iterative. The iterative process removes clutter and "noise" that distract from the UX Mission, for example, unnecessary or confusing element that might distract the User.

- Context, Not Generalities: If a button is not reachable by a thumb on a mobile device, you have context. Saying the button looks to be in the wrong location provides no context.

- Comments Aren't Confrontations: A comment that says "This button is all wrong" starts a confrontation. Instead, consider starting a conversation with a comment like "Why does this button not look different from the other buttons?" At this point, the recipient can reply with a rationale for the change or admit to a mistake.

- Comments in Figma Are Not Threads: Being able to comment on a file in Figma requires concision on the part of both the sender and the person replying. If you need to have a fuller discussion, then common tools such as the Slack plug-in for Figma or a team meeting might be a better forum.

If you are looking for a more robust way of providing comments or feedback in Figma, the Feedback Kit by Mixpanel (Figure 4-29) is a Figma plug-in that should help kickstart the process.

Figure 4-29. *The Feedback Kit from Mixpanel is a Figma plug-in you might want to check out*

Your Turn: Create a User Flow Diagram in FigJam

Earlier in this chapter we created a User Flow diagram that followed a login sequence. The diagram, as you may recall, used Figma's drawing tools. In this exercise, you are going to leverage the tools in FigJam. We are also going to approach this in a more efficient manner than creating each element and moving them into place. Let's get started.

1. From your Dashboard, create a new FigJam board. When it opens, close the AI dialog box.

2. Select the Circle tool and click once on the board. Click once in the text area and enter the word "Yes".

3. With the circle selected, use these properties:

   - Color: Green

   - Text: Extra Large

4. Press Command/Ctrl-D to create a duplicate.

5. Create another duplicate but this time change the color to Red and the Text to "No".

6. Create two more duplicates of the No element. This is an example of one of our core design principles: "Let the software do the work." In this case, you created one circle, added a color and some text, and duplicated the circle to create the five circles needed for the chart (Figure 4-30).

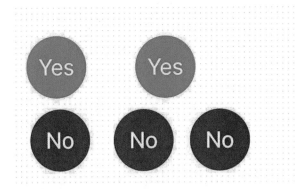

Figure 4-30. *Let the software do the work*

It is not exactly a best practice to create flowcharts in Figma. Figma is the last step. These charts start life on paper either drawn freehand, using a stencil (Figure 4-31), or a series of Post-it notes on a wall or whiteboard. These drawings are then subjected to feedback and iterated to ensure no unnecessary steps will interfere with the process. Once they are finalized, they can be reproduced in FigJam and added to the project's documentation.

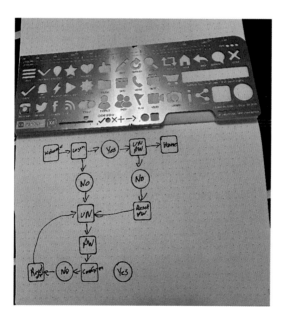

Figure 4-31. *Flowcharts always start on paper using, as shown, a stencil to keep it neat*

7.   Add a black box to the board and change the text to "Welcome" and set the text as Extra Large.

8. Create seven duplicates and change the text to

- Login

- User Name/Password

- Home

- User Name

- Password

- Reset PW. Duplicate this box.

- Confirm PW.

What you have done is to create and assemble the elements (Figure 4-32) that will be used in the flowchart, and they were created efficiently.

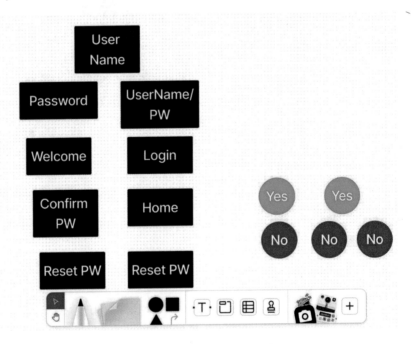

Figure 4-32. *The chart's elements are assembled*

Build the Chart in Figma

With the elements assembled, we can create the flowchart. Here's how:

1. Using the drawing shown in Figure 4-33, move the elements into position.

2. Add the Connectors (Figure 4-33), being sure to add an arrow to the Connector's end point.

3. Save the file as Flowchart.

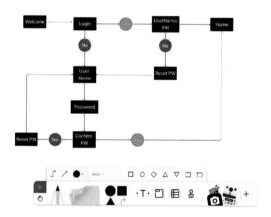

Figure 4-33. *The flowchart is created in FigJam*

Add the Chart to Figma

As you learned earlier in this chapter, FigJam files have their own format, .jam, which needs to be copied and pasted into a Figma frame.

1. Open your Figma Dashboard and select Design File.

2. Add a frame and select Slide 16:9 in the Properties panel. Name the frame User Flow.

3. Open your FigJam User Flow document, select it, and press Command/Ctrl-C to create a copy.

4. Return to your Figma file, right-click the frame, and select "Paste Here".

   The chart appears but is seriously larger than the frame. You could scale the chart, but you will discover that the elements don't scale all that well. The solution is to make the frame larger, but if you look at the Properties panel, the Width and Height values are shown as "Mixed". Here's how to fit the chart.

5. In the Layers panel, make sure all the element layers are selected.

6. Group them and name the group User Flow. With the group selected, you will notice the chart now displays values for width and height.

7. Change the dimensions of the frame to be a bit larger than the group's dimensions. Move the group into position on the frame as shown in Figure 4-34.

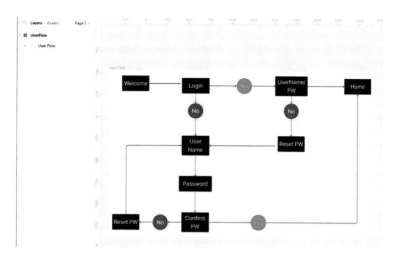

Figure 4-34. _The FigJam file is pasted into Figma, and the elements are grouped_

So there you have it: how to quickly create charts and diagrams using FigJam. You might perceive the Figma file's dimensions as overly large; it should not be a concern. Remember, this chart could be added to the Documents page and made available to the team and stakeholders. As reference material, it is the content, not the dimensions, that is important.

You Have Learned

- How to create a page to hold all of a project's documentation

- How to create a slide presentation in Figma

- When and how to use FigJam

- How to use the new FigJam AI module to create brainstorms

- How to use the tools and features found in FigJam

- Where to find and edit a Persona template

- To use Figma's shape tools to create Flow diagrams, user journeys, and other documentation based on the Research.

- The intimate relationship between feedback and iteration.

- How to quickly create a User Flow diagram in FigJam and add it to the team's documentation page in Figma.

With the documentation completed, the team has a great overview of the users, their journey, and how they will, for example, create an account and login. Armed with that knowledge, the team's next step in the process is to answer a simple question: What does it look like? That process starts in the next chapter.

CHAPTER 5

Building Low-Fidelity Prototypes

"Lo-fi wireframes don't ask for much content. They are meant to communicate a visual idea and explore possibilities rather than document a design."

−Sergio Nouvel
Ditch Traditional Wireframes
UX Magazine

To this point in the UX Design process, you have created a number of documents that identify the typical user, what users need and don't need in the app or website, and a host of other documents that support the project's intent. With all that information available to you, the time has arrived to answer the next important question: What does it look like?

Consider what it takes to build a house. The construction team does not dig a hole in the ground and start building. The process starts with the architect consulting with the client to understand what they need and don't need. Once that process is completed, the architect draws up a set of blueprints outlining, among other things, the placement of windows and doors and where the rooms are located. The blueprint is handed over to the construction team, and following the blueprint, they build the house according to the blueprint's specifications. At this point, the house is a

© Tom Green and Kevin Brandon 2024
T. Green and K. Brandon, *UX Design with Figma*, Design Thinking,
https://doi.org/10.1007/979-8-8688-0324-6_5

shell with holes in the walls for the windows, plywood for the floors, and holes in the interior where doors will be added. The final construction phase is adding the final details that were specified. The house is inspected, and the keys are turned over to the new homeowner.

Let's now relate this process to UX Design because building a website or app follows the same process as building a house. The consultation with the client is the Research phase of the project. The blueprints are the wireframes. The initial construction phase is building the static screens or pages, and the final phase is where interactivity brings the project to life. The house inspection is User Testing before the product is released.

The prototyping process is based on "fidelity," which moves a product from boxes and arrows (a low-fidelity (Lo-Fi) prototype), to content placement (medium fidelity (Mid-Fi)), to a fully interactive high-fidelity (Hi-Fi) prototype. In this chapter, we are going to focus on the low-fidelity wireframing process and where Figma plays a rather significant role.

What Is a Low-Fidelity Wireframe?

A wireframe connects the research documentation to the visual design (where required areas of the website or app are defined in dimensions and location within the wireframe). Wireframes should be regarded as visual representations of an interface that not only establishes the information architecture but also answers a few questions:

- How will this app or website be structured?

- What content will be used?

- How will the information be organized?

- What is an intuitive user flow for the content?

- How will a user get from here to there in an efficient manner?

- How does this thing work?

The biggest mistake one can make about a Lo-Fi wireframe is that it is a "rough idea of where stuff goes." Not quite. Wireframes are the best method of starting the visual design of a website or app because everyone involved is more concerned with the layout than images, videos, color, type, and other design elements. By concentrating on what goes where and determining the size of each area, you are defining the information hierarchy. A Lo-Fi wireframe becomes the skeleton or blueprint upon which the product will be constructed. In many respects, wireframes are a foundational framework for the design that explores both structure and content during the project's design formation.

As the screens, pages, or frames are drawn on paper or whiteboard, a sitemap starts coming into focus along with the User Flow. The team also gets to consider how users get from here to there. Toss in light interactivity when the wireframes are reproduced in Figma and User Testing becomes necessary.

Finally, wireframing is an iterative process. A reason to start with paper is to allow for quick changes, everyone involved in the process has the same access to the tools, and parts can be recycled when they are not needed – if the concept doesn't work, crumple it up, toss it in the recycling bin, grab your pencil, and start over. Wireframing is also not something you make up as you go along. The wireframes visualize the research, personas, User Flows, and other documents and move it from a theoretical space into a tangible working space. Along the way, the sketches are refined and refined again to achieve the essence of the User Experience Mission: focus on the user, not the technology.

The Case for and Against Wireframing

The decision to create wireframes is made during the project's planning phase. The reasons not to use wireframes include the following:

- They Aren't Even Close to the Final Product: This is a valid objection because the team – including stakeholders – must translate an abstract concept into a visual idea of what the project may look like.

- Constant Changes to the Layouts: Wireframing is an iterative process that tosses concepts into the trash can. Naturally, those constantly changing and redrawing the wireframes stake out ownership of the concept, which can hinder the process if not push back deadlines.

- They Can't Be Subjected to User Testing: Wireframes hint at structure and can be seen as nothing more than yet another addition to the documentation.

- Agile and Rapid Prototyping Workflows Don't Need Them: In these workflows, the aim is to get as close to the final product as fast as possible.

These are all valid objections, and we are not advocating that you incorporate a wireframing phase into your project planning. Still, there are a few advantages to wireframing. They include the following:

- Design Structure: A wireframe is the skeleton of an app or website that shows what goes where and prevents the tendency to "make it up as you go along." They bring structure to the Design phase.

- Something vs. Nothing: You can explain it better when you have something to show. Wireframes visually communicate the page's structure or the screen. It is challenging to say: "The menu bar is at the top, and right under it is a Hero image with a key message." How did you picture that when you read it?

- Content, Not Design: Everyone involved concentrates on where stuff goes without being concerned with things like images, text, etc. They also establish an information hierarchy.

Creating Wireframes

There are many different types of wireframes. Some are not digital because the process started on paper before they are reproduced in Figma. Again, we have no intention of telling you what method is most suitable to your workflow; instead, here are a few of the common wireframing methods:

- Sketching: By simply drawing your ideas on paper (Figure 5-1), you have the opportunity to fail fast. By that, we mean you may decide a series of cards are needed. You sketch it out and realize the cards need to be a bit smaller and moved up in the information hierarchy. The solution is to either erase the big cards and sketch smaller ones or throw the sketch into the wastebasket and start over. The best aspect of sketching is that you work fast and intuitively.

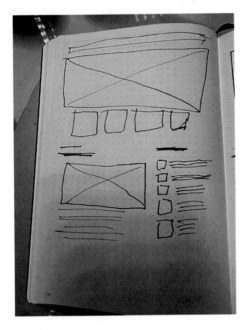

Figure 5-1. *Sketching is fast and intuitive*

- Paper Cutouts: Paper prototypes (Figure 5-2) take a bit more time, but they offer one advantage you don't get with sketching: they can be user tested.

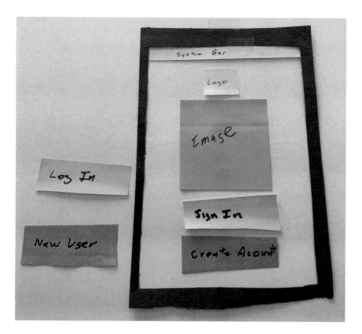

Figure 5-2. *Paper cutouts can be user tested*

- Digital Lo-Fi Wireframes: Adobe Photoshop, Illustrator, and Sketch (Figure 5-3) are commonly used. If the design team has expertise with these applications, they can be created in short order. If this method is used, the designers should resist the temptation to add graphic detail. We also should add Figma does have the ability to import Sketch documents containing layers and symbols, which could make the process more efficient.

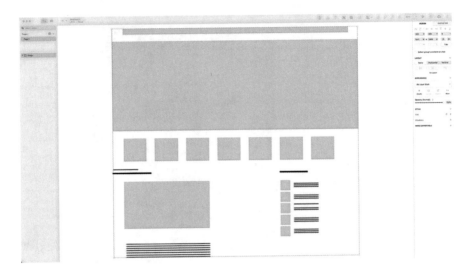

Figure 5-3. *You can use drawing software such as Sketch to quickly create the wireframes*

Wireframing and the UX Design Process

As we have said, when and how to create wireframes is dependent upon your workflow method. Here are the three most common situations:

- Traditional: The wireframe moves from paper, to a Lo-Fi prototype in Figma, to a Hi-Fi prototype. With this process, the wireframes show the information hierarchy using what we call Boxes and Arrows. In Figma, the wireframes become more focused, adding more visual details such as text and color. The prototype is where interactivity and usability are determined.

- Rapid Prototyping: If you use an Agile workflow, the path is Wireframe to Prototype as multiple iterations quickly lead to a Minimum Viable Product. There is a misconception that wireframing impedes the speed of the workflow. This is not true. Add interactivity to the wireframes and the same usability data from User Testing is available.

- Straight to Code: In this workflow, the wireframes lead to a coded prototype. If the project has unique technical requirements, then coding as soon as possible is important. Just keep in mind, wireframes provide a visual guideline for web and app prototypes. Producing a set of carefully considered wireframes and layout considerations will make the development process much more efficient.

What Is a Content Wireframe?

Wireframes are based on the team determining what content will be needed, which really is nothing more than establishing a content inventory. This is where the concept of creating a Content Wireframe is a useful first step before digging into drawing out the wireframes. We first came across this concept in 2012 when Stephen Hay presented the concept at the Beyond the Desktop Conference in 2012 (`https://vimeo.com/47171001`). His concept was succinct: "Build from the content outwards."

That phrase is important. Wireframes aren't created out of nothing. The team needs to decide what they need before they decide what goes where. "What they need" is a content inventory, and once that is established, the inventory becomes a hierarchical list with the most important content blocks at the top and the least important blocks at the bottom of the list. With that list created, a Content Wireframe can be constructed that establishes content precedence, not page flow.

Using the wireframe depicted in Figure 5-1, the content inventory could be

- Hero image, or main image

- News about current events available in Bern

- Social Media comments

- Cards that suggest activities

- Header and footer areas of the design

It may surprise you to see the header and footer at the bottom of the list. The header and footer are there to provide simple navigation. The Hero image is there to get the user's attention. The News area provides information, and the list of Social Media comments is there to provide third-party influence.

Having negotiated the content hierarchy, we can now create the Content Wireframe. Following the UX Design Best Practice of "Mobile First," we start with the mobile version, which, in many respects, follows the "Content Outwards" philosophy. In this case, it is "Mobile Outwards."

Using the list as a guide, here is how you would create the Content Wireframe:

1. Create a new Design file from the Figma Dashboard. When the new Design file opens, click the Frame tool, and in the left-hand Properties panel, select the option for Android Large to create a new frame.

2. With the frame selected, add a four-column grid with a 16-pixel margin using the right-hand Grid properties.

3. We now have the underlying structure for a four-column Android screen. We can now turn our attention to creating the hierarchy from the list.

4. Select the Rectangle tool. Draw a box at the top of
    the frame and across the columns with a height of
    440 pixels. Fill the rectangle with a dark gray color
    (#464646). In the Layers panel, name the rectangle
    layer "Hero".

5. Draw another rectangle below the first, from the left
    edge of the first column to the right edge of the last
    column with a height value of 120 pixels. Change the
    Fill color to #464646 and name the layer Cards.

6. Draw another box, below again, the same width as
    the last one; apply a height value of 180 pixels. Fill it
    with that dark gray and name the layer News.

7. Select the Text tool and label inside each of the
    rectangles to match the layer name. If Grid is visible,
    turn it off (Shift-G).

What you have done, as shown in Figure 5-4, is to create a Content
Wireframe for a mobile website. As you can see, space restrictions
compromise what goes on that first screen. In this case, the Hero, Cards,
and News areas will appear on that screen. The Social area is missing
because it is low in the hierarchy.

The screen is the viewport that also could lead to a discussion of
whether that screen is scrollable to accommodate a larger News section
and the Social section. It could also be that the Social section could be
moved to a different screen or not added to the project. These are all issues
arising from the creation of that Content Wireframe, and none of them
are locked in. For example, the team may decide the Hero image should
be full screen and that the Cards and News area should be moved to
separate screens. What you have learned from this is a Content Wireframe,
especially for mobile, forces the team to concentrate on Content
placement based on the information hierarchy, not the actual content that
will be placed in those areas.

Figure 5-4. *Content wireframes focus on the "where" of content, not the "what"*

Let's now turn our attention to a desktop website Content Wireframe.

1. Create a new Design file from the Figma Dashboard. When the new Design file opens, click the Frame tool and draw a frame that is 1440 × 1200 pixels.

2. With the frame selected, use the Properties panel, Grid to add a 12-column grid with a 20-pixel margin.

3. We now have the underlying structure for a 12-column web page. We can now turn our attention to creating the hierarchy for the list.

4. Select the Rectangle tool. Draw a box at the top of the frame, across the columns, with a height of 30 pixels. Fill it with a dark gray color (#464646). In the Layers panel, name the rectangle layer "Header".

5. Draw another rectangle from the left edge of the first column to the right edge of the last column with a height of 430 pixels. Change the Fill color to #464646 and name the layer Hero.

6. Draw another rectangle, the same width as the last one and a height value of 180 pixels. Fill it with dark gray and name the layer Cards.

7. Draw another box that is 808 × 436 pixels. Move it to the left edge of the first column, fill it with dark gray, and name the layer News.

8. Draw another box that is 572 × 436 pixels. Move it to the left edge of column 8 and fill it with dark gray and name the layer Social.

9. Duplicate the Header Layer. Name the layer Footer; then move it to the bottom of the frame.

10. Select the Text tool and add a label matching the layer name to each of the rectangles. If Grid is visible, turn it off (Shift-G).

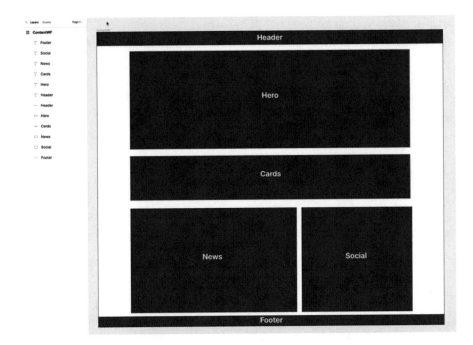

Figure 5-5. *The Content Wireframe lays out the content areas for a web page*

What you don't want to do is to get "locked in" to those box sizes. They basically show where "stuff" goes, and it just may be that "stuff" could be larger or smaller than the content boxes. The boxes are to define a general location for the area as well as dimensions.

What you have done, as shown in Figure 5-5, is to concentrate on content hierarchy. Bigger boxes are more important than smaller boxes – you have applied the idea of starting by building from the content outward. The other benefit to this technique is these can be iterated by the team to the point where the content areas are settled, meaning you can now concentrate on what goes in those areas.

There is one final advantage to this technique. Starting with a mobile web design and building out to a desktop version (Figure 5-6) provides the UX Design team and the development team with a visual guide to planning for Responsive Design as the content moves from mobile screens, to tablets, to web pages.

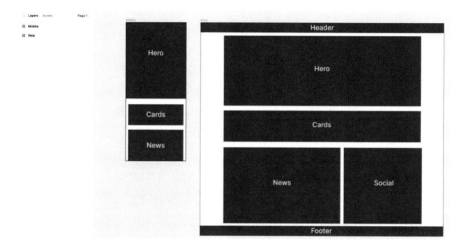

Figure 5-6. *Building from Mobile Outwards starts the Responsive Design process*

From Content Wireframe to Lo-Fi Wireframe

Although a Content Wireframe is a good first step in the UX Design process, it really is nothing more than a rough guide to the order or placement of the content areas to establish an information hierarchy. The next step in the process is to flesh out those areas with a Lo-Fi wireframe.

Lo-Fi wireframes are, in many respects, the blueprint for your design. They connect the structure from the Content Wireframe with a smartphone, tablet, or web app. What they don't do is to represent the visual design or brand identity. This explains why Lo-Fi wireframes use grayed-out boxes for various elements such as cards. Boxes with image icons or an "X" to represent images and repeated lines for text.

What we don't need to know is what images will be used, what text will be entered, the colors, etc. The goal here isn't depth; it's content breadth, because the wireframes are the skeleton of the app or website. Even something as benign as adding colors or shades of gray will add detail, which leads to confusion because those viewing them won't know, for example, what they communicate such as a variation of an element.

Wireframes are also a communication vehicle. What they need to communicate is behavior, which means showing how an element interacts or behaves with the user, which is where affordances and signifiers come into play.

If you are unfamiliar with those two terms, think of the chair you are sitting in. That chair affords sitting because, when you look at it, you instantly know what it does. The same thing applies to wireframes. If you see a button on an app or web page, you know it requires tapping or clicking. When it comes to wireframes, a gray box does not exactly scream, "Yo, this is an image!" Adding an image icon to that box signifies it is an image. That image icon is what is called an Explicit Signifier, which makes that gray box instantly understood as an image.

With that out of the way, let's turn this sketch (Figure 5-7) into a wireframe.

Figure 5-7. *Move a sketch on paper into the digital realm*

Creating a Low-Fidelity Wireframe in Figma

Though you could start using the Shape tools in Figma to create the various
wireframe elements such as images, text, and video, in a collaborative
environment, everybody on the design team will have their own way of
creating these elements. It would be a good idea to gather the team and
come up with a uniform set of these elements and add them to a Library
of wireframing components available to those responsible for creating the
wireframes for each page or screen in the project.

In this exercise, we are going to wireframe a web page using a rudimentary collection of components. Here's how:

1. Open the WFLibrary.fig file found in your chapter download. If you open the Assets panel (Figure 5-8), you will see it is a collection of local components. This means the only person with access to them is you, which tends to negate collaboration.

Figure 5-8. The wireframing components

2. What is missing are two elements indicating the header and the footer of the web page. Select the Rectangle tool and draw out a rectangle that is 1300 × 50 pixels. Fill it with a dark gray (#6B6B6B). Select the Text tool and enter "Header". Change its color to white and move it into the rectangle. That text is the "Explicit Signifier."

3. Group the text and the rectangle and name the group "Header".

4. Duplicate the Header Group. Change the Text to "Footer" and rename the group Footer.

5. The next step in making these two new elements available to everyone is to convert them to components.

6. To create a component right-click on the Header element and select Create component from the pop-down menu shown in Figure 5-9. You could also use the keyboard command – Ctrl-Shift-K (PC) or Cmd-Shift-K (Mac) for this conversion. You can also create components by selecting them in the Layers panel.

7. Convert the Footer group to a component.

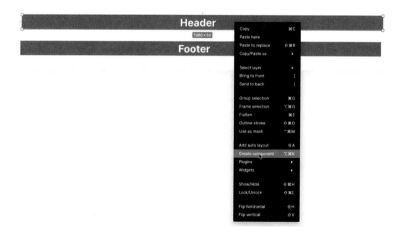

Figure 5-9. *Converting a group to a component*

Components are "create once, use many times" elements that can speed up your workflow. There is a lot more to creating components than this example, and we'll get into them later on in the book.

Creating a Team Library

The current roster of components is restricted to your computer. This is where a Team Library will make that component roster available to the rest of the team and ensure design consistency across all the pages or screens. Before we start, you need to know the ability to publish styles and components to a Team Library is only available to Professional or Enterprise versions of Figma.

Follow these steps to create a Team Library:

1. Click on the Assets tab. In the upper right corner of the panel is an open book icon. This is the Library button. Click it and the Libraries dialog box, as shown in Figure 5-10, opens.

Figure 5-10. *Clicking the Library button in the Assets panel creates a new Library*

2. Click the Publish button. If you are not working in a Team, you will be asked to move to a team and publish there. To do that, you need to return to your Dashboard and open the team project. Otherwise, the Publish button shown in Figure 5-11 will be grayed out. You can also add a description of this Library. Clicking the blue Publish button will publish this Library to your Team project.

Figure 5-11. *When creating a new Team Library, you can add a description*

With the Library created, here's how team members access it.

3. Select the Team project in your Dashboard and create a new Design file.

4. Select the Frame tool, and in the Desktop choices, select Wireframe.

5. Open the Assets panel and click the Library button, which opens the Libraries panel. Notice the Library is in the list. Click the "Add to file" button.

6. Close the Libraries panel and open the WFLibrary. All of the components created earlier are now attached to this document (Figure 5-12).

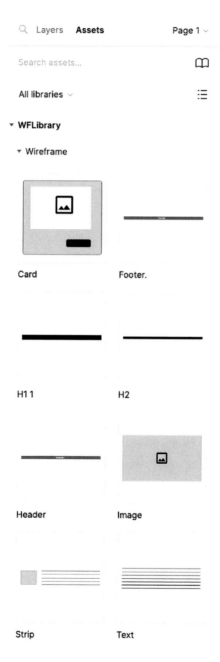

Figure 5-12. *All of the assets in the Team Library are added to the document*

A Quick Word About Shared Libraries

We have to admit that Shared Libraries in Figma are a killer feature allowing designers to maintain and create styles and components across multiple team files. They also add consistency to the design process, foster collaboration, and create a single source for a Design System. Though you may think Libraries are "carved in stone," this is not true. Library assets can be added to and edited, and those additions and edits will instantly be reflected in the Shared Library.

There are many benefits to a Shared Library. Among them are as follows:

- They promote consistency across multiple files and projects.

- They increase efficiency and productivity by reducing the time to create styles and components used across team projects. The design team can focus on content and functionality rather than appearance and layout.

- They enhance communication and collaboration by allowing the design team to share and reuse styles and components from other contributors, provide feedback, and rapidly iterate designs based on feedback.

- Finally, Shared Libraries in Figma add an efficiency boost to the normal workflow. All of the assets needed for a project are found in the Library, meaning there is no need to recreate them. When a Design System is in place, all of the styles and components for that Design System are not only available but the Design System is scalable as new elements and styles are added to the Design System.

Build the Wireframe Using a Shared Library

Accessing and using the elements in a Team Library is relatively simple: Select your team, open a new Design file or the team project, and open the Library in the Assets panel. Here's how:

1. Open a new Design file. When it opens, select the Frame tool and select Wireframe in the Desktop section of the Properties panel.

2. With the Wireframe selected, add a 12-column grid with a 20-pixel gutter.

3. Click once on the Assets tab.

4. Click on the Explore libraries link when the Assets panel opens. The Libraries dialog box opens (Figure 5-13).

Figure 5-13. *Clicking the Explore Libraries link opens the Library used by the Team*

5. Click the Add to file button for the Library to be used. When the dialog box closes, the Library is added to the Assets panel and is ready for use.

   If you twirl down the Library, all of the components in that Library are there. We can now construct the wireframe using these components. Here's how.

6. Select the Header component to open the Details
    dialog box. The component is shown. To add an
    instance of the component to the design surface,
    drag the image of the instance into the frame or click
    the Insert instance button (Figure 5-14). An instance
    of the Header component is added to the page.

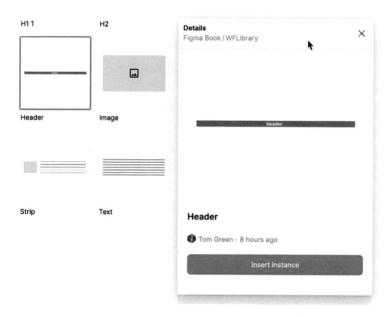

Figure 5-14. *Instances of the components in the Library are added to the page*

Using Figure 5-15 as your guide, build the wireframes. As you do, you
will discover the instances can be scaled to fit the grid. You also don't need
to add multiple instances of the Card component. Scale the first instance
to the size you need. Select the instance, and with the Option/Alt-Shift keys
held down, drag out a copy.

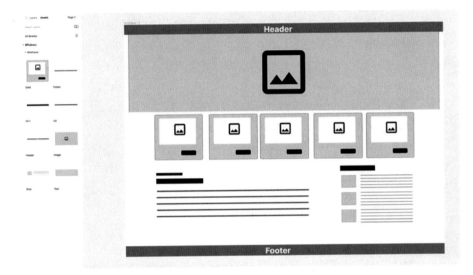

Figure 5-15. *The wireframe is created by adding instances to the page and scaling them as needed*

Yes, the wireframe looks a bit rudimentary. That isn't important. What you have discovered is you can wireframe an entire page or screen in under ten minutes.

Create Wireframes Using a Wireframing Kit

Now that you understand how to use a Component Library, there is another approach to wireframing that doesn't require creating your own components. There are a number of free wireframing libraries available to you through the Community Resources site. One of our favorites is Wireframer by Tony Allsopp. Follow these steps to access the Wireframer Library:

1. From your Dashboard, click the Explore Community link to open the Figma Community site. When it opens, enter Wireframes into the Search area.

2. Select Wireframer by Tony Allsopp to open the Description page.

3. Click the Open in Figma button and the Library will open and the Layers will appear.

4. Click the Assets tab to view the Local components contained in the Library.

5. Click the Library icon and publish the kit.

6. Return to your Dashboard and create a new Design file. When it opens, click the Frame tool and select Wireframe from the Desktop selections. Change the Height value to 2200 pixels and add a 12-column grid with a 20-pixel gutter.

7. Add the Wireframer Library by clicking the "Explore libraries..." link in the Assets panel.

8. When the Libraries dialog box opens, click the Add to file button for Wireframer. The components are now in your Team Library (Figure 5-16).

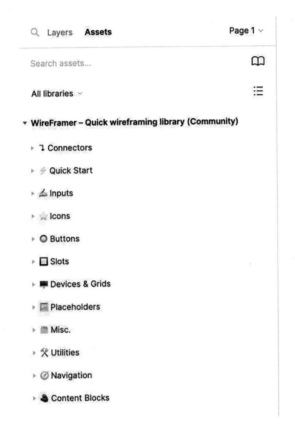

Figure 5-16. *The Wireframer components are added and ready for use*

Use the Wireframer Library

With the components available, let's build a wireframe.

1. Twirl down the Navigation components and add a Header instance to the top of the page and a Footer instance to the bottom of the page.

2. Resize both instances to run across the columns (Figure 5-17).

Figure 5-17. *The Header and Footer instances are in place*

3. Twirl down the Placeholders section and add an
    Image Placeholder instance. Use these Property
    values for the Image placeholder:

    - X: 20

    - Y: 100

    - Width: 1400

    - Height: 717

4. Twirl down the Content Blocks area and add a Card instance. Use these property values for the Card:

   - X: 20

   - Y: 850

   - W: 453

   - H: 493

5. Copy this instance two times and place the instances (Figure 5-18) in the remaining eight columns.

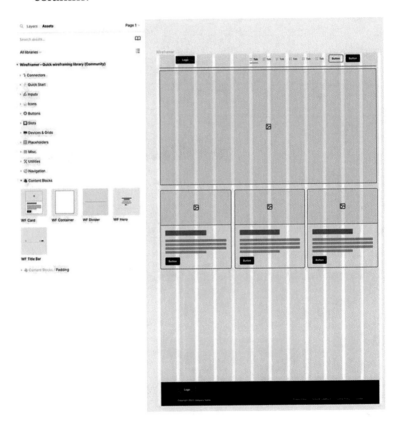

Figure 5-18. *The Image and Card instances have been added*

The remaining pieces to be added to the wireframe are the News section and the Social links. Start with the News section.

6. To add the Headline, twirl down the Placeholders section and then twirl down the Placeholders/ Headings/Left section. Add a 1-line M instance to the page.

7. With the instance selected, use these properties:

   - X: 20

   - Y: 1400

8. To add the Body text, twirl down Placeholders/ Body text/Left and add a Paragraphs-4 instance (Figure 5-19). Apply these properties:

   - X: 138

   - Y: 1495

   - W: 572

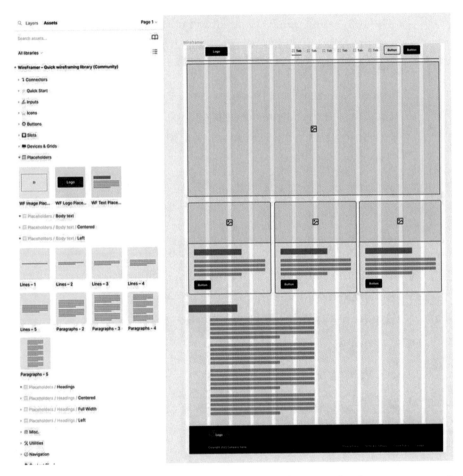

Figure 5-19. *The News section uses a Heading and a four paragraphs*

The Social section requires a Headline and a list of people and their comments.

9. To add the Headline, add a 1-line instance. Change its X value to 852 pixels and the Y value to 1400 pixels.

We only need one list element that contains an image and a text instance.

10. Add an Image Placeholder instance and use these properties:

    - X: 970

    - Y: 1495

    - W: 97

    - H: 66

11. Add a 3-line Body text/Left instance and use these values:

    - X: 1087

    - Y: 1495

    - W: 333

12. Select both the image and text instances, and with the Option-Shift (Mac) or Alt-Shift (PC) key held down, create four more copies by dragging the section downward. As you create the copies, make sure there is 24 pixels of space between each copy.

The wireframe is complete, and to turn off the grid, press Shift-G.

In this exercise, you completed a wireframe that looks a lot more professional than the one using custom wireframe components (Figure 5-20). When it comes to UX Design, we firmly believe in letting the software do the work, and a wireframing kit like Wireframer does a lot of the work for you.

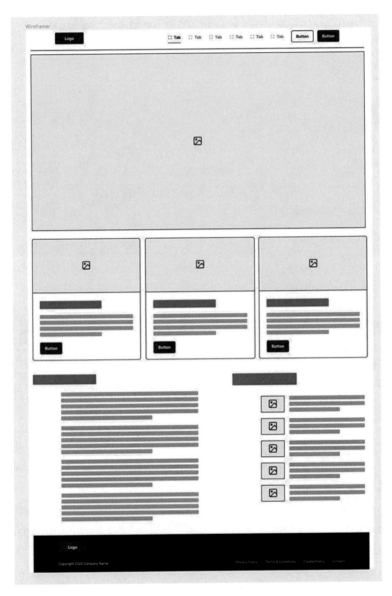

Figure 5-20. *The wireframe is composed of Wireframer components from the Library*

The Interactive Wireframe

The wireframes for the various sections of the app are complete. To get to this point, there have been multiple iterations of the screens. Each screen has been created in Figma, and based on feedback, there have been multiple iterations of the Content Wireframes and the wireframes. They have been approved, and they are now being presented to the stakeholders and the full team. At this point, the whole thing grinds to a halt when someone asks, "What happens when I tap that button on the first screen?" (Figure 5-21).

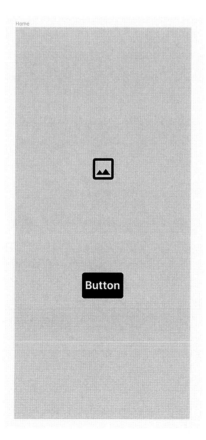

Figure 5-21. *"What happens when I tap that button on the first screen?"*

This is where you should consider adding interactivity to the wireframes.

To some, this may seem to be "overkill." To others, it may be regarded as a waste of time because that button is just a "thing." It isn't going to be the robust element that changes color when rolled over in the Prototype or that vibrant blue with "Let's go" replacing the word "Button". These objections are valid, but they don't answer the question, "What happens when I tap the button on the first screen?" You could try answering the question verbally such as "It goes to the next screen." Here's the issue with that: everybody listening will form a different mental impression of "how" it goes to the next screen. The question can be best answered by adding "light interactivity." By that, we mean interactions that move from page to page and nothing else. Remember, the focus of a wireframe is "where" content will be placed. Add light interactivity and you show "how" a user will interact with the content.

The wireframe stage is also the ideal time to start brainstorming interactivity to answer the "What" questions the team will ponder. These would be such questions as

- Does the button change color when rolled over?

- Does the button grow or shrink when rolled over?

- Are the buttons on the second screen in a dialog box?

There are a ton of questions that can be asked, and depending on the complexity of the project, this stage of the UX Design process is the ideal place to start exploring them. Interactions could be added to

- Call-to-action buttons or other elements

- Navigation menus

- Modals and pop-up or pop-down menus

- Alerts and dialog boxes

With nothing but primitive boxes and arrows, these low-fidelity wireframes give the team permission to play what we call "What if..." games. By this, we mean such things as "What if the second screen slides in from the right when the button of the first screen is tapped?" Try and if it doesn't work, remove it.

In today's UX Design discipline, Lo-Fi wireframes no longer provide a rough idea of "where stuff goes." It is the start of the visual design process allowing everyone from the design team to the stakeholders and developers to focus exclusively on the layout without being distracted by color, type, images, or other design elements.

At the same time, low-fidelity wireframes provide a low-risk opportunity to start examining interactivity and the user experience.

Add Interactivity to a Wireframe

Before we start, we are going to be concentrating on "going from here to there" and nothing else. By that, we mean we are going to add simple button clicks. We will be getting deep into the process of interactivity in Chapter 7. With that out of the way, let's get started:

1. Open the InteractiveWF.fig file found in your chapter download. When it opens, there are four screens (Figure 5-22).

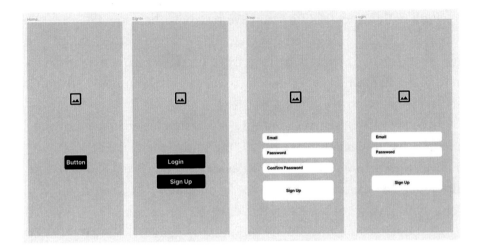

Figure 5-22. *We start with four wireframed screens*

Here's the plan:

- When the user taps the "Button" element on the Home screen, the User is taken to the Signin screen.

- If the User taps on the Login button, the User is taken to the Login screen.

- If the User taps on the Sign Up button, the User is taken to the New screen.

Did you happen to notice how we presented the interactivity? It is a story focused on the User. This is a great way of planning interactivity.

---

2. Click the top-right Prototype tab in the Properties panel. The panel changes (Figure 5-23) to the prototype Settings, which show you the device, the orientation (Portrait or Landscape), a preview of the device, and the background color. There is also a Flow category, which we will get to later.

Figure 5-23. *The prototyping panel is where you add interactivity*

3. Select the Button on the Home screen. If you move
    the mouse to either side of the button, you will see a
    circle with a + sign. Click on that circle and drag the
    mouse to the Signin screen. You will see an arrow
    (Figure 5-24) pointing to that screen when you
    release the mouse. That arrow shows the "here" to
    "there" path. The arrows are commonly referred to
    as "wires."

245

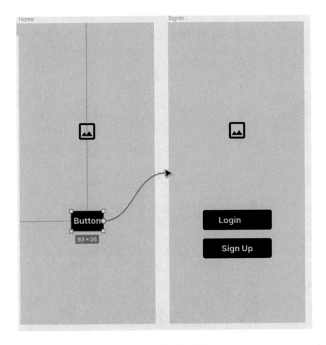

Figure 5-24. *When the button is clicked here, it moves to there*

When you release the mouse, you will also see the Interactions dialog box (Figure 5-25), which points to the arrowhead and answers the common "What," "Where," and "How" questions that bring your interactivity story to life. At the top you will see On tap. This is the event that answers the "What" question. The Navigate section answers other two questions:

- Where does the Tap event go? Signin screen

- How does that screen appear? Instantly when the mouse is released

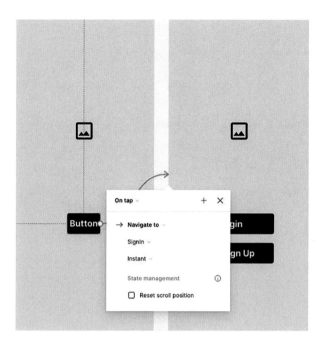

Figure 5-25. *The Interactions dialog box*

4. Click away from the Interactions dialog box to
    accept the interaction. You also should know this is
    the default state of the Interactions dialog box.

5. To test your interaction, click on the blue Flow icon
    attached to the Home screen. A separate window
    opens, and when you click the button, the Signin
    screen appears instantly. This is a handy way of
    quickly seeing if the interaction was what you
    expected.

6. To finish up, connect the Login button to the Login
    screen and the Sign Up button to the New screen as
    shown in Figure 5-26.

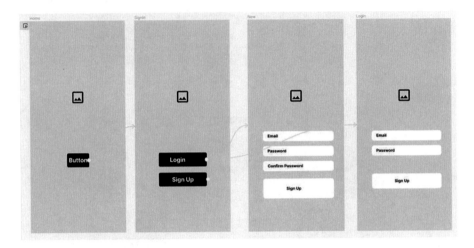

Figure 5-26. *The sequence is "wired up"*

Testing an Interactive Wireframe

The Flow button is a great way of ensuring the interactivity does what it is supposed to do. When you are confident everything works, you can share the prototype with the team and the stakeholders. Here's how:

1. Click the top-right Figma Play button. The wireframe appears in the device (Figure 5-27), and you can click the buttons to navigate through the project. Except for one glaring error: when you land on the New screen or the Signin screen, there is no way of getting back to that second screen. We also should add this error would also become evident when you test the Flow.

Figure 5-27. *Testing the Interactive Wireframe*

This error can be solved in one of two ways: Add a Back Button to the two screens or use the Image wireframe in the screens to link back to the Signin screen.

Having addressed the interaction issue the prototype can now be tested, click the Share button and choosing the desired sharing options.

There are a couple of advantages to sharing the Interactive Wireframe:

- The team can test it and comment on issues they perceive.

- The stakeholders can try it out.

- The prototype can be sent out for User Testing.

Though User Testing is something to be discussed, we can assure you users will find issues the team never even considered. For example, users may find it difficult to tap the button on the first screen. This is due to the way users actually use their smartphones. They use their thumbs to tap elements such as buttons. In this case, the issue is easily solved by moving that button closer to the bottom of the frame. Another issue could be the size of the button. If the button is small, the user may not be able to access it. These are all issues that don't have major implications. Test it when the sequence is a high-fidelity prototype and that button issue will ripple through the entire project, especially if it is a key component in the Design System.

Your Turn: Wireframe a Login Sequence Using FigJam

FigJam is not a wireframing tool. Where it absolutely shines, though, is it presents the team with the opportunity to get together and consider the user flow of such things as a login sequence. In the previous chapter, we worked on the user flow for a login sequence (Figure 5-28). In this exercise, we are going to use FigJam to turn those boxes, arrows, and circles into a wireframe in order to learn how many screens will be needed.

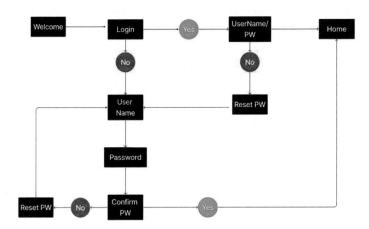

Figure 5-28. *We start by turning this diagram into a wireframe*

1. Open a new FigJam board. Select the Square tool and draw a rectangle. Fill it with dark gray.

2. Make four copies of this rectangle and space them out.

3. Select the Text tool and add "Welcome" above the box. Select Extra Large as the font size and select Black as the color. Repeat this step for the remaining four rectangles and name them, from left to right, Login, User, New User, and Home (Figure 5-29).

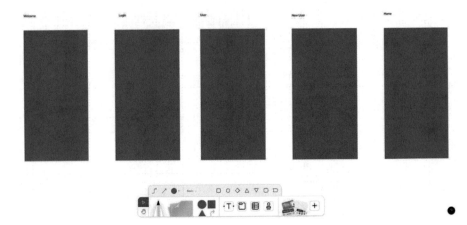

Figure 5-29. *The screens are in place*

4. Create a Rounded Rectangle filled with light gray.
    Click the text inside the rectangle and enter the
    word Welcome. Set the text as Extra Large and select
    Black as the color.

5. Create four copies of this shape and change the text
    to read Login, New Account, and Submit for the last
    two. Move the Login shape onto the Welcome page,
    Login and New Account onto the Login page, and
    move the Submit buttons to the bottom of the User
    and New User pages as shown in Figure 5-30.

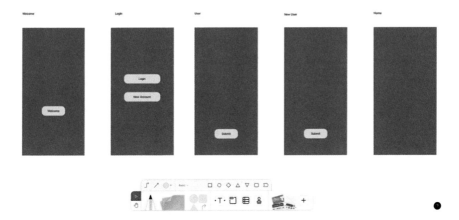

Figure 5-30. *The buttons are added to the screens*

6. Select the Square tool and draw out a rectangle filled with white. Click once inside this box and enter New User as the text. Set the text to Extra Large and black as the Fill color. This will be a text input box.

7. Make four copies of this rectangle. Move the first and second rectangles to the User page. Change the text in the second one to Password.

8. Move the remaining three rectangles to the New User page. The text should be User Name, Password, and Re-enter Password (Figure 5-31).

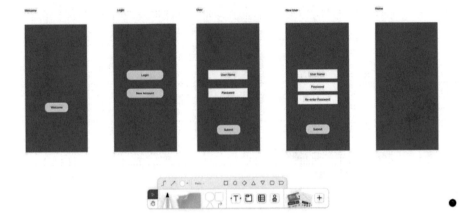

Figure 5-31. *The text input areas are identified*

One of the neater aspects of brainstorming using FigJam is the team can consider solutions to such questions as "What happens if the user enters either the wrong User Name or Password?" A possible solution would be the use of a Modal, which will appear if the incorrect information is entered.

9. Select the Rounded Rectangle shape, draw out a square shape, and fill it with black.

10. Create copies of the User Name and Password boxes and add them to the shape. Add a copy of the Submit button to the shape. Select the Text tool and enter Error Modal. Format the text as Extra Large and filled with black. Move this text above the Modal and move both the Text and the Modal under the User page.

11. Select both the Text and the Modal. Make a copy and move it under the New User page (Figure 5-32).

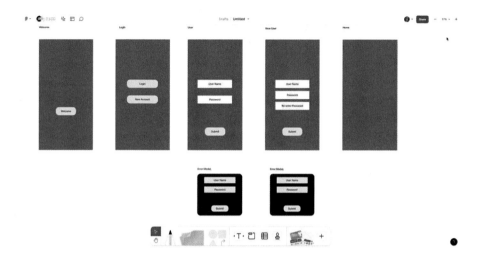

Figure 5-32. *The Modals are placed under the User and New User pages*

12. The final step is to add the Connector wires to the screens as shown in Figure 5-33.

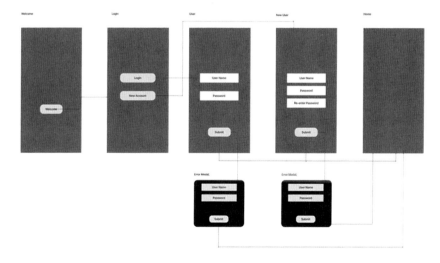

Figure 5-33. *Connector wires are added to the board to show the flow*

Once everybody is happy with the board, it can be converted to a section and added to the Documents pages.

You Have Learned

- The importance of wireframing in the UX process

- Why low-fidelity wireframes connect the research to the visual design

- Various methods for creating wireframes

- How to create a Content Wireframe in Figma

- How to create a low-fidelity wireframe in Figma

- How to create a Team Library

- How to access a Team Library

- How to use the Wireframer Library

- How to create an Interactive Wireframe

- How to use FigJam in the wireframing process

CHAPTER 6

Building Medium-Fidelity Prototypes

"Never go to a meeting without a prototype."

−Boyle's Law
Tom Kelley, IDEO

Creating a set of wireframes that map out a UX Design project is a good start, but they only provide a rough idea of "where stuff goes." Eventually, someone is going to ask, "So what does it look like?" This is where the next step in the UX Design process gets underway. A medium-fidelity prototype or mockup brings to life the "experience" behind "user experience." They help to provide "proof of concept" and start the process of exposing the usability and accessibility issues that can only be revealed at this stage of the process.

The UX Design process is undergoing some profound changes. Though wireframes are a common first step, it is what happens after the wireframes are locked in that is changing. The process we outline throughout this book is the "traditional" method of Sketch, Wireframe, Prototype, Interactivity, and Development. We are now in a time where such workflows as Lean UX, rapid prototyping, Agile, and even straight to code are replacing the traditional workflow. They all follow the traditional workflow with the

© Tom Green and Kevin Brandon 2024
T. Green and K. Brandon, *UX Design with Figma*, Design Thinking,
https://doi.org/10.1007/979-8-8688-0324-6_6

focus on finding the shortest time possible to move a project from concept to development. Having said that, prototyping is an incremental, iterative process that refines the screens, pages, or frames to meet and test the project's intent (Figure 6-1). Before we dig into Figma, let's look at a few of them.

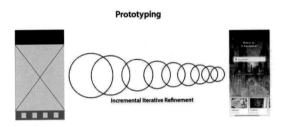

Figure 6-1. *The time between a wireframe to an Interactive Prototype design is compressing*

Lean UX

This workflow focuses on the shortest time between you and the code. Sometimes referred to as "rapid prototyping," advocates state some of the following advantages:

- Time: The time between wireframe to code is compressed as steps are skipped to get the project out the door.

- Efficiency: By concentrating on only what is important, the time spent on non-essential tasks is minimized.

- Experience: Deliverables focus on the experience, not the prototype. Pull the team together, present the design vision, and get to work.

This is a messy process because it is all about quickly iterating and updating the prototype based on feedback. That being said, it's also a tremendous way of helping the team to visualize the design as they work together toward the final product.

Agile

Agile and UX Design don't play well together because the Agile method tends to work ahead of the UX Designer, which could introduce friction to the collaboration between the UX Designers and the Development crew. This friction is disappearing because Agile has become the methodology for development.

Agile works best in a rapid prototyping environment. The product milestones are broken into manageable pieces of the UI. They are designed, developed, tested, and iterated upon regularly.

Straight to Code

It is common knowledge that the shortest distance between two points is a straight line. The concept of moving from wireframe directly to code is efficient. That is the good news. The bad news is this methodology only works if there is a clear direction. Starting with paper or whiteboards, concepts can be fully explored and either accepted or rejected. Once everything is approved, the development team starts writing the code based on the defined device platform.

What Is a Medium-Fidelity Prototype

In basic terms, a medium-fidelity prototype starts adding details and information to the wireframes, without interactions. By information, we mean the boxes and arrows become components: images or text.

259

They aren't interactive because they are designed to communicate their purpose. They also come in two forms: low detail, high functionality or high detail, low functionality.

An example of a low-detail, high-functionality prototype is shown in Figure 6-2. As you can see, the wireframe moves from a series of boxes to a series of elements that are vague enough to encourage pointed feedback but have enough detail to explore user flows. The elements used are also primitive enough that they can be converted to components and added to a Library. For those of you in a rapid prototyping environment, interactivity can be explored without the distraction of color palettes, type, images, and so on. Another key aspect of this prototype is that it can be subjected to multiple iterations with minimal budget implications.

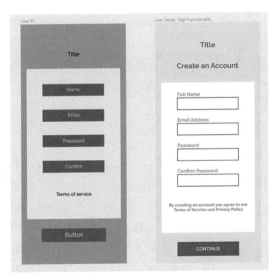

Figure 6-2. *Low-detail, high-functionality prototypes are ideal for rapid prototyping*

High-detail, low-functionality prototypes (Figure 6-3) validate your project's hypothesis because they have been fully examined and the wireframes iterated with an eye to the information hierarchy and content structure. It also presents the visual design and not the core interactions.

From an interaction point of view, these prototypes are treated more as clickthroughs than anything else. The advantage of this form of prototype is the stakeholders get their first glimpse of the user interface. We should caution you that creating this prototype without sketching the wireframes on paper and fully examining them is dangerous.

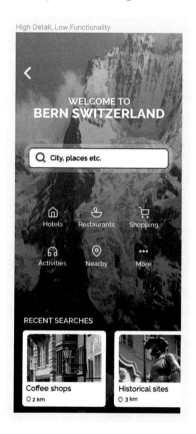

Figure 6-3. *High detail, low functionality*

Which type of medium fidelity (Mid-Fi), and workflow to use, is something that should be determined during the planning phase of the project. You may even choose to start with the low detail prototype, and once the screens are approved, the content for the high detail prototype can be flowed in.

When searching the Figma Community for UI blueprints you will be presented with both templates and plug-ins that can speed up your workflow. You will also find the latest UI kits for both Google Material Design and Apple iOS.

Choosing a Platform

When the planning process gets underway, the first issue to be decided is: Which platforms will be used? The reason is you have no control over how the project or product will be viewed. You have no control over the iPhone, Android phone, tablet, desktop or laptop monitor screen size/resolution, and even a television that the users will choose to view the product. It is important, therefore, for the team to clearly determine their base platforms and target devices.

If you open a new document and click the Frame tool (f), the first thing you will notice in the right-hand Properties panel is the number of iPhone models available but only two Android versions (Figure 6-4).

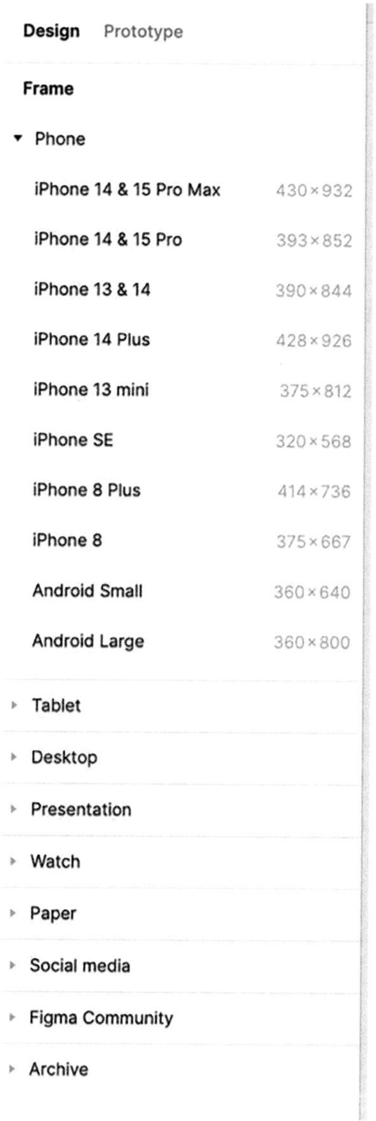

Design   Prototype

Frame

▾ Phone

    iPhone 14 & 15 Pro Max   430×932

    iPhone 14 & 15 Pro   393×852

    iPhone 13 & 14   390×844

    iPhone 14 Plus   428×926

    iPhone 13 mini   375×812

    iPhone SE   320×568

    iPhone 8 Plus   414×736

    iPhone 8   375×667

    Android Small   360×640

    Android Large   360×800

▸ Tablet

▸ Desktop

▸ Presentation

▸ Watch

▸ Paper

▸ Social media

▸ Figma Community

▸ Archive

Figure 6-4. *The default device frames*

These frames are the size of the viewport in pixels, not the physical dimension of the device.

Apple is commonly referred to as a "Walled Garden," and with Apple, "consistency" is the guiding principle. You get what you get, and that is that. The great advantage of this philosophy is common frame sizes. Not so much with Android. You only have two frame sizes. Why only two Android frames? The defaults are based on the Google Pixel smartphone, which is not exactly helpful. As we like to say, "Android is the wild west."

Android is an open source OS, and the phone manufacturers have taken advantage of that by competing on cameras, screen size, and the number of pixels they can jam into that screen for differing resolutions. Walk by any smartphone kiosk in any mall and the odds are pretty good you will encounter devices from Samsung, Huawei, OnePlus, and others. Which to choose?

Based on worldwide market share, according to Statista.com, at the time of writing this book Samsung and Apple are neck and neck at 18.7% and 17.7%, respectively (Figure 6-5). It is a completely different picture for North America. According to Statcounter (https://gs.statcounter.com/vendor-market-share/mobile/north-america), the numbers are skewed toward Apple with a 56% market share and Samsung with a 25% market share. Our advice is to look at the global picture because you have no control over where your users are located. Obviously, Samsung and Apple are the logical choices. Though the Google Pixel devices are the default frames, the Pixel global market share is less than 1%, and in North America, it has 4% of the market. Think of the Android Small and Android Large as more of a starting point when considering the Android platform.

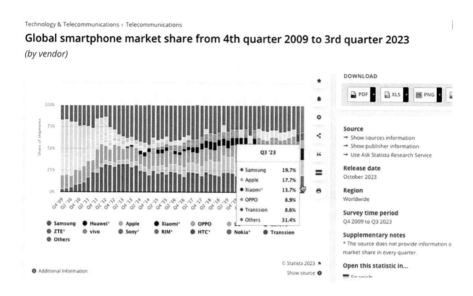

Figure 6-5.   Samsung and Apple lead the global smartphone market

When it comes to choosing your Android target devices and viewport size, you need to do some research. For example:

- IC Web Design (`www.icwebdesign.co.uk/common-viewport-sizes`) has a rather concise chart containing the common Android devices and their viewport sizes.

- Find the viewport dimensions of your screen or device by using the website ViewportSizer (`https://viewportsizer.com/devices/`).

- The Worship Agency has been creating yearly articles on screen sizes showing the top and most popular mobile screens viewport sizes (`https://worship.agency/mobile-screen-sizes-for-2023-based-on-data-from-2022`).

- Manually adjust the Android frame to match the viewport for the device targeted.

- Download an Android template from the Community site. There are quite a few, though, such as the Android UI Kit from Google (Figure 6-6).

Figure 6-6. *The Android UI Kit contains various device frames*

Having decided which devices and their viewports to target, let's now look at how content arrives in those frames and is manipulated or edited.

Graphics and Figma

For the balance of this chapter, we will be concentrating on the use, addition, and manipulation of the assets you will use when creating high detail prototypes. These assets include images, text, and vectors. Figma is an Assembly application. Assets are prepared elsewhere and added to Figma shortly thereafter.

When it comes to UX Design, the "need for speed" is the prime driver. These assets have to quickly load into a browser or app. The reason is users need it now. They are not prepared to wait for something that takes more than a second or two to appear on the screen. It is critical, especially with images, that they be optimized for minimal download times.

The reason images are potential download choke points is they are bitmaps or raster graphics. Each pixel in a photograph, for example, needs 3 bits of color information: red, green, and blue. That may not seem like much, but a color image that is 100 × 100 pixels in size contains 10,000 pixels. Toss in the color information and that image requires 30,000 bits of information to render properly.

It isn't all sweetness and light when it comes to vectors. Some of this art can be extremely complex with thousands, if not millions, of points. Though vectors are device independent, rendering a complex image could also cause issues with download times.

Images destined for smartphones need to have the device scaling factors applied. These scaling factors, based on screen resolution, range from .75x to 4.5x depending on the device. All images used in Figma have a scaling factor of 1x, meaning you really don't have to use the other versions of the image when preparing a prototype in Figma.

What types of graphic objects can be used in Figma? Figma can handle four types of graphic objects:

- Primitives: Rectangle, Line, Arrow, Ellipse, Polygon, and Star are vector graphics created using their respective tools in Figma.

- Drawing Objects: These are another type of vector shapes you can draw using the Pencil tool in Figma.

- Shapes: These are generally more complicated vector graphics created using the Pen tool in applications such as Adobe Illustrator, Affinity Designer, or Figma.

- Bitmaps: Pixel-based images in either the .JPG or .PNG format usually created in Photoshop or other imaging applications.

The .JPG format is "lossy" in that images are compressed based on areas of contiguous color. By "losing" color information with minimal impact on image quality, there is a reduction in file size. The .PNG format is a lossless compression file type that does compress an image, which makes the file size larger compared to a .JPG image. Where .PNG shines is that it allows for alpha transparency.

IMPORTING IMAGES INTO FIGMA

There are two ways of importing an image into a Figma artboard. Here's how:

1. Open a new Figma file and select the Android Large frame in the Properties panel.

2. Open your chapter download and drag the Alps.jpg image onto the pasteboard area outside the frame. The image is significantly larger than the frame (Figure 6-7), which means it will have to be scaled to fit the Android frame.

Figure 6-7. *Drag and drop an image onto the pasteboard*

3. Drag the image onto the frame. The frame (Figure 6-8) now
    acts as a method of cropping the image because of the option
    in the Properties panel to "Clip content." You can select the
    image and move it around inside the frame. You can still scale
    the image, as parts of the image are outside of the frame.

Figure 6-8. *The areas of an image larger than the frame will be hidden*

From a UX Design point of view, this is a rather messy way of working with images in a UI. There is a better way.

4. Delete the image, select the Frame tool, and draw out a frame that is 320 by 450 pixels on the Android artboard. Name the frame Alps in the Layers panel.

5. Select the Alps frame and open the Fill properties.

6. Click the color chip, and when the Color Picker opens, click the image icon. The frame will fill with a checkerboard pattern.

7. Click on the checkerboard in the Color Picker and click select image.

8. When the dialog box opens, navigate to the Alps.jpg image and click open. The image fills the frame as shown in Figure 6-9.

Figure 6-9. *Images can be imported into a frame using the Fill property*

When it comes to UX Design and the quest for pixel-perfect placement, the technique of filling a frame with an image is a best practice.

GENERATIVE AI: A WARNING

Prompt: Summer mountain meadow landscape with tree.

Figure 6-10. *From prompt to image with one easy click*

The rise of Generative AI has been regarded as either a blessing or a curse or both. The AI Large Language Models (LLM) have been trained on the billions of images found on the web and can create astonishingly complex images with nothing more than a simple text prompt. When looked at from a purely UX Design lens, there should be no issue with including Generative AI images in your websites or apps.

The issue many have with this technique lies with the creation of the image. If it is based purely on a prompt, the critics rightly point out there may be some serious copyright issues. For example, the photographer in which the eyes from one of his images appear in a generated image did not give permission for its use for this purpose. In fact, Stock Photography sites such as Getty and Newgrounds have banned the upload of and sale of AI images. Shutterstock and Adobe are in the process of considering how to compensate those with images in their collections whose work was used in the creation of an AI image.

The potential for abuse, not to mention outright fraud, is also there. One of the authors raised this point in an article titled "The ethics of generative art" published through the UX Collective (https://uxdesign.cc/the-ethics-of-generative-art-159453feaac4). The example given was based on a theoretical ad campaign. The final image was right on brand, but the actual artwork was created in Photoshop using a prompt and started with two fills and a stick tree. As shown in Figure 6-10, did the agency pay for the image or the stick tree?

We are not suggesting you ban the use of AI art. We do, however, suggest it is incumbent on you to have a corporate policy regarding the responsible use of Generated AI images.

Installing and Using Imaging Plug-ins in Figma

The use of images in websites and apps is commonly tied to budget. Images can be obtained by hiring a photographer, paying for images from a Stock Photography site, or using an image plug-in through Figma. The cheapest option, of course, is obtaining images through a plug-in. Before you start installing them, be aware not all of the images are royalty-free. Be sure to check the usage information beforehand. The exception is for documents, such as personas or image used "For Position Only," which are used internally.

If you do a search for Photos in the Figma Community, dozens of suggestions will appear. Which to choose is up to you, but we are going to focus on Unsplash, which is among the most popular Figma plug-ins.

To install either one:

1. Open the Community site or the Resources button in the Figma Toolbar.

2. Enter Unsplash as the Search criteria.

3. When the description appears, click Run to install the plug-in.

4. To save the plug-in, click the Save icon (Figure 6-11) in the Resources pop-down.

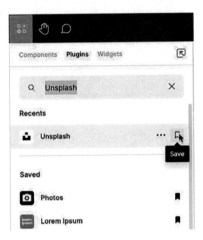

Figure 6-11. *After you install a plug-in, save it*

Here's how to use the Unsplash plug-in:

1. Open a new Design file and add a frame.

2. Select the frame.

3. Click the Resources icon on the toolbar and select Unsplash to open the Unsplash dialog box (Figure 6-12). You are presented with three choices: Editorial, Presets, and Search. The Presets choice offers you the opportunity to add a Random image based on a number of categories.

Figure 6-12. *The Unsplash dialog box offers three options for image selection*

4. Select Search and enter Bern into the Text Input area. A number of images that meet that criteria are presented.

5. Click on an image and it is added as a Fill for the selected frame (Figure 6-13).

Figure 6-13. *Click an image to add it to a Figma frame*

When you search Unsplash for an image, you will see an All Licenses pop-down above the images. If you open the pop-down, the choices are Unsplash+ and Free. Unsplash+ images are not royalty-free.

Color Correcting Images in Figma

Open the Fill panel containing an image and you can do a bit of color correction (Figure 6-14). The sliders allow you to do minimal color correction. We use the word "minimal" because if significant corrections are required, they are best done in such imaging applications as Photoshop, Lightroom, or other imaging applications.

Along the top are four icons that, if selected, will replace the image with a solid color or gradient or replace the image in the frame with another image or a video.

The Fill pop-down offers you the choice of Fitting a large image to the frame dimensions, Cropping the image, or Tiling the image.

Figure 6-14. *The Fill options for a frame containing an image*

Manipulating Image Content in Figma

When it comes to image manipulation in Figma, the choices are limited. You can, as shown in Figure 6-14, perform some rudimentary color correction. The remaining choices are Crop an image, Scale an image, or Mask an image.

Crop an Image in Figma

Cropping an image allows you to not only change the dimensions of the shape the image is inside of but also scale and reposition an image inside the shape.

Here's how to crop an image:

1. Open the Fill mode and select Crop from the pop-down. Crop handles (Figure 6-15) will appear on the corners and sides of the frame.

2. Drag the top-left handle down to crop more of the image. The cropped portion of the image displays as opaque. You can also drag a corner handle upward. This has the same effect as dragging a side handle upward or inward.

3. Drag the image within the crop area to change the focus of the image.

4. Press the Enter (Windows) or Return (Mac) key to accept the crop.

An alternative cropping technique is to hold down the Ctrl (Windows) or Command (Mac) key, select the frame, and drag the corners. One disadvantage to this technique is you are not able to move the image inside the crop area.

Figure 6-15. *Cropping an image using the Fill mode*

Scale an Image in Figma

There will be occasions where the image content is a bit too large to meet the specification. Scaling an image is the obvious solution, and there are a couple of ways to approach this. Here's how to fill a frame with a scaled image:

1. Open the Crop.fig file found in your chapter download. It is nothing more than a frame named Image.

2. With the Image frame selected, open the Photos plug-in and select Random in the side menu and select the People category. An image (Figure 6-16) will fill the frame. This is a great way of avoiding scaling an image. If you select Fit in the Fill mode, the actual image proportions will be applied in the frame.

Figure 6-16. *Adding an image from a plug-in fills the frame with a scaled image*

3. Press Command/CtrlCtrl (Windows) or Command (Mac) + Z to undo this change. This time, with the empty Image frame selected, open the Fill mode and select image and Fit. The frame fills with a checkerboard.

4. Click on the checkerboard in the dialog box and select Choose image. Navigate to your chapter download, select the Bern.jpg image, and click Upload. The image will fit the frame. Change the option to Fill and the image (Figure 6-17) fits the frame.

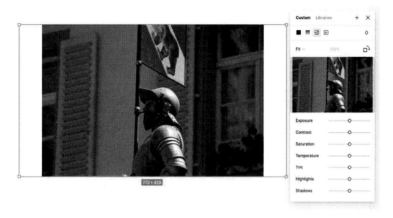

Figure 6-17. *Adding an image to a frame without scaling the image*

Now that you know how to add an image to a frame without scaling, let's look at working with an image that hasn't been scaled when dragged into a frame.

5. Open the NoScale.fig file found in your chapter download. If you double-click the image, you will see it is quite a bit larger than the frame. If you drag the image around inside the frame, you will see the frame acts as a mask.

6. To scale the image in proportion, hold down the Shift key and drag the upper left corner toward the lower right corner. The image fits but doesn't fill the Image frame.

7. Undo the scale and this time select the image layer and change its height value in the Properties panel to 429. Before you do, make sure the values are linked. Doing it by the numbers (Figure 6-18) is far more precise than using a mouse.

Figure 6-18. *For accurate image scale, do it by the numbers*

Obviously the image doesn't fill the frame. Here's how to fix that.

8. Select the frame and drag the left edge horizontally to the right. All that does is shift everything over, which isn't what we were trying to accomplish. Undo the change.

9. Hold down the Ctrl (Windows) or Command (Mac) key and drag the left edge of the frame to the left edge of the image. When you release the key, the frame is resized. Again, a more accurate method is to match the Frame size to the Image size in the Properties panel.

Let's now assume you want the frame with the image to be smaller or larger. What you can't do is resize the frame by holding down a modifier key and dragging a frame handle. Instead, here's how to resize a frame with an image.

10. Select the Image frame, and in the Toolbar, change the Selection tool to the Scale tool (Figure 6-19), or press the K key.

Figure 6-19. *Use the Resize tool to scale a frame containing an image*

11. With the Ctrl (windows) Command (Mac) + Shift key held down, scale the image to make it larger or smaller.

Masking in Figma

Common artifacts for UX Design include badges and avatars. They are usually circular in shape and have a head shot of an individual inside the circle. These are created using a mask. Here's how:

1. Insert an image from the Photo's plug-in and resize it to fit the canvas. The image should be on its own layer, not the fill for a frame.

2. Select the Ellipse tool, and with the Alt (Windows) or Option (Mac) + Shift key held down, draw out a circle that covers the area to be included in the avatar. Don't worry about the color of the circle.

3. Move the shape to the layer below the image, select both layers, and click the Create Mask tool. The image (Figure 6-20) now resembles an avatar.

Figure 6-20. *A mask has been applied using the Use As Mask tool*

The key to masks in Figma is the shape, including type, to be used as a mask must be the bottommost layer of the layer stack. Any layers above the mask layer will be masked as well.

Creating a masked object doesn't always require the use of the Mask tool. Right-click on the mask layer and "Use as mask" will be one of the options in the menu. To release a mask, right-click on it in the Layers panel and select Remove mask from the menu or click on the Mask tool.

You can also adjust the object being masked by clicking and dragging it within the mask.

To add a stroke around the avatar:

1. Create the shape and add a stroke, then duplicate the shape. Move one of the duplicates under the image.

2. Select the image and bottom shape layer, then group them. Create a Mask using the shape in the group. The filled shape with the stroke is still visible.

3. Select the Filled shape with the stroke, and in the Fill
    panel, delete the Fill or set the Fill's opacity value to
    0 (Figure 6-21).

Figure 6-21. *The Circle contains a stroke and a Fill opacity value of 0%*

Fonts and Figma

A medium-fidelity prototype changes wireframe-defined text areas
to formatted text. At this point in the prototype, the text areas can be
placeholder text such as Lorem Ipsum or authentic text. Regardless of the
form of the text, it will have to be formatted, and this is where the display
medium becomes critical. Web pages can use both serif and sans serif
fonts due to the fact they will be viewed on large screens.

It has become a best practice when designing for mobile to use a sans
serif font. There are a number of reasons, apart from Apple iOS suggesting
the use of SF Pro and Google recommending the use of the Roboto font for
Android devices, both fonts included in Figma's font set. Reasons for using
sans serif fonts include the following:

- Readability: Sans serif fonts have clean, simple lines that enhance character recognition.

- Legibility: These fonts are designed to maintain legibility even at smaller sizes. This is especially important for readability of text. The varying screen sizes for these devices make it crucial to choose fonts that are readable across all devices.

- Consistency: The use of the same sans serif font across all devices results in a consistent user experience across both iOS and Android devices.

Figma's default font is Inter, which is a custom sans serif designed by Figma's Rasmus Andersson. It is a fascinating story, and you can learn more here: `www.figma.com/blog/the-birth-of-inter/`.

That last point, consistency, is the key to the use of fonts in all prototypes right up to development. Consistency is applied through a hierarchy of different font sizes, weights, and styles, which helps users quickly understand the information hierarchy. The hierarchy is applied either through the use of a Style Guide or a Design System. There will be occasions when you might wish to change or create a text style. If you are working with a Design System or Style Guide, consider the implications of the changes not to the frame you are working in but to all frames in the prototype. One change you consider to be relatively minor will ripple through every document that uses the Design System or Style Guide.

It is not uncommon for the use of fonts, other than those included with Figma, to be used. These fonts can come from a variety of sources and, as long as they are properly licensed, can be used in Figma... sort of. If you are using the desktop version of Figma, fonts installed on your computer can be used and accessed through the font menu in Figma. If you are using the browser version, you need to install either the Mac or Windows version of the free Figma Font Installer (`www.figma.com/downloads/`). Once installed, your fonts will be available in the Font Picker. If multiple people are working on the same project, they will also need to install the font and Figma's Font Installer to view and access the fonts.

Color and Figma

Working with color in any application is risky. We use color to communicate; for example, red can mean an error or blue, underlined, text indicates a link. We also use color when users click on an object, roll over a button, or when an element gains focus. Use the wrong mix of color meanings and users "won't get the message," for example, a green button displaying an error message. As educators, the authors are constantly dealing with color contrast and harmonies. Our advice can be rather blunt: "Look out the window or go for a walk. Nature never messes up color." Unfortunately, computers do. The Adobe Color website offers some good examples of color harmonies applied to a color theme and even offers support for accessible color themes (`https://color.adobe.com/`).

The colors of the leaves on a tree or a flower in the garden can't be reproduced on a computer. This is due to the fundamental difference between color in nature and color on the computer and how different color gamuts are displayed. The natural light spectrum can be broken down into seven colors based on wavelength. They are red, orange, yellow, green, blue, indigo, and violet. The computer uses three colors from that spectrum: red, green, and blue. The color you see in a green tree leaf is because all of the colors that aren't green have been absorbed and the green is reflected back to you. On a computer, that green leaf is a mixture of the three colors being transmitted to you.

When it comes to UX Design, Figma uses four different color models (Figure 6-22) to describe that green tree leaf:

- The Hexadecimal Color Model: Commonly used on the Web. Hex color is defined as a mixture of pairs of numbers ranging for 0 to 9 and letters ranging from A to F. For example, a pure blue color would be #0000FF.

- The RGB Color Model: The colors are expressed as three pairs of values 0–255 for each of the colors: red, green, and blue. For example, a pure blue color would be R: 0, G: 0, B: 255.

- The RGBA Color Model: This model is based on the RGB values of 0–255 and adds a fourth value for alpha transparency. For example, a pure blue color at 50% would be R: 0, G: 0, B: 255, a: 0.5.

- The HSB Color Model: Represents Hue, Saturation, and Brightness. Hue is the color, Saturation is the color's purity, and Brightness is the color's intensity. The values in this model are quite different. Hue ranges from 0 to 360 around an imaginary wheel. Red starts at 0. Green starts at 120, and blue starts at 240. Brightness is expressed as a percentage. For example, a pure blue would be 240, 100, 100, 100%.

- The HSL Color Model: Represents Hue, Saturation, and Lightness. Hue is the color, Saturation is the intensity of the color, and Lightness is how light or dark the color is. Lightness values range from 0 (Black) to 100 (White). For example, a pure blue would be 240, 100, 50, 100%.

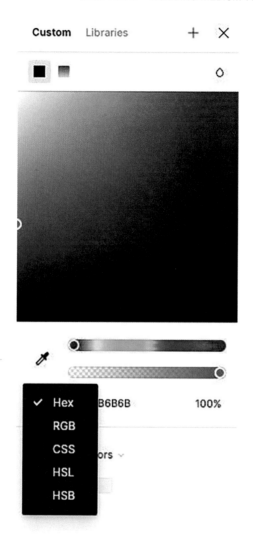

Figure 6-22. *The Figma Color Picker*

Create a Scrim Using a Gradient

It is not uncommon when designing a screen to encounter a situation where a full screen image completely dominates the content on the screen. For example, in Figure 6-23, the image of the Alps overpowers the text and the two cards at the bottom of the screen. One possible solution would be to darken the image by changing the frame's background color to black and reducing the image's opacity. Another would be to select image and, in the Fill options, use the Exposure, Contrast, and Saturation sliders to do a bit of color correction. Neither of these options would work.

Figure 6-23. *The background image is overpowering the content*

This is where a technique borrowed from the theater could apply. In the theater, a scrim is a drop that appears opaque when a scene is lit from the front or transparent or translucent when lit from behind. It is commonly used to hide actors or props in a scene. When applied in UX Design, a scrim is a design technique that uses a semi-transparent gradient layer to make objects more noticeable when they are over background images. Here's how to create a scrim using a gradient:

1. Open the Scrim.fig file found in your chapter download. When it opens, select the Home frame. In the Properties panel, you will see that the frame has an image for the Fill.

2. In the Fill properties, add a new fill to the frame. Set the 20% transparency to 100%. Click on the black color icon to open the Fill Colour Picker (Figure 6-24).

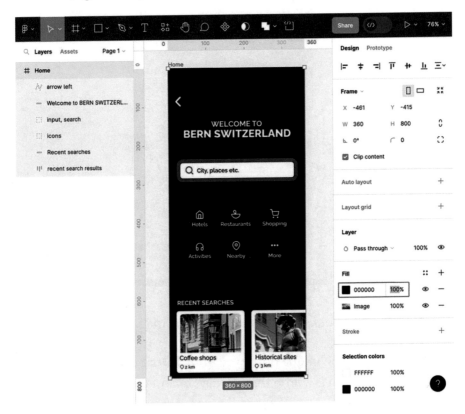

Figure 6-24. *Add a new solid color fill to the frame set to 100%, above the image fill*

3. Click the Gradient choice to open the Gradient
    options (Figure 6-25). Those two boxes below are
    the Gradient stops and are used to create the start
    and the end colors for a gradient. The bar below
    them is called the ramp.

Figure 6-25. *The Gradient options*

4. Click on the box on the left and change the color to White. Click on the box on the right, change the color to Black, and change the opacity from 0% to 100%.

5. Now apply a blend mode to the gradient fill. Click the teardrop icon in the top right of the Fill Colour Picker, and from the drop-down menu, choose Multiply (Figure 6-26).

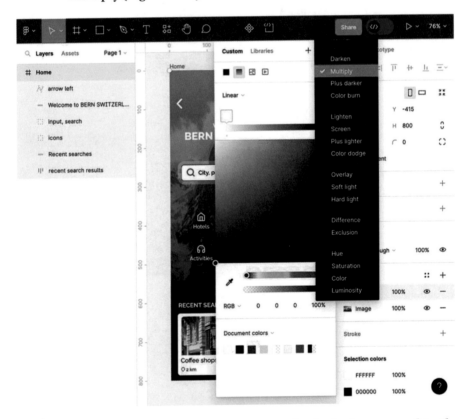

Figure 6-26. *The gradient stops appear on both the image and in the Color Picker*

6. Change the position of the colors in the gradient by either clicking and dragging the white or black gradient stops in the Fill Color Picker. Top and bottom gradient handles appear on the gradient tool slider as well, and they can be repositioned by moving them up, down, or on an angle.

7. Let's drag the white box to the right and lighten the top of the image and drag the black box to the left and darken the bottom of the image.

8. To better control the gradient blend change, click between the white and black gradient stops and a new mid-gray color will be added. This new gradient stop can be repositioned to control where the gradient changes from dark to light (Figure 6-27). New gradient stops can be removed by selecting the color square and pressing Delete on your keyboard.

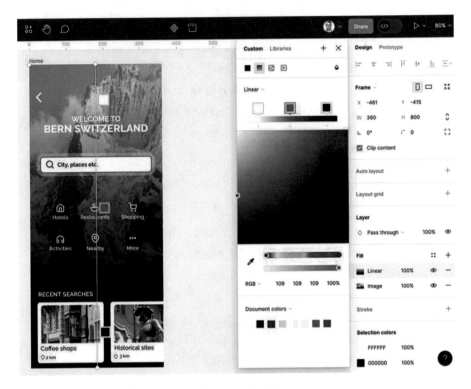

Figure 6-27. *Gradient from dark to light*

So there you have it, how to create a scrim using a gradient to provide contrast for the elements above a background image.

Paying attention to details is important in UX and UI Design. Working with the placement and opacity in a gradient can add the contrast needed to create a focus for the main content.

Adding Effects to Graphics

Graphics elements don't just sit on a screen as flat elements. They can be manipulated in a number of ways to create dimension. For example, a drop shadow implies an object is sitting above the design surface. Apply a blur to have the user focus on important content such as a modal. Apply an Inner Shadow to give the illusion of 3D. Have a button change color using a Blend mode on a rollover. All of this and more can be accomplished in Figma.

Though you can manipulate objects to create some stunning changes, keep the word "subtle" in mind. Here are a few effects that you can apply to graphic elements.

Apply a Drop Shadow

Drop shadows give the illusion of an element rising off of the design surface. They also indicate a light source's direction. A common UX Design use is when a Floating Action Button is rolled over, the drop shadow increases in size.

1. Open the Effects.fig file found in your chapter download.

2. Select the Drop Shadow button in the Shadow frame.

3. Select Effects in the Properties panel. Click the pop-down and the four effects – Inner Shadow, Drop Shadow, Layer Blur, and Background Blue – appear. Select Drop Shadow.

4. To manipulate the Drop Shadow, click the Star Burst to open the Shadow properties (Figure 6-28).

5. Use these values:

- X: 0

- Y: 10

- Blur: 10

- Opacity: 25%

Figure 6-28. *The Drop Shadow properties*

You can also change the color of the blur by clicking the color chip and choosing a different color. The light source can be changed by changing the X, Y, and Blur values. You may notice the Spread value is grayed out. This effect can only be applied to shapes. Open the Drop group and select the Rectangle layer. If you open the Drop Shadow properties, you can apply a spread to the shadow.

Instead of entering a value for the Spread property, click and hold on the word spread. The cursor changes to an arrow, and if you drag left or right, the value changes. These are affectionately known as "Scrubby Numbers" because you can scrub the value.

Apply an Inner Shadow to Create a 3D Effect

For the longest time, Flat Design has been a standard. Flat Design came about as a reaction to Skeumorphic design in which objects mimic their real-world counterparts. This was especially prevalent during the early days of iOS. Once users got used to buttons and icons and understood their purpose. Flat Design, introduced by Microsoft in 2010, emphasizes the minimalist use of simple elements. We are starting to see a slow movement away from Flat Design to one that introduces subtle 3D effects. In this exercise, we will use the Inner Shadow effect to give a button a subtle 3D appearance.

1. Select the Inner Shadow button in the Shadow frame and apply an Inner Shadow. The same properties as a Drop Shadow can be applied. You should notice an Inner Shadow is applied to the top of button (Figure 6-29).

Figure 6-29. *Applying an Inner Shadow*

One interesting feature of the Figma Shadow Effects is they can be applied multiple times to the same object, and you can also apply Blend modes to the shadow. Here's how:

With the Inner Shadow properties open, use these values:

- X: 0
- Y: 4
- Blur: 4
- Opacity: 20%
- Color: #000000

We are going to add a Multiply Blend mode to this shadow.

2. Click the teardrop beside the close icon to open the Blend modes. Select Multiply. The shadow darkens. Close the dialog box.

3. With the button still selected, click the plus sign to add a new effect. Select Inner Shadow and use these values in the dialog box:

- X: 5
- Y: 4
- Blur: 4
- Opacity: 20%
- Color: #FFFFFF
- Blend: Screen

This new shadow runs around the left and bottom edges, and the Screen Blend lightens the Inner Shadow to give the 3D effect shown in Figure 6-30.

Figure 6-30. *A Black Inner Shadow and a White Inner Shadow combine to subtly create a 3D effect*

Applying Blur Effects

Blurs are used to give focus to objects on the screen by blurring out the content behind them. For example, when a side menu slides onto the smartphone screen, the UI under it is blurred out. Figma contains two Blur effects: Layer Blur and Background Blur. Here's how to apply them.

1. Twirl down the Blur frame and select the Cow image.

2. Add a Layer Blur to the cow and open the properties. Scrub the numbers, as shown in Figure 6-31, and you control the intensity of the blur.

Figure 6-31. *A Layer Blur is applied. Note the cursor allows for Scrubby Numbers*

The Background Blur effect is not what you may assume it to be. It does not blur the background layer. It blurs out the background behind a selected object. A common use for this is applying it to cards appearing over colorful backgrounds. This technique is known as "glassmorphism." Here's how:

1. Select the Cow image and remove the blur by clicking the - button in the effects properties.

2. Turn on the visibility of the Rectangle in the Blur frame. An opaque rounded rectangle appears over the cow.

3. Select the Rectangle and apply a Background Blur. The area of the cow behind the rectangle is blurry.

4. Open the Background Blur dialog box, and using Scrubby Numbers, increase the blur (Figure 6-32).

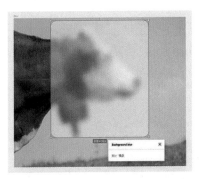

Figure 6-32. Applying the Background Blur effect

Applying a Blend Mode to a Layer

The Figma Blend modes are the standard Blend modes used by many imaging and drawing applications. They affect the color of pixels overlaying each other, and as you may have guessed, they are math driven and are applied in a top-down manner. Here are a couple:

1. Open the Blend Frame and select the Text Layer.

2. Open the pop-down in the Layer Properties panel and the Blend modes are listed.

3. Select Multiply. The text darkens. The math behind this one is easy to explain. The color values of text pixels directly over the image pixels are multiplied and then divided by 256. The result is the text gets darker.

4. Select Color Burn. The text changes color because the mode increases contrast to darken the image colors before blending it with the text colors. The result is a much darker image than Multiply.

5. Select Difference. The text turns blue. This mode is a comparative mode that subtracts the darker pixels from the lighter pixels and what you see if the blue colour change in Figure 6-33 is the absolute value of the result.

Figure 6-33. *The Difference blend mode is applied to the text*

6. Select the Luminosity frame and select the image in
    the Layers panel.

7. Apply the Luminosity blend mode. Think of this
    as a very quick way of converting a color image to
    grayscale using the frame's fill color (Figure 6-34).

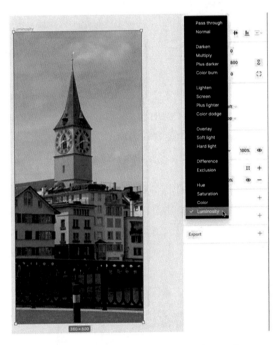

Figure 6-34. *Applying the Luminosity blend mode*

Create a Mesh Gradient in Figma

Earlier in this chapter, we showed you how to add a gradient fill and how
to use a gradient to create a scrim. In this exercise, we are going to create
a Gradient mesh using colored shapes and a Layer Blur. This technique is
a good way of adding a 3D effect to a logo, creates a colorful background
for a web page, and is used to highlight the key message in a call-to-action
button. Here's how:

1. Scroll over to the Gradient Mesh frame in the
    Effects.fig file. You will see it is nothing more than a
    series of random shapes created with the Pen tool
    and the various shapes. Underneath the frame are
    six colored boxes. These will be the colors to use to
    fill the shapes.

2. Select a Shape and open the Color Picker. When
    the Color Picker opens, select the Eyedropper and
    click on one of the six colors. Repeat this for the
    remaining shapes (Figure 6-35).

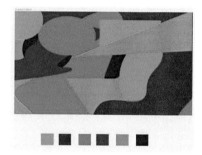

Figure 6-35. *The shapes have all been colored using the chips below
the frame*

3. Select all of the Shape and Vector layers in the
    Gradient Mesh Frame and add a Layer Blur. Be
    aggressive. The Blur value applied in Figure 6-36
    was 175.

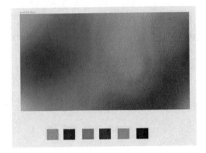

Figure 6-36. *The effect uses a Layer Blur value of 175*

Using Auto Layout in Figma

The auto layout feature of Figma is designed to make your life easier
by allowing you to create designs that adapt to their screen size and
orientation. For example, auto layout can structure a frame in such a way
that it can automatically grow and adapt the contents to that change.

You can use auto layout to

- Create buttons that resize as you edit the text label

- Build lists that adjust as items are added, removed,
  or hidden

- Combine auto layout frames to build complex
  interfaces

To use auto layout, you apply it to a frame or selection of objects on the
page. This is done in one of three ways:

- Press Shift-A.

- Select Auto layout in the Properties panel.

- Right-click on the selection and select Add auto layout
  from the pop-down menu.

You can then customize the properties of the auto layout frame, such as the following:

- Direction: Choose whether the objects will flow vertically, horizontally, or wrap to the next line.

- Spacing: Set the amount of space between the objects and the edges of the frame.

- Alignment: Align the objects within the frame to the left, right, center, top, bottom, or middle.

- Resizing: Choose how the frame will resize when the content changes.

- Absolute Position: Exclude an object from the auto layout flow and position it relative to the parent frame.

To start, let's explore the features of auto layout.

1. Open the Auto layout.fig file. When it opens, select the Button frame.

2. With the Button selected, click the + sign beside Auto layout in the Properties panel. The Auto layout properties (Figure 6-37) open.

Figure 6-37. *The Auto layout properties*

Let's go through what you are looking at:

- The three arrows at the top-left are Vertical Layout, Horizontal Layout, and Wrap.

- The doted Box on the right sets the Alignment options.

- The brackets indicate spacing between elements.

- The bottom three brackets are Horizontal Padding, Vertical Padding, and Individual or custom padding values.

- The Ellipsis opens the Advanced options.

When an auto layout has been applied to an element, the Layer icon in the Properties panel changes to the one shown in the Alignment option **‖‖**. This is a visible clue that auto layout has been applied.

3. Roll over the button. Those highlighted areas (Figure 6-38) indicate the padding, and the blue lines allow you to manually adjust the padding by dragging the mouse. As you drag the mouse, the button will resize to accommodate the padding increase.

Figure 6-38. *The Padding area is shown and can be adjusted manually*

4. Select the Scale tool (K) to make the button smaller.
    Notice how the text automatically reduces in size
    while the padding remains constant.

5. Switch back to the Move tool (V) and you will see
    the padding values have also changed.

The values for padding and spacing are also Scrubby Numbers or you
can do it by the numbers by changing the values manually.

Let's now look at how auto layout works with a number of items. What
we are going to do is to create a card and apply auto layout. Along the way
you will discover how to align and space objects and that everything is in a
container. Let's get started.

Below the button are the three elements: Kate's avatar from the People
plug-in along with the Head and a Subhead, an image of Bern, and along
the bottom are five icons that could be used to let visitors check out various
locations in Bern. We'll start with the Head and Subhead.

1. Select the Head and Subhead and press Shift-A to
    apply auto layout. Name the container "text". If you
    check out the spacing in the Auto layout properties,
    there is 25 pixels of space between them. Change
    the spacing value to 14 pixels (Figure 6-39).

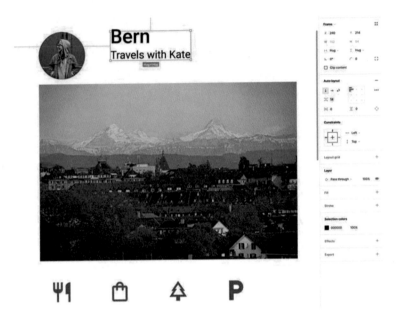

Figure 6-39. *Change the spacing values in the Auto layout properties to increase or decrease the spacing between elements in an Auto layout container*

2. Select the Avatar and the Text container and apply auto layout. Name this container Avatar and reduce the vertical spacing between the text and the image to 10 pixels in the Auto layout properties. To line everything up, select Center Align in the Auto layout properties (Figure 6-40).

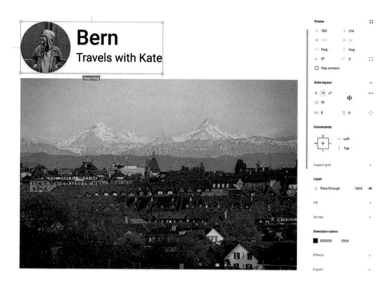

Figure 6-40. *Applying Align center in an Auto layout container*

3. You may have noticed the icons are in their own container. To turn this into a card, select all of the elements and apply auto layout. Name this new container "Card".

4. The canvas is still showing through. Select the Card container and change its Fill color to a light gray (#F0EFEF).

5. Everything is a bit spaced out. To deal with this, select the Card container and set the vertical spacing to 0. As shown in Figure 6-41, this jams everything together but also gives us the opportunity to apply proper spacing.

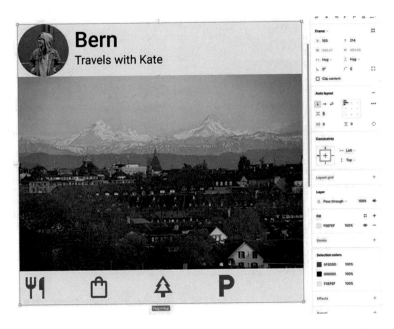

Figure 6-41. *The card's background color has been changed and vertical spacing is set to 0*

6. Let's fix the Avatar. Select the Avatar container, and in the Auto layout properties, select the Individual padding icon. Add 16 pixels to the left, top, and bottom of the Avatar container (Figure 6-42).

Figure 6-42. *Padding can be applied to individual sides of a container*

7. We don't want the image to look distorted when the Card container is resized. Select the image and set its horizontal resize value to Fill. Leave the vertical value at Fixed.

8. Next, we have to deal with the Icons. Select the Icons container and change the resize values to Fill.

9. Select the Car container and make it larger or smaller. One issue is the Icon container does not behave as expected. Press Ctrl (Windows) or Command (Mac) + Z to undo and move the Card back to its original size of 380 × 500 pixels.

10. Select the Icons container and apply these Individual padding values:

    - Top: 16

    - Bottom: 16

    - Left: 20

    - Right: 20

If you select the Card and resize it, it behaves as expected.

To finish up, select the Card container and change the Corner roundness value to 5 pixels and add a drop shadow (Figure 6-43).

Figure 6-43. *The Card container's corners are rounded and a drop shadow is applied*

Your Turn: Create a Medium-Fidelity Mobile App Location Card

We started the chapter by talking about wireframes and moving into the next stage of design, developing medium-fidelity prototypes. It's time to put much of what we have covered in this chapter into practice. In this exercise, you are going to create a location card highlighting the Zytglogge Clock Tower in Bern. As you move through this exercise, keep in mind that wireframes are nothing more than a guide as to where content will be placed. Your challenge here is to use the Medium-Fidelity-App.fig file and, following the instructions, create a medium-fidelity prototype. Let's get started:

1. Import and open the Medium-Fidelity-App.fig file found in your chapter download. When the file opens (Figure 6-44), you will see a Section containing the vector icons to be used in this exercise and a wireframe of the screen containing the card. We have also included guides to help you along. If you can't see them, press Shift-R to turn on the guides and rulers.

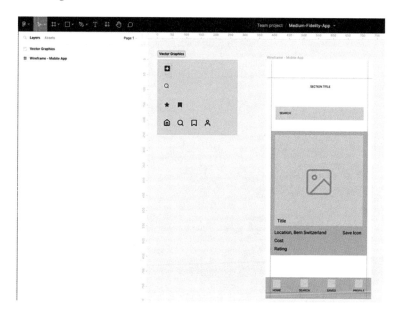

Figure 6-44. *We start with a wireframe for a mobile app*

2. Duplicate the frame "Wireframe - Mobile App", Ctrl (Windows) or Command (Mac) + D. Rename the duplicated frame "Medium-Fidelity".

315

3. From the Vector Graphics section, copy the "logo switzerland sm" logo. Right-click on the Medium-Fidelity page between the text and the top guide and select Paste Here from the Context Menu. With the Logo selected, clicking Align horizontal centers the icon in the Properties panel. The logo is centered on the page. Use the up or down arrow key to vertically position the icon if needed.

4. Select the Text tool and select "SECTION TITLE". Change the selected text to "EXPLORE BERN, SWITZERLAND". (Note the use of capital letters.)

5. Set the text in Roboto, Black, 18 px. Fill the text with the color #436EAE (Blue).

6. Select the text "BERN SWITZERLAND" and change the font to Roboto, Light (Figure 6-45).

Figure 6-45. *Create the medium-fidelity title section*

Create the Top Search Bar

Having added the main header and logo, we are going to use auto layout to create the top Search bar using just the text box. Here's how:

1. Delete the input search background layer in the Layers panel.

2. Select "SEARCH" and change the font to Roboto, SemiBold, 14 px.

3. Switch to the Move tool (V), select SEARCH, and apply an auto layout (Shift A). The text is now in a Container.

4. In the Layers panel, change the name of the Frame 1 layer to Search.

5. Set the Fill to #FFFFFF (White) and add a 1-pixel stroke with a color of #000000 (Black).

6. In the Auto layout area or the Properties panel, add the following Individual padding values: Left: 15, Right: 220, Top 12, Bottom: 12.

7. In the Frame area of the Properties panel, set the Corner Radius value to 7.

8. Copy the search icon – icon search – and paste it onto the pasteboard. In the Layers panel, drag the icon into the Search container. Notice how it automatically appears beside the text in the Auto layout.

9. In the Properties panel, Auto layout, change the Individual padding Right value from 220 to 195 as shown in Figure 6-46.

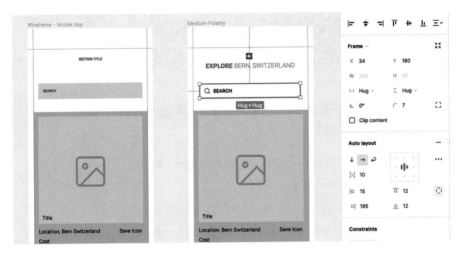

Figure 6-46. *Creating the Search input area using Figma's Auto layout*

Creating the Location Card

Having created the Search bar, we can now work our way down the page and turn our attention to changing the wireframe to a medium-fidelity design. Let's get started:

1.   Select the "card background" layer and add a Corner Radius value of 14 and change the Fill color to #FFD700 (Yellow).

2.   To make the background color a little more interesting, click the + sign in the Fill area to add a second Fill. Change the opacity of the new fill from 20% to 100%, and click the black color square on the left to open the Color Picker. When the Color Picker opens, click the linear gradient icon. Set the left

stop gradient to #FFFFFF (White) and the right stop gradient to #000000 (Black) and change the opacity to 10%. In the Color Picker, click the teardrop and set the Blend mode to Multiply (Figure 6-47).

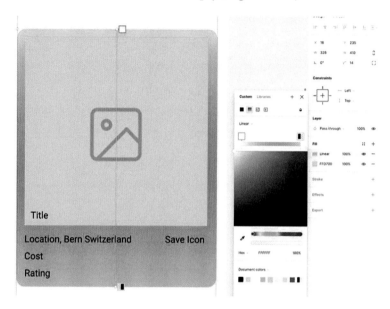

Figure 6-47. *Adding a gradient layer to the background layer*

3. With the Background layer selected, from the Properties panel, Effects, add a drop shadow using the following values: X: 5, Y: 5, Blur: 5, Spread: 0, Opacity 10%.

4. With the background of the card dealt with, let's add the image to the main image layer. Select the layer "main image". Delete the "image" Fill layer in the Layers panel.

5. Select the Fill layer, and in the Color Picker, select Image. Click the Checkerboard in the Color Picker and add a new image Fill using the supplied image "Clock_Tower.jpg".

6. In the Color Picker, choose Crop to reposition and scale the image.

    The text is a bit lost in the image. We are going to add more contrast between the image and the Zytglogge text by coloring the text white and add a gradient to the "main image" layer.

7. Select the layer "Title" and change the text properties to Roboto ExtraBold, 15 px, with a Fill of #FFFFFF (White).

8. Replace the text "Title" with "Zytglogge Clock Tower".

9. Select the image; add a gradient Fill layer. Set the gradient layer to 100% opacity. Set the left stop gradient to #FFFFFF (White) and the right stop gradient to #000000 (Black) and change the opacity to 100%. Set the teardrop, Blend mode, to Multiply.

10. Move the left stop gradient square to the right so that the gradient starts and stops behind the text. As you do this, the gradient will move down the image allowing control of where the gradient is applied.

11. Add an effect, Inner Shadow, to the image with the following values: X: 10, Y: 15, Blur: 30, Spread 0, Opacity 50%.

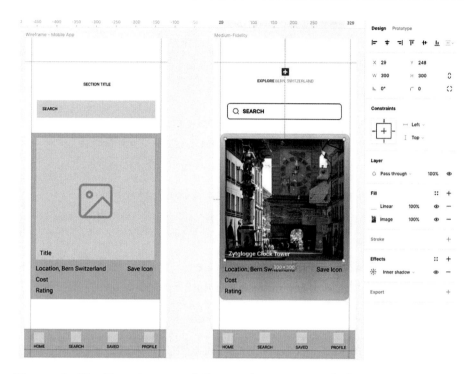

Figure 6-48. *Creating a mobile app location card element and image. Designing contrast between the text and background image using multiple fills*

With the image in place, we can now concentrate on the text under the image by putting it in an auto layout container. This will also give you the opportunity to create nested Auto layouts.

1. Select the Location and Cost Layers, and in the Properties panel, change the font and change the Properties to Roboto, Medium, 15 px.

2. Change the text "Cost" to "Cost: Free".

3. With the Shift key held down, select the Location, Cost, Rating, and Save icon layers in the Layers panel and place them in an Auto layout container. Name the container CardText.

4. Delete the Save Icon text layer and drag a copy of the icon saved filled under the Location layer in the CardText container.

5. Delete the text "Rating".

6. Drag the "icon filled star" under the Cost: Free layer in the Card text container. Using Ctrl (Windows) or Command (Mac) + D, create four copies of the star.

7. Change the Fill of the last star to #FFFFFF (White) and add a 1 px stroke and change the stroke color to #0229FF (Dark Blue).

8. Select all the Star icons and create an Auto layout (Shift A) and name the container Stars.

9. In the Properties panel, Auto layout, set the Horizontal Gap to 2, and change the Horizontal and Vertical Padding to 0.

10. Select the Location, Cost, Saved icon, and Star icon, and create a new Auto layout (Shift A) and name it "Card".

11. In the Properties panel, Auto layout, change the vertical gap value to 15.

Figure 6-49. *Use Figma's Auto layout to organize spacing in the card content text and star rating area*

We are going to finish up by creating the navigation bar at the bottom of the page.

1. Delete the text and boxes for the Search, Saved, and Profile icons in the BottomNav group.

2. Copy the nav icon home vector. Select the Home rectangle and zoom in (Shift 2).

3. Pasting the Home icon will position in the center of the light gray rectangle. Delete the rectangle. Move the Nav icon home layer above the Home text layer.

4. Zoom out and select the Home icon and the text HOME. Create an auto layout (Shift A) and name the container NavHome.

5. Copy and paste the Search, Saved, and Profile icons below the NavHome Container.

6. Duplicate the Nav home container three times. Drag the copies out and space them so the last one is roughly the same distance from the right guide as the first one. This can be quickly done by choosing Tidy up in the Properties panel. Name the new containers NavSearch, NavSaved, and NavProfile.

7. In the Nav search Container, delete the home icon and drag the search icon into the container. Change the text to SEARCH. Repeat this step with the remaining two containers.

8. Position the Nav profile, in bottom nav to the right, with similar spacing as the Nav home icon on the left. Delete the nav bottom background rectangle layer.

9. Select all the bottom navigation, icons, and text, and create an Auto layout container named NavBottom.

10. Add a Fill of #EFEFEF (Light Gray), with an opacity of 95%.

11. In the Properties panel, Auto layout, use the following Individual padding values: Left: 25, Right: 25, Top: 8, Bottom: 23. Align the NavBottom container with the left edge of the page (Figure 6-50).

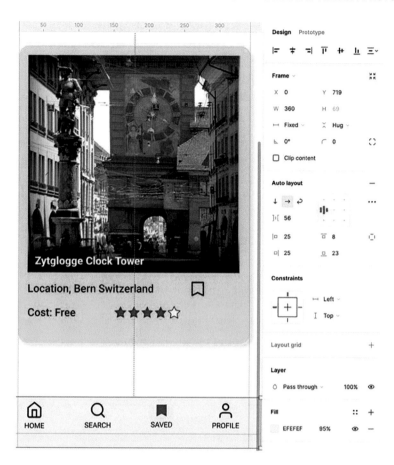

Figure 6-50. *Complete the layout for the bottom icon navigation using a nested Auto layout in Figma*

You Have Learned

- How to duplicate a wireframe frame and create a medium-fidelity prototype frame in Figma

- How to apply type properties to the title creating contrast between the font weights

- How to create the search input area by applying an auto layout to text – not requiring a text and a rectangle shape

- How to create a location card, including multiple fills to a shape: solid fill and a linear gradient with a Blend mode and opacity

- How to create contrast between text placed over the top of an image using a gradient fill over the top of an image

- How to create consistent spacing between text and graphics in the location card information area

- How to create a consistent bottom icon navigation bar

- How to use a nested auto layout to create the background and spacing for the bottom icon navigation layout

CHAPTER 7

Interactivity Fundamentals

"Experience is critical, for it determines how fondly people remember their interactions."

−Don Norman,
The Design of Everyday Things

Planning for interactivity establishes two relationships. The first is the relationship between the designer and the user. The second is the relationship between the designer and the developer.

The relationship between the designer and the user is murky. You don't know much about a user beyond the personas and the research. You must make some pretty broad assumptions regarding how much a user can interact with your product. If your assumptions, based on the research, are close, you will have enhanced the experience by making the product more engaging, responsive, and personalized. If the assumptions are wrong, users will vote by deleting the app or simply giving up and moving on.

The relationship between the designer and the developer is critical. You don't just hand over the prototype with a cheery "Here you go" and assume the developer knows what to do. Developers don't know what to do because they don't know what the designer is thinking. By developing a collaborative relationship with the developers, they can give you technical direction and suggestions that give you an insight into the reasoning for certain interaction design decisions. In short, they intimately understand your interaction design intent.

When planning for interactivity, we suggest you read Gillian Crampton Smith's four dimensions of interactive design article, "What Is Interaction Design," in Bill Moggridge's book *Designing Interactions* (www.interaction-design.org/literature/topics/interaction-design). In straightforward terms, Smith's dimensions refer to the language we use to communicate with users instead of how we communicate ideas within the design process. The language dimensions are as follows:

- Words: This is the first dimension because they impart information. Text, labels, menus, and instructions are words that communicate directly with the user. Using the word "Submit" in a button is more concise than "Send", send where?

- Visual Representation: Typography, images, icons, diagrams, and other graphic elements are critical because users, being exposed to these elements, intuitively extract their meaning. For example, a button containing the word "Submit" with a border and a color background is an excellent example of this dimension.

- Physical Space: This third dimension is not where the user interacts with the project. It is what device is being used. For example, a critical button placed in the middle of a smartphone screen makes it difficult for the user to interact because users use their thumbs to tap buttons on a screen.

- Time: This fourth dimension includes animations, audio for feedback, and transitions between screens that show progress and changes. Audio may strike you as a bit of a surprise. Simple things like a click sound when a button is tapped indicate that something will happen and enhance the user experience.

- Behavior: Ken Silver, in his 2007 article, "What Puts the Design in Interaction Design" (www.uxmatters. com/mt/archives/2007/07/what-puts-the-design- in-interaction-design.php), suggested this fifth dimension. This language dimension includes action or reaction. We are familiar with our smartphone or watch vibrating to indicate a notification (Action). We will open our phones or tap our watch to see what was delivered (Reaction). According to Silver, Behavior is multidimensional even though it is commonly visual. For example, an animation that walks a user through an app or for preloading purposes "can give the necessary pause in an interface to create a greater sense of change or affordability."

Considering these high-level design thinking concepts. Planning interactivity is not something you make up as you go along, that is a recipe for disaster. Instead, go back into the research to discover how users will interact with the project. The other aspect of planning interactivity is those five dimensions presented in the medium-fidelity prototype. All of the elements in the prototype will, in some form or other, be driven by the dimensions. The text is there. Decisions around buttons, such as stroke thickness and color, will have been made. Auto layout addresses the physical space. Menus, alerts, and so on will have been designed and refined. What hasn't been applied are the Time and Behavior dimensions. It is through planning interactivity that brings them into play.

Planning interactivity to bring the Time and Behavior dimensions to life will enhance the user experience by making it more engaging, responsive, and personalized. When planning interactivity, consider the following:

- Define how a user can interact with the site or app. This could include the number of times a user clicks on something before a message appears. It could be scroll depth or the amount and type of text a user enters when creating a password.

- Provide users with clues about their subsequent actions or expected behaviors. Clicking a submit button is a clue as to the following action. A Home icon lets users know they can access the Home page or screen with one click. A message tells users to enter a custom code sent to their email or phone if two-factor authentication is used.

- Predict and prevent errors. What does the user see if they enter the wrong password? How many times can they make this mistake before you suggest they create a new password?

- Determine how fast the system will respond to input. This will be determined between the designer and the developer.

- Rationalize the overall design and the page elements in the design. Most of this will have been dealt with when constructing the medium-fidelity prototype. Still, things like state changes for buttons, how modals or other changes such as swipes or drags will function now have to be considered.

- Simplify the design and information flow to make it easily digestible and memorable for the user. For example, the medium-fidelity prototype may have information spread out among a number of pages, which could be consolidated into one page element such as a carousel or modal.

The Basics of Adding Interactivity in Figma

In this exercise, we are going to explore the basic interactions. All interactions, in Figma, involve two things: a trigger and an event. A trigger is what initiates the event. In Figma, the triggers are as follows:

- On Click: The user clicks on something.

- On Drag: The user clicks on something and, with the mouse pressed, drags it somewhere.

- While Hovering: When the cursor is over something.

- While Pressing: When the cursor is pressed but not released. There are always three states for the mouse: Mouse Over (Hovering), Mouse Down (Pressing), and Mouse Up (Click).

Events answer the "What happens?" question. For example, when the object is selected, it gets dragged to another position. In this scenario, the trigger is On Drag and the event is something is dragged from here to there.

We will start with a basic click. Click an element and move from Here to There. Though it may sound rather rudimentary, this is where the interactivity dimensions of Time and Behavior are added. This is all done through the Prototype panel, and simple clicks can get rather complicated rather quickly.

1. Open the Triggers.fig file found in your chapter download. When it opens, you will see two frames labelled "Here" and "There". The plan is to go from here to there with a mouse click.

2. Select Prototype mode. You will notice that first frame is labeled Flow 1. Double-click and change the name to Here it on the pasteboard, but we'll leave with this one for now. Click on Show prototype settings. A panel asks you what device is being used, the background color, and which Flow to use. Click on Flow 1 in the panel (Figure 7-1), and three options appear. The first icon, Select Frame, is asking you to establish the start of the interaction. Click on the Here frame.

Figure 7-1. *Select your starting point in the Prototype panel*

This really is an unnecessary step for simple interactions. You can open the Prototype panel and select your start point instead.

3. When a frame is selected as the starting point, the Prototype panel adds an Interactions section. Click on the word Interactions and a side menu

(Figure 7-2) appears with the click action. Click on None to open a drop-down menu and select Navigate to....

Figure 7-2. *You are asked what to do when a click action is triggered*

4. The dialog box will change and ask you which frame to go to with a click. Select "There" from the pop-down (Figure 7-3).

Figure 7-3. *The final step is choosing the destination*

5. Click on the pasteboard and an arrow now points to the "There" frame.

   One of the fundamental rules of interactivity is: "If you send someone somewhere, you need to take them back." Here's how.

6. In Prototype mode, select the "There" frame.

7. Roll the mouse along one of the frame's edges and you will see a circle with a plus sign.

8. Drag an arrow, called a wire, from the circle to the "Here" frame. Notice how the dialog box shown in Figure 7-4 shows the path with a Click event.

Figure 7-4. Drag a wire to the finish point of the interaction

   The second rule of interactivity design is: "Do a bit. Test it." Nothing is worse than discovering a mistake with a complex interaction and having to start all over again or it comes back from development and you notice your mistake.

9. With the "Here" frame selected, select the playback preview or press Shift-Spacebar.

10. Click once in the preview to go to the There frame and click the There frame to go back. As you navigate from Here to There, notice how the frame that starts the interaction is selected on the pasteboard.

Now that you know how to create a simple click interaction, let's assume you don't want the user to get back to the start. To accomplish this, select the wire and either drag it off of the Here frame or press the delete key.

One of the authors would show this mildly complicated technique, to his students. They would inevitably struggle, but after a couple of minutes, they were creating the interaction. Then he would say, "Here's the easy way." And drag a wire to the destination. Of course, the complaints started, but as he explained, "You have to know the decisions to be made and the hard way walks you through those decisions."

Create a Drag Interaction

A common interaction is dragging something from here to there on a screen. A typical example of this technique would be something like a slider. Here's how:

1. If it isn't already open, open the Triggers.fig file found in your chapter download. We will be creating a slider in the Drag frame.

2. Select the Drag frame and duplicate it. Rename the duplicated frame Drag 2 and move the red ball to the end of the Base in the duplicated frame. We have now established how the ball will be dragged from here to there.

3. Select the Drag frame and open Prototype mode. Select the red ball, add the On Drag trigger, and drag a wire to the Drag 2 frame (Figure 7-5).

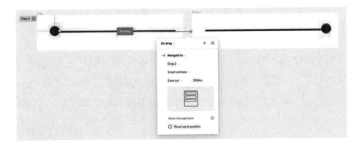

Figure 7-5. *The Drag event is set*

4. Still in Prototype mode, select the red ball in the Drag 2 frame and attach an On Drag event back to the Drag frame. Test.

Create a Hover Interaction

The most common use for this trigger is to indicate to the user that something is interactive. Here's how:

1. If it isn't already open, open the Triggers.fig file found in your chapter download. We will be creating a hover effect that changes the red ball's color to blue.

2. Switch to Prototype mode. Select the red ball in the Hover frame and drag a wire to the Hover 2 frame.

3. Select While hovering and close the dialog box. Test the interaction. One thing you should notice is when you move off of the blue ball, it reverts back to the red ball (Figure 7-6).

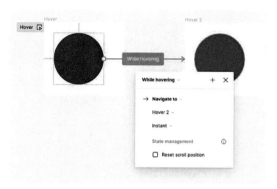

Figure 7-6. *Adding a Hover effect*

Create a While Pressing Interaction

There are three common events that a mouse can trigger during a simple mouse click. They are Mouse Up, Mouse Over, and Mouse Down. The While pressing event is actually a Mouse Down event, and we are going to use these events to create a simple interaction. Let's get started:

1. If it isn't already open, open the Triggers.fig file found in your chapter download. We will be using mouse events to turn the red ball blue.

2. Switch to Prototype mode and select the red ball. Drag a wire to the Press 2 frame.

3. This time select Mouse enter as the trigger (Figure 7-7). Instead of a hover, the ball will turn blue when the user moves the mouse over the red ball.

337

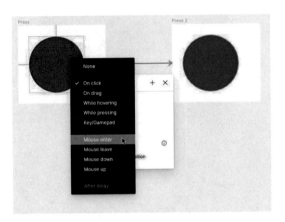

Figure 7-7. *Using a mouse event as a trigger*

4. Select the blue ball and drag a wire to the red ball.
    Add a While pressing event. Test. The blue ball
    changes to the red ball when you release the mouse.

5. Close the preview and select the While pressing wire
    and change it to Mouse Down. Test. Notice how the
    color doesn't revert to blue. This is due to the mouse
    event. As you can see, there is a difference between
    a While pressing event and a Mouse Down event.

Create a Component in Figma

In the previous exercise, you discovered how to apply triggers that
initiate interactions. They really didn't do much other than moving
between frames. Unfortunately, using separate frames for button presses
is not a best practice. It messes up the workspace and tends to irritate
the developers. In this exercise, we are going to convert a button into a
component. Then we are going to create a button component that is used
to navigate from one frame to another.

Components are reusable elements that can be applied across multiple frames and designs. Being able to reuse instances of a component is a huge value for workflow speed as well as design consistency. Create once and it can be used many times within a local document, a or a shared Team Library. This is critical for a consistent Design System. A key aspect of components is a simple change to a component, such as a background color, will ripple through every document that uses that component. Another neat aspect of components is you can make changes directly to the instance of a component in your prototype without affecting the master component. Here's how to create a component:

1. Open the Component.fig file found in your chapter download. As you can see, it is nothing more than a frame with the word "Up" in it. You should also notice the frame has had auto layout applied to it and the frame has rounded corners, which are common to buttons (Figure 7-8).

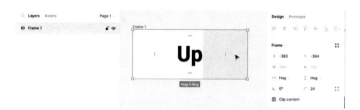

Figure 7-8. *We start with a frame containing Autolayout and rounded corners*

2. To create the component, select the frame, and with the frame selected, click on the Create Component button, the icon with four diamonds(⬥⬥), on your toolbar. Your frame turns purple and there is an icon composed of four diamonds both over the frame and in the Layers panel (Figure 7-9). That icon represents the master component, and if you open the Assets panel, you will also see the component.

339

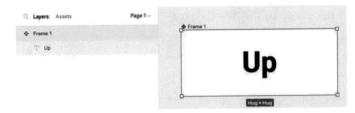

Figure 7-9. *The Four-Diamond icon and the Purple color indicate a master component*

This component resides in the local Assets library, meaning it can only be used in the document you currently have open. If you have a Team Library, a Shared Library, or a Design System, this component can be added to them. If you feel compelled to add this component to the Design System, it would be a good idea to first check with the UX Designer managing the project and the development team. You can also edit the component by right-clicking it in the Assets panel and selecting Go to main component in the pop-down menu. Again, editing components in the Library or Design System should only be done in consultation with the UX Designer and the developer.

---

3. Open the Assets panel and drag the component onto the pasteboard. You should notice the component icon is missing, but the frame is still purple. This indicates you are using an "instance" of the Master component (Figure 7-10). If you open the Layers panel, you see another visual clue: an instance of the component is on the pasteboard. The layer icon changes to a hollow diamond.

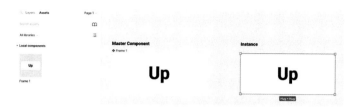

Figure 7-10. *The difference between a Master component and an Instance*

4. Drag an instance of the component from the Assets panel to the pasteboard. Change the Fill color of the instance. Change the Fill color of the text. As you can see, none of these changes were applied to the Master component.

5. Select the master component and increase or decrease the margins. The instance instantly reflects that change. This explains why there has to be a solid reason to edit a master component.

Add States by Creating Variants

Now that you understand how to create a component, edit an instance, and discover changes to the master component rippled through the instances, let's add interactivity to our component.

1. To start, delete the instance on the pasteboard.

2. Select the Component on the pasteboard and make the following changes:

    • Width: 200

    • Height: 100

- Corner Roundness: 100

- Stroke: 2 point black

- Text Size: 36

We are now prepared to add the various states of the button. This is accomplished through the use of "variants" within the component. For example, you may wish to have Light Mode and Dark Mode variations of the button. They can all be contained in the component. For this button, we are going to add Down and Pressed variants of this button that change the background color of the button. Let's get started.

3. With the component selected, click the Add variant button. When you select the component, the Create Component icon changes to a hollow diamond containing a + sign (⬖). The variant is added, and a dashed bounding box surrounds the component (Figure 7-11), showing you this is a component with two states.

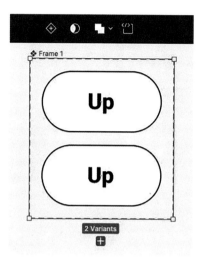

Figure 7-11. *Add a component variant by clicking the diamond-shaped Add variant icon on the toolbar*

4. To add the third state of the button, click the + sign under the dashed bounding box.

5. If you look at the Layers panel, the states are there, but they don't say what they do. Select the Middle button, and over in the Properties panel, the state is named in the Current variant section. Double-click the name and change it to Hover. Rename the third variant to Click. If you open the Variant pop-down, the variants will be listed (Figure 7-12).

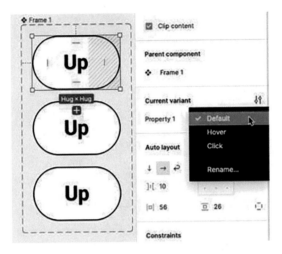

Figure 7-12. *Give each variant a unique name*

6. Select the Hover variant and change its background
    color to blue (#03B1FB). Select the text in the Hover
    state and change its color to white (#FFFFFF).
    Change the Click state's background color to green
    (#0BEE07).

Adding Interactivity to a Component

With the states created and named, we can make this button interactive.
Here's how:

1. With the component selected, open the
    Prototype panel.

2. Select the Default variant and drag a wire to the
    Hover variant. When the Interactions dialog box
    opens, select While hovering, and just to be sure,
    select the Hover instance in the Property drop-down
    (Figure 7-13).

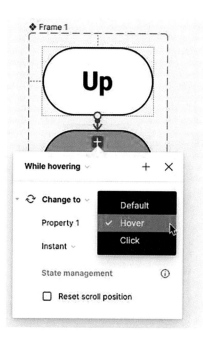

Figure 7-13. *Adding Hover to a variant*

3. Select the Hover variant and drag a wire to the Click variant. When the properties open, choose While pressing and set the Click variant in the Property area. On click is used to go somewhere, which we will get to in the next exercise. Using While pressing will return to the Hover state when the mouse is released; On click won't.

4. Rename the Component to Button.

5. Press the F key and draw out a new frame that is slightly larger than the button.

6. Open the Assets panel and drag an instance of
    the Button component to the new frame you have
    just created. Test the interactions. To return to the
    default state, just move the mouse out of the button
    (Figure 7-14).

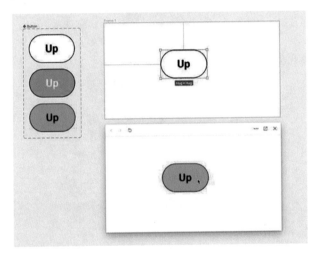

Figure 7-14. *The click state is showing when the button is tested*

It is not unheard of for a button to go through multiple iterations
based on user testing or in consultation with the design team and the
development team.

Create Interactivity Using a Component

To this point, you have created a component, added triggers to a
component, and created component variants to show the various states of
a component. In this exercise, we are going to create a component and put
it to work. Let's get started:

1. Import the Bern.fig file found in your chapter
    download. When you open the file, you will see
    three layers: Button, Card, and Valley (Figure 7-15).
    The plan is to convert the Button layer to a
    component and place it on the card. When the
    button is clicked, the user will be taken to the Valley
    layer. To go back, the user will click on the Back
    button at the top of the Valley layer to return to the
    Card layer.

Figure 7-15. *We start with three rather simple frames*

2. Select the Button frame on the pasteboard and
    convert it to a component.

3. Add one variant and rename it Click.

4. Select the Click variant, and in the Properties
    panel, change its background color to a light blue
    (#D0F0FA) (Figure 7-16).

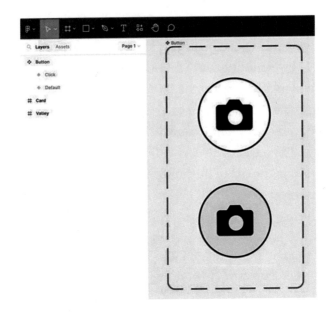

Figure 7-16. *The button states are established*

5.   Switch to Prototype mode, select the Default variant, drag an arrow to the Click variant, and add a "While hovering". Change to Click event.

6.   Select the Click variant and drag a wire to the Valley frame as shown in Figure 7-17. You should also note the event has changed to On Tap and you are asked where to navigate. In this case, it is Card, but if you had a number of frames, they would appear in the Navigate to pop-down.

Figure 7-17. *Tapping the Click variant opens the Valley frame*

Where did the On Click event go? When custom frame sizes are created, Figma will assume this is a mobile project and On Tap is the default trigger. If you use Presentation as the Preview, the project will appear in an iPhone skin.

---

7. Open the Assets panel and drag a copy of the Button component to the bottom right of the Card frame.

8. In the Valley frame, select the Back icon and drag a wire to the Card frame. Test.

One of our cardinal rules is: Test early. Test often. With this exercise, the prototype could be shared with both the design and development teams. The design team may suggest different colors for the Click variant or the icon should be different or scaled up or down or its Fill color changed to provide contrast. This is the ideal time to iterate components until you get the various states "just right." Sharing the component with the developers won't require their input but demonstrates your intent to the development team.

Your Turn: Create Interactivity Using Components and Variants

In this chapter, we focused on interactivity fundamentals. Now let's apply the interactions to a website design for a Switzerland tourism Home page and a Swiss Alps Adventure page. We will start with creating the main navigation titles at the top of the page, creating one main navigation title as an auto layout element, and then converting that into a component with different variants, one for each button state: default, hover, and click. By creating one main interactive navigation button, you will see how easy it is to create all the required main navigation titles. We will also learn how to apply a Text property to the component. Let's begin.

1. Import and open the Interactive-Website-Navigation.fig file found in your chapter download. When the file opens (Figure 7-18), you will see three frames: Components, Swiss - Home page, and Swiss - Adventure, Alps page. We will create the main navigation component and apply the interactions. Then, we will add the main navigation component to the Swiss - Home page to create the full main navigation, copy the main navigation from the Swiss - Home page to the Swiss - Adventure, Alps page, and link the pages together.

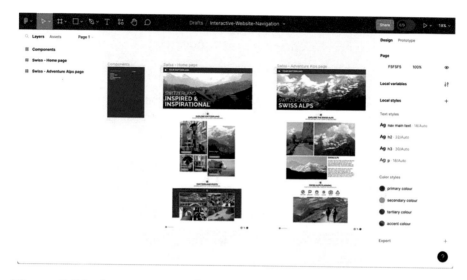

Figure 7-18. *Interactive-Website-Navigation.fig showing three frames: Components, Home, and Swiss Alps page*

Create a Component for the Home Button and Create a Text Property

The first step is to create the button component. By doing this, you make the interactive elements more efficient and reusable. We'll start with the Home button:

1. In the Components frame, select the text "HOME" and zoom in so you can see the text easily (Shift 2).

2. With the text selected, create an auto layout (Shift A).

3. In the Properties panel, select auto layout and apply the following values:

    • Horizontal Gap: 0

    • Horizonal Padding: 12

- Vertical Padding: 3

- Change the Fill color to #FF0000 (red)

4. With the HOME auto layout selected, create a Component Option – Command-K (Mac), Alt-Control-K (PC).

5. Select the text in the component. Below the alignment icons, you will see the text "HOME". Right-click the diamond icon with the arrow pointing right (Figure 7-19).

6. A new window will pop up, "Create component property." In the Value input area, change the word HOME to BUTTON. This will allow you to replace the button text using the Properties panel faster than having to highlight and change each button text in each frame (Figure 7-19).

Figure 7-19. *Component Text property*

All components have properties, and by switching the Text property value in the component from "Home" to "Button," you are able to switch the text without digging into the component and its variables, selecting the text, and manually entering the text. It can be done right in the Text properties.

Create the Variant States for the Main Navigation Button

Having created the component and changed the Text property to the more general button, we can now concentrate on creating the variants.

1. Create a Variant of the BUTTON by clicking the top diamond icon with the + sign; this will be our hover state.

2. In the Properties panel, select Current variant, double-click on "Property 1", and change it to "State".

3. To the right of "State", double-click on "Variant2" and change it to "Hover".

4. At the bottom of the purple dotted component set, click the + icon, creating a third variant. This will be our selected state.

5. In the Current variant area, change "State3" to "Selected". We now have a component with three states for the navigation button: Default, Hover, and Selected.

6. In the Layers panel on the left, change the Component frame title to "Nav Main Button" as shown in Figure 7-20.

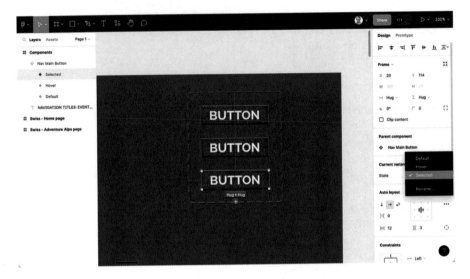

Figure 7-20. *Three button component variant states*

Design Each of the Three States for the Main Navigation Home Button

Having created the variants and identified the states, you can now concentrate on what the button looks like for each of the three states.

1. Select the top BUTTON variant, Default, and remove the Fill from the Properties panel by clicking the - sign in the Fill area. This makes the button transparent.

2. Select the middle BUTTON variant, Hover state, and change the Fill in the Properties panel to #FFFFFF (White), with a 40% transparency.

3. Select the bottom BUTTON variant, Selected state, and change the Fill to #FFFFFF (White), 100% transparency.

4. In the bottom HOME variant, double-click the
    text and change the Fill to a dark green (#113A12)
    to match the website header background color
    (Figure 7-21).

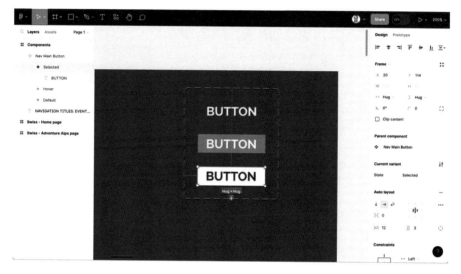

Figure 7-21. Three button variant states designed

Apply Interactions to Each of the Three Button States

There are two ways to add interactive triggers: by dragging a wire from
each variant and selecting the trigger from the Interactions dialog box or,
as we now demonstrate, adding them right from the Interactions panel
when in Prototype mode. Here's how:

1. Switch to Prototype mode.

2. On the canvas, select the Default state and
    click once in the Interactions area to open the
    Interactions dialog box. You will see the default "On
    click" trigger has been applied.

355

3. Click on the trigger, and when the Interactions dialog box opens, change the trigger from "On click" to "While hovering".

4. Though we have selected While hovering as the trigger, we still need to tell it what to do. Click on the word None to open the Actions pop-down. Select Change to and select Hover in the variants pop-down as shown in Figure 7-22.

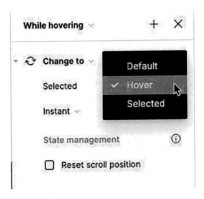

Figure 7-22. *Navigation can also be established using the Interactions dialog box*

5. Select the middle BUTTON variant, Hover state, and from the blue circle + icon on the right, drag a flow path to the bottom BUTTON variant.

6. Select the bottom BUTTON variant, Selected state, and drag a wire or flow path back to the Default state(Figure 7-23).

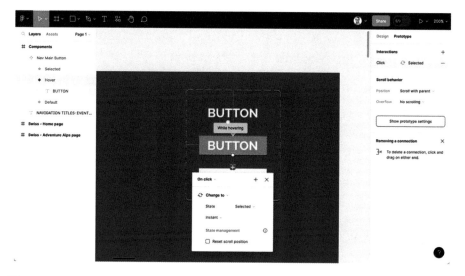

Figure 7-23. *Variant states defined interactions*

Add the Main Navigation Button to the Header of the Swiss - Home Page

With the Navigation component created, it can now be added to the Home page frame. Here's how:

1. Select the frame "Swiss - Home page" and zoom into the top green bar, the header section of the website.

2. Open the Assets panel and twirl down the Local components to access the Button component.

3. Select the "Nav Main Button" and drag the component from the Assets into the green bar in the Swiss - Home page. This creates an instance of the component.

4. Open the Header layer in the Layers panel and drag
    the instance to the top of the Header layers. Center
    the button vertically in the green bar.

5. In the Properties panel, select the Nav Main Button
    instance and change the Text from BUTTON
    to HOME.

6. Test by pressing Shift-Spacebar. Roll over the button
    to see the state change.

Figure 7-24. *Applying a component instance for the HOME button*

Creating the Main Navigation Buttons

Having tested the component on the Home page and determined it is
working as expected, we can now use that component to create the Header
navigation. Here's how:

1. In the right-hand Properties panel, click on Design.

2. Select the HOME button in the Swiss - Home page, and with the Option-Shift (Mac) or Alt-Shift (PC) key held down, drag out five copies of the component along the header. By keeping the Shift key held down when dragging the copy, the component stays horizontally centered.

3. Select each of the new buttons, and in the Properties panel, change the Text to EVENTS, ADVENTURES, DINING, ACCOMODATIONS and CONTACT.

4. With the component instances selected, apply auto layout to and add consistent spacing between them in the Header as shown in Figure 7-25.

5. Select the Home button, and in the Properties panel, change its state from Default to Selected.

6. Test the navigation by pressing Alt-Control-Enter (Windows) or Option-Command-Return (Mac).

7. Change the auto layout name in the Layers panel to Nav.

Figure 7-25. *Applying multiple instances for the main website navigation and changing the text in the Component properties*

Adding the Header Navigation to the Adventures Page

Obviously, the Navigation on the Home page will be added to the other pages in the site. The main difference will be the state of the button will change to Selected to provide the user with a visual clue they are on that page. In this case, the user will click the Adventures button to navigate to that page. At the same time, the Adventures button will change its state to indicate the page. Let's get started:

1. Select the Nav Autolayout layer and copy it to the clipboard.

2. Scroll over to the Adventures page, select the header layer, and paste the Nav copy into the Header. By doing this, the copy will be put in the same position as the original.

3. Select the HOME button, and in the Properties panel, change its state from Selected to Default.

4. Select the ADVENTURES button, and in the Properties panel, change its State from Default to Selected (Figure 7-26).

Figure 7-26. *The main website navigation is pasted into the Swiss Alps page, with the ADVENTURES button in the Selected state*

5. Zoom out to 50% in order to see the two pages and change to Prototype mode.

6. On the Home page, select the Home button and drag a wire to the ADVENTURES page.

7. On the Adventures page, select the ADVENTURES button and drag a wire back to the Home page as shown in Figure 7-27.

8. Test, Alt-Control-Enter (Windows) or Option-Command-Return (Mac).

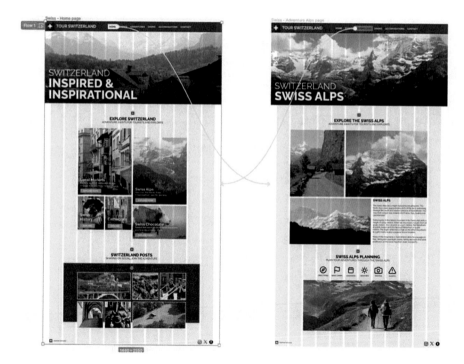

Figure 7-27. *Using one component to link to multiple web pages*

You Have Learned

This is an important chapter because as you have discovered, the Time and Behavior dimensions of an interaction are how we communicate directly with the user through interactivity. This is why we constantly use the word "iterate." Only through iteration can you achieve a harmony between Time and Behavior. In this chapter, you have learned the following:

- Interactivity involves a trigger and an event.

- How to add interactivity to elements on a screen.

- How to create a Drag interaction.

- How to create a Hover interaction.

- How to create a While pressing interaction.

- How to create a component and its variants.

- How to edit component variants.

- The difference between a component and an instance.

- How to add interactivity to a component and its variants.

CHAPTER 8

Microinteractions in Figma

Motion is essential part of the language that designers use to communicate with users. It is used to describe spatial relationships between states and functionality of individual elements. Thoughtful motion in design can enhance the user's experience.

–Nick Babich
Motion in UX Design
UX Planet
`https://uxplanet.org/motion-in-ux-design-90f6da5c32fe`

If ever there was a process in UX Design that required full collaboration between the design and development teams, it would be the incorporation of motion in a project. Motion incorporated into a Figma prototype is nothing more than the designer showing, "Here's what I think should happen." It is the developers' responsibility to write the code that makes it happen. Let's assume there is a hamburger menu that appears when the icon is clicked. The designer can easily prototype that interaction in Figma, toss it over to development, and be done with it. Due to space limitations, we are not going to enumerate all of the things that could go wrong.

© Tom Green and Kevin Brandon 2024
T. Green and K. Brandon, *UX Design with Figma*, Design Thinking,
https://doi.org/10.1007/979-8-8688-0324-6_8

Let's change it up. There are issues that should be resolved between the designer and the developer before the prototype is handed over to development. These issues would include the following:

- How big is the menu?

- Where does it appear from? Top, left, right, bottom?

- How long does it take to appear?

- How far does it travel?

- Is there a transition instead of motion? Which transition and for how long?

With that basic information in hand, the developer knows what to expect.

You should also be aware this sort of thing is not a one-and-done workflow. There are usually several iterations of the interaction and motion to get it just right. Then, it can be handed off to development. One company, Intercom, uses a design-build-beta workflow (Figure 8-1), where the design is built. The development team makes suggestions as they iterate through the build, and once everyone is on board, the beta phase starts until it is approved and the design/build cycle restarts. By locking down the interactions and motion, you build a Motion language where such things as transitions, animations, and motion can be moved into the Design System and/or documented by the developers.

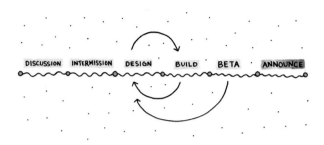

Figure 8-1. *The Intercom process is a collaborative effort between the design and development teams*

Interactivity and Motion

These two items are inseparable. As you saw in the previous section, they require careful planning and execution from the developers' perspective because it is the developer that makes the idea a reality. As such, here are a few things your developer should know when interactivity and motion are involved:

- Interactivity involves clicking, dragging, swiping, and so on.

- Motion is how those elements change or move through the use of a transition or animation.

- Interactivity and motion must follow the fundamental principles of UX Design such as consistency, affordance, hierarchy, and clarity. The motion must include principles of motion design such as timing, easing, and direction.

- Interactivity and motion must be optimized and tested for different platforms, devices, and browsers. They should also be accessible and inclusive.

There is one other aspect of motion you need to clearly understand before we move on. Motion is not animation. Animation falls into the realm of what Google calls "delightful details." They are "nice to have" but offer no value. In his groundbreaking essay "The UX in Motion Manifesto," Issara Willenskomer is quite clear about the differences between tools and the principles of UX motion. "Animation is all about tools." He writes, "Principles are the practical applications of ideas that guide the usage of tools and as such, Principles provide high leverage opportunities for designers."

Again, you may think of UI motion as being a delightful detail. You couldn't be more wrong. UX motion is something that can be designed, and that includes, as Willenskomer so neatly put it, "the temporal behaviour of interface objects during realtime and non-realtime events."

We have all experienced what has become to be known as the "ripple effect" when a button is clicked.

A colored circle or other shape moves across the button to indicate the state change. Just the creation of this simple button requires a lot of decisions, such as the following:

- What color is the shape?

- What opacity value is applied?

- How long does it take for the shape to move into place?

- Where does it come from? A side? The center?

Those are the design principles. The UX principles would be the following:

- Does it drive the user's attention to the object and hint at what will happen?

- Does it provide guided focus through the use of icons or words?

- Does it provide the user with visual feedback?

Once all of those decisions have been made, that simple button can then be converted to a component and added to a Shared Library or Design System for consistent reuse in your Figma prototype.

Let's loop back to our description of a ripple because there is a fundamental aspect of motion that needs to be explained: "A colored circle or other shape moves across the button." When you read just that sentence, you form, in your mind's eye, your concept of a ripple effect. We are willing to bet those of you that read that sentence all have a different concept of that motion. This brings us to the fundamental principle of UX motion: "You can't describe it. You have to show it." Let's do just that:

1. Open the Ripple.fig file found in your chapter download. When it opens, you will see we have created the effect in a component. If you open the Layers panel and open the Default component, you will see (Figure 8-2) that it is a 150 × 150 pixel circular frame filled with a Light Blue (#7FA2FC). There is a stroked shape in the top layer and a dark blue circle sitting outside of the frame. In the Ripple Layer, the dark blue circle moves under the Stroke layer. In the Assets panel, you will see the Button component. An instance of the component has been placed in the Home frame.

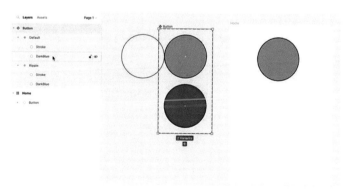

Figure 8-2. *The ripple effect is designed*

2. Preview the component. The ripple is the dark blue circle sliding into the Ripple variant.

3. Let's see how that happened. Switch to Prototype mode and select the wire between the variants to open the Interactions panel shown in Figure 8-3.

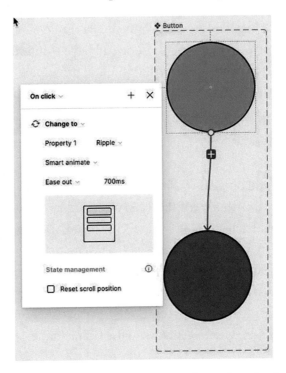

Figure 8-3. *The Interactions panel shows how the ripple effect was created*

There are two things that are somewhat new. The motion interaction uses Figma's Smart animate feature to move the Ball. This feature is not important right now, and we will dig deeper into it later in this chapter. The Ease out number, 700 ms, is what's important. That number represents the amount of time it takes for the circle to move into its final position.

When you clicked the button, did you happen to notice how slowly the ball moved? The number 700 indicates how many milliseconds (ms) the circle takes to move into place. What we would like you to do is to imagine 700 ms. You can't because your personal experience of time starts with seconds. Even though the circle was moving quite quickly in real time, it seemed to be moving rather slowly.

Your perception of that motion reinforces Willenskomer's contention that the UX of motion is created by "the temporal behaviour of interface objects during realtime and non-realtime events." That 700 ms is the "temporal," and the circle moving in from the left is the "behavior." Let's play with the temporal and behavioral properties.

4. With the Interactions dialog box open, change the time value to 300 ms.

5. In the Layers panel, select the dark blue circle in the Default variant and move it down, as shown in Figure 8-4, to a point just below the center of the Light Blue circle. Test. The circle moves up to its final position in a much shorter time.

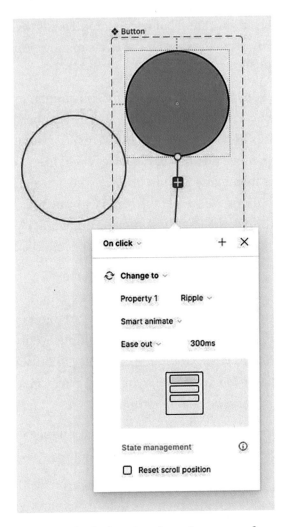

Figure 8-4. *Changing the behavioral and temporal properties of a circle in motion*

This rather simple exercise is extremely important when it comes to motion. Creating an interaction involving motion requires you to undertake several iterations of that simple interaction until it is good enough to send off to development or to add to a Team Library or Design System. It involves playing with time and the location of the object in motion. The last thing you need when the product is in the hands of your users is to start getting complaints about how slowly everything moves. Users want instant gratification because they have no conception of milliseconds.

This exercise is based on a technique Joshua Davis, a brilliant Digital Artist, demonstrated in 2002 at a Macromedia Flash seminar. Josh explained how all of his work involved painstakingly iterating the temporal and behavioral properties of the objects in his work. If you have ever seen his work, it is a riot of colorful shapes moving and interacting with each other. The first step in his creative process was to use primitive shapes – gray circles, squares, triangles, and so on in order to get the time and behavior to meet his high standard. He called these first iterations "Machines." This also explains why in earlier chapters we used gray boxes to create a wireframe to focus on the design, not the content. We will be using "Machines" in a number of subsequent exercises for that very purpose: to focus on the interactions, motion, and transitions, not the content.

Playing with Time and Motion in Figma

Motion, in very simple terms, is how something moves from "Here to There." That blue circle started in the Default variant position Here, moved to its final position There, in the Ripple variant. There is a lot more to it than that. We, as humans, are hard-wired into detecting motion, and we use time to determine how fast an object is moving. When you thought the circle was moving too slowly, you saw how a simple time change changed your perception of the motion.

There is another aspect of motion in UX you may not know. It is that nothing moves at a constant speed. If your car started moving at 30 mph or 50 kmph when you started the car, the odds are that you will be heaved into the back seat or through the back window. In order to reach that speed, the car needs to accelerate, and to stop the car, it needs to decelerate.

Microinteractions Overview

The term "microinteraction" was first coined by Dan Saffer in his book *Microinteractions: Designing with Details* published by O'Reilly in 2013. He defined microinteractions as "product moments that revolve around a single use case – they have one main task." That interactive button you just worked on falls squarely into that description. Its main purpose is to do something or go somewhere when it is clicked. Another microinteraction is one you may be familiar with. Have you ever had your smartwatch inform you it is time to stand? Its use case is simple: to get you to stand up from your reclined or seated position.

Saffer also demonstrated the four parts of a microinteraction (Figure 8-5). They are as follows:

- Trigger: This is what prompts the microinteraction to start. Triggers are user activated events such as a mouse hover, a mouse click, or from a system notification "It's time to stand."

- Rules: What happens when the event is triggered. It could be something simple such as being navigated to a web page, submitting your username and password, or having a menu slide in.

- Feedback: This is anything a user sees, hears, or feels when a microinteraction is triggered. That ripple effect falls into this category.

- Loops and Modes: These two factors determine what happens when circumstances change. Loops determine the duration of the microinteraction.

An example of this is Amazon; it keeps an eye on your search history. You spend some time looking at camera lenses. Each time after that, Amazon will present you with camera suggestions. A couple of weeks later you are looking for printer ink refills. The "mode" has changed to ink refills, and the loop will be in effect until you search for an office chair.

Figure 8-5. *The four parts of a microinteraction (Microinteractions: Designing with Details, Dan Safer, 2013, O'Reilly)*

As a UX Design tool, Figma lets you control the first three parts of a microinteraction. Loops and modes fall squarely in the realm of development, but it is the wise designer who collaborates with the developer to determine the loops and modes.

The Principles of UX in Motion

In his 2017 UX in Motion Manifesto, Issara Willenskomer postulated there are 12 principles behind UX motion that have come to be accepted as the standard for motion. The principles are as follows:

- Easing

- Offset and Delay

- Parenting

- Transformation

- Value Change (think timers)

- Masking

- Overlay

- Cloning

- Obscuration

- Parallax

- Dimensionality

- Dolly and Zoom

You may not have noticed it when we did that ripple, but the principle of easing was applied. Remember that blur you created earlier in an earlier chapter? It used Obscuration. When you drag images in a carousel, one image gets bigger and one gets smaller. That is Dimensionality.

Putting things in motion in Figma uses a technology called Smart animate, but to use it effectively, one or a combination of those principles will apply. Let's examine how those principles apply when you choose Smart animate.

We are not going to demonstrate all of them. Instead, we will look at how four UX motion principles are used.

Easing and Smart Animate

A fundamental rule of UX in motion is nothing moves at a constant speed. Think of your car. You accelerate to hit the speed limit and decelerate when the car stops. You are experiencing the principle of easing every time you get into your car. The technology that allows this principle in Figma is Smart animate. Here's how the Easing principle applies:

1. Open the Easing.fig file found in your chapter download. There are two frames. The box will fall from the top of the frame to the bottom when it is clicked.

2. Switch to the Prototype mode and drag a wire from the box in the Start frame to the End screen to the Down frame.

3. When the Interactions dialog box appears, select Smart animate and choose Ease in and out in for the easing. Change the time to 1,000 ms (Figure 8-6).

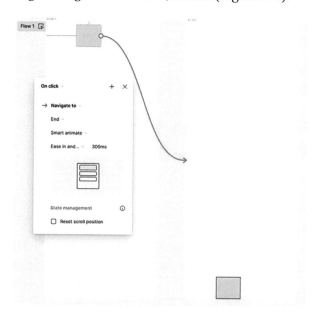

Figure 8-6. *Applying easing to motion using Smart animate*

When you test this, you will see the box accelerate and decelerate. One reason you can see this is we have set the duration, the temporal behavior, of this motion to 1 second (1000 ms). Always apply easing to any object that moves from here to there.

Easing, improperly applied, can present usability issues. In this example, timing will be a huge issue because users will complain that it seems to take a lot of time to travel down the screen or distract the user's attention.

There are some rules regarding the application of easing. The three most important are as follows:

- Apply Ease out when an object placed outside a screen moves inside a screen.

- Apply Ease in when an onscreen object moves off-screen.

- Apply Ease in and out if the motion is contained to the screen.

The Eases Available in Figma

When you select Ease in, the Interactions dialog box displays the eases available to you (Figure 8-7):

- Linear: There is no easing.

- Ease in: Acceleration

- Ease out: Deceleration

- Ease in back, in and out, and out: Applies what is called an overshoot. The object seems to move backward or upward when it starts moving and moves past the end position when it comes to rest.

- Custom: We will deal with this in the next section.

The next grouping are the Spring animations:

- Gentle: A very slight overshoot is applied at the end of the motion.

- Quick: A slightly more pronounced overshoot is applied at the end of the motion.

- Bouncy: As implied, the end of the motion bounces.

- Slow: A very obvious deceleration occurs.

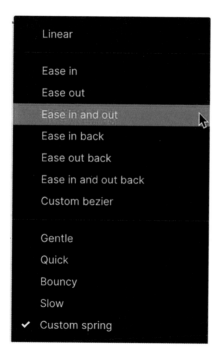

Figure 8-7. *The Figma eases*

Editing an Ease

At the bottom of the ease options is the category: Custom bezier or Custom spring. Select this category and you can edit the ease or apply your own custom ease. Let's see how this works with the Ease in and out applied to the motion of the box.

When you select Custom bezier, the graph shown in Figure 8-8 opens.

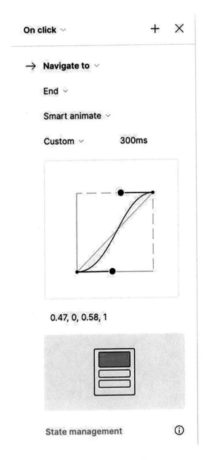

Figure 8-8. *Customizing an ease using the Bezier curves*

The X axis is time. The Y axis is the motion, though it could also be a change such as Rotation, Scale, or, in this case, Position. The motion or change starts at the bottom of the graph and ends at the top. In this case, the curve at the bottom is the acceleration, and the one at the top is deceleration. The dots are the handles. Pull the bottom handle to the right and you have sped up the acceleration and the opposite is true if you move the top handle. In this way, you can "tweak" the animation as you iterate the interaction. Those numbers at the bottom – 0.47, 0, 0.58, 1 – are the CSS values your developer will use when the project moves into development.

The Spring curve, shown in Figure 8-9, is quite a bit different. A car spring and a toy spring are totally different beasts, and by adjusting the Stiffness, Damping, and Mass values, you can turn a car spring into a toy spring.

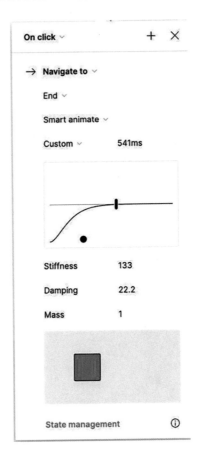

Figure 8-9. *Spring curves use Stiffness, Damping, and Mass to determine the animation*

Moving the dot or the line will change the Stiffness and Damping values. To increase or decrease the Mass value, you need to input a value. Here's what each parameter does:

- Stiffness: Increase the stiffness and the number of bounces will decrease.

- Damping: This value affects "springiness." A big number would be a car spring. A small number would be a toy spring.

- Mass: This is where physics comes into play. This value influences the speed and height of the bounce. This value can only be added manually and will change the animation's duration.

Spring animations should be used sparingly or not at all. There needs to be a valid justification or use case if it is to be applied. This is one of those animations that will require collaboration with the development team especially when Mass is applied. What you can't do with a custom spring animation is save it for future use.

Applying the Transformation Principle in Figma

We have all created a slide deck. As you move between the slides, you have seen or used a transition. In fact, the effect is a transformation where an object or screen changes. Transformations are important because they stand out. Users will notice them. It could be something as simple as a button with a plus sign rotating when it is clicked and the + becomes an X that tells the user the transformation is complete. It grabs the user's attention and tells the user something is happening as it rotates, and the motion is complete when the X appears. In short, transformations smoothly move users through a variety of UX states that result in a desired result.

In Figma, these are the transformations:

- Instant

- Dissolve

- Smart animate

- Move in

- Move out

- Push

- Slide in

- Slide out

They are all, with the exception of Smart animate, self-explanatory. Click a hamburger menu and its appearance uses the Instant, Dissolve, Move, Push, or Slide transformations. Let's take a deeper look at how Smart animate facilitates the transformation principle. We will create three transformations: Dissolve, Move in/Move out, and a rather complex transformation that uses Smart animate. Let's get started.

Create a Dissolve Transformation

1. Open the Transforms.fig file found in your chapter download. When it opens, you will see we have set up the Transformations in separate frames – Dissolve, MoveIn, MoveOut, and Animate. There is also a component named Dissolve, and the three dots and blue circle will be used in the Animate frame (Figure 8-10).

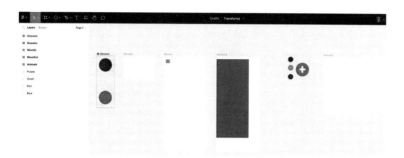

Figure 8-10. *We start with four frames for the transformations*

2. Open the Assets panel and right-click on the
    Dissolve component. Select Go to main component
    from the pop-down menu. Figma will zoom in on
    the component.

3. Switch to Prototype mode and drag a wire from the
    red ball to the green ball.

4. Change the Trigger to While hovering.

5. Open the Instant pop-down and select Dissolve.

6. Select Linear from the Eases pop-down and change
    the duration to 700 ms (Figure 8-11). If you roll over
    the preview, you can see the transformation.

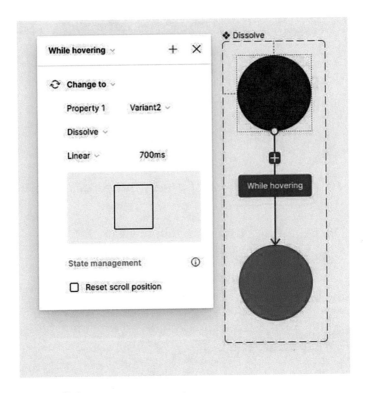

Figure 8-11. *Editing a component*

7. Open the Assets panel and drag the component into the Dissolve frame. Test. That was a bit slow; feel free to go back into the component to try out different durations.

Create a Move Transition

Move transitions are ideal for those situations where one object moves into a screen from off screen. A common move transition is creating a slide menu. Here's how:

1. Select the MoveIn layer and you will see there is
    a hamburger menu and a solid gray rectangle.
    As you can see, the rectangle is visible in the
    MoveOut frame.

2. Switch to Prototype mode, select the hamburger
    menu and drag a wire to the MoveOut frame.

3. In the Interactions dialog box, change the Trigger to
    On click, the ease to Ease out, and the duration to
    500 ms, which is 1/2 second. You will notice there
    are four arrows beside the Move in. They determine
    the direction of the motion. Our gray element is
    to the left of the MoveIn frame, meaning the right
    arrow (Figure 8-12) should be selected. Why an
    Ease out? The motion starts off-screen, meaning
    acceleration is really not needed.

Figure 8-12. *The arrows indicate movement direction*

4. Still in Prototype mode, select the gray box in the
    MoveOut frame and drag a wire to the MoveIn
    frame. Change motion to Move out, the ease to Ease
    in, and the Direction is to the left. Test.

385

If this were a slide in menu, clicking it would shoot it back to the menu's start position, meaning the user would not be able to access the menu items. A common best practice in this situation is to attach the interaction to the frame or to the right of the menu through the use of a transparent rectangle.

Create a Complex Interaction Using Smart Animate

In this exercise, we are going to create the following interaction: "When the Blue button is clicked, it rotates to turn the + sign to an X. At the same time, the Red, Green, and Purple circles move to their final position. Click the button again and the circles move back to the start position and the button rotates." Here's how:

1. Select the four circles on the pasteboard and align their centers vertically and horizontally. This will be the start position for the circles. Move the Blue layer to the top of the Animate frame's layer stack.

2. Select all four layers and convert them to a component.

3. Make a variant of the component.

4. Select the component in the Layers panel and drag out a bottom handle to make room for the animation.

5. Open the Variant2 layer in the Layers panel and turn off the visibility of the Blue layer.

6. Drag the three circles to different positions. If a circle gets moved out of the component, drag the layer back into Variant2.

7. Turn on the visibility of the Blue layer, select it, and in the Properties panel, set its rotation value to 45 degrees. You have created the end position of the interaction as shown in Figure 8-13.

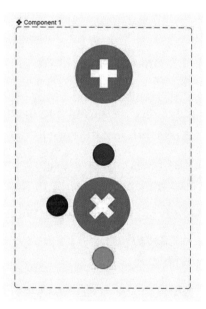

Figure 8-13. *The start and end positions of an interaction that uses motion*

8. Switch to Prototype mode and select the Default variant.

9. Drag an arrow from the Default variant to the Blue circle with the X. That circle is the variant, not the small one.

10. When the Interactions panel opens, use these values:

    - Trigger: On click

    - Transition: Smart animate

    - Ease: Ease out

    - Duration: 500 ms

11. Open the Assets panel and add the component to the blank Animate frame.

12. Test. The circles smoothly move out as the circle rotates.

13. Select Variant2 to reverse the animation and add an On click; only this time, set the ease to Ease in.

14. Test. The circle rotates back to a + sign button, with the small circles moving behind the button.

This exercise is a more complex example of Willenskomer's Transformation and Easing principles and employs three parts of Saffer's four parts of a microinteraction:

- Trigger: On click.

- Rules: Rotate the Blue circle and move the small circles out from behind.

- Feedback: The cursor changes to a pointer finger when it is over the Blue circle.

Create a Scrolling Behavior

Scrolling behaviors, whether text or other content, are one of those ubiquitous UI behaviors. It allows the UI Designer to keep the content within a manageable space. Though it is a common technique, there are some advantages and disadvantages when creating scrolling content. The advantages are as follows:

- Users can use their mouse or finger to smoothly move through the content.

- User engagement is a big advantage. By scrolling, the user will be looking for new content that might interest them.

- Scrolling is ideal for projects where the content is current and dynamic and where each bit of content such as a friends list or cards is of equal importance.

The disadvantages are as follows:

- Impatient users looking for specific information and having to wade through a lot of unimportant information first.

- It can create performance issues such as loading times, memory usage, and bandwidth. This is where a focused discussion with your developers will avoid these issues.

- When designing scrolling content, always keep the user in mind. For example, providing scroll bars and back-to-top navigation is extremely useful. Also, provide them with visual clues or, when creating the elements that control scrolling, don't get creative, which tends to force users to decipher which button to drag to scroll through content. Also, users can ignore the scroll bars and drag the content. Keep this one in mind as you work on creating scrolling content.

In this exercise, we are going to use Overflow to enable scrolling, employ Saffer's fourth aspect of a microinteraction, Looping, and use Smart animate to create a Scroll component. Let's get started.

Create Scrolling Content

Figma makes it rather uncomplicated when it comes to scrolling. The key to creating scrolling content is to understand Figma applies it to a frame and the scroll is set in the Prototype panel.

1. Open the Scrolling.fig file; when it opens, open the Scroll page. As you can see in Figure 8-14, the Content frame contains an image and a paragraph from this exercise, and the contents of the frame are a lot longer than the Scroll frame.

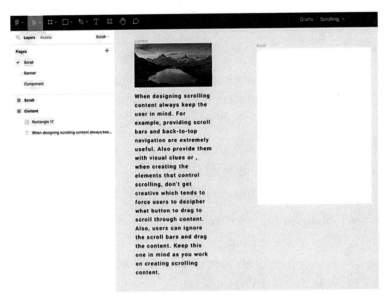

Figure 8-14. *Scrolling content should be in a frame*

2. Drag the Content frame into the Scroll frame. Drag the bottom of the Content frame up to a point where some of the text is cut off. From the Properties panel, Frame check the Clip option. The overflow disappears. This is the first part of this technique.

3. Select the Content frame, then switch to Prototype mode. In the Scroll Behavior area, open the Overflow pop-down and select Vertical (Figure 8-15).

Figure 8-15. *Scrolling direction is determined by choosing a Scroll behavior, Overflow option*

4. Test. The scroll works and stops when you reach the bottom of the text block. You also might want to consider adding Up and Down arrows to indicate the scrolling direction.

Create a Scrolling Loop Animation

In this exercise, we are going to apply both Saffer's feature of Looping and Willenskomer's Delay principle for microinteractions. Looping content is ideal for such features as Alerts and Breaking News in a website or mobile app. Here's how:

1. In the Scrolling.fig file, select the Banner page. The text is in a frame named TextFrame. This text is what will be scrolling across the screen.

2. Select the Text layer and apply Auto layout (Shift A), change frame name to TextFrame, and change the Alignment to Align Left (Figure 8-16).

Figure 8-16. *The Auto layout will use Left Alignment*

3. Open the TextFrame Auto layout; select the text. Copy and paste the copied text at the end of the first text block as a separate text block and new layer. At the end of the second text block, paste again. This will expand the text well beyond the boundaries of the Banner frame.

4. Select the TextFrame and press Command/Ctrl-G to group the layers into one object. Name the group TextGroup.

5. Select the group and convert it to a component. Name the component TextScroll. This component will be where the motion happens.

6. With the component selected, zoom out and move the right edge of the component just to the other side of the word "city" (Figure 8-17).

Figure 8-17. *The width of the component is set to show the message*

7. There is still a bit of text showing, and the content showing is the middle content; we need to deal with this. Open the component and select the Auto layout layer. Click left aligned in the Properties panel. The first bit of text is showing. Select the TextGroup component in the Layers panel and select Clip content.

8. With the component selected, add a variant and we are ready to put the text in motion.

    We have defined the start of the animation. The variant will be the end of the animation. Open the variant and select the TextFrame Auto layout. With the Shift key held down, press the left arrow on your keyboard until the last sentence lines up with the one above it (Figure 8-18).

Figure 8-18. *The TextFrame Auto layout layer is moved to align the end of the text to match the start*

9. We can now create the scroll using the Delay principle. Switch to Prototype mode and select the Default variant in the Layers panel.

10. Drag a wire to Variant2, and when the Interactions panel opens, use these settings:

    - Action: On Delay with a delay value of 1 ms

    - Motion: Smart animate

    - Easing: Linear

    - Duration: 7500 ms

    We have just applied the Delay principle (Figure 8-19) of a microinteraction.

Figure 8-19. *The scrolling starts after a delay of 1 millisecond*

11. Select Variant2, and in the Interactions panel, set the delay to 1 ms. But change Smart animate to Instant. This will immediately restart the scroll and make it seamless.

12. Open the Assets panel and drag a copy of the TextGroup component to the Banner frame. Test.

Create a Scroll Control

In this exercise, you are going to create a Scroll Control. Here's how:

1. Open the Component page in the Scrolling.fig file. If you look at how it was put together, it follows much of what was covered in the previous exercise. The key aspect of this component is the use of Clipped Content when the component was created and moving the Cards group up, using the Shift-Up

arrow technique to show the bottom three cards.
The red circle is the "Thumb" layer (Figure 8-20)
and will be used for scrolling.

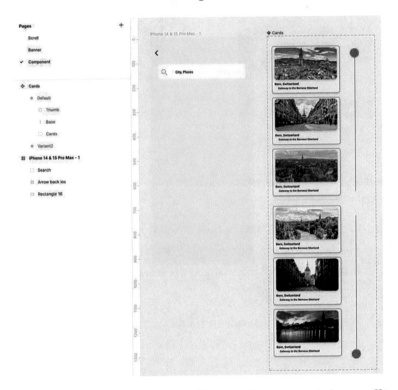

Figure 8-20. *The Thumb layer will be used to control the scrolling microinteraction*

2. Switch to Prototype mode, open the Cards
   component, open the arrow to the left of the Default
   variant, and select the Thumb layer.

3. Drag a wire to Variant 2, and when the Interactions
   panel opens, select On Drag, turn on Smart animate,
   and select an Ease out with 300 ms.

4. Select the Thumb layer in Variant2 and add the
    same drag interaction.

5. Open the Assets panel and drag an instance of the
    Cards component into the iPhone 14 layer. Test.

Applying the Obscuration Principle

Obscuration is one of those techniques that follow the whole point of a
microinteraction: do one thing. The one thing it does is focus the user's
attention on the item that just appeared by obscuring everything behind.
In this exercise, we are going to apply this principle in a couple of ways.
Let's get started:

1. Open the Obscuration.fig file found in your chapter
    download. You will see it is a Home screen with
    a menu sitting on the pasteboard. The plan is to
    have the menu slide in when the hamburger icon is
    clicked and for the image to be obscured when the
    menu slides in.

2. Switch to Prototype mode and select the
    hamburger icon.

3. Drag a wire from the icon to the menu to open the
    Interactions panel.

4. This is where we will add the obscuration. Open
    the Navigate to pop-down and select Open overlay.
    The panel will change to allow you to manage the
    Overlay (Figure 8-21).

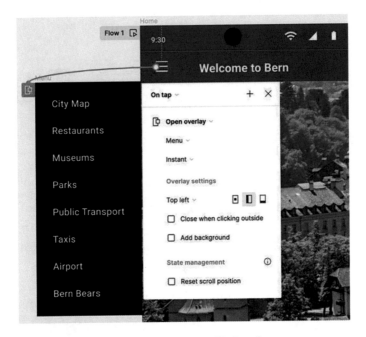

Figure 8-21. *The Overlay Interactions dialog box*

5. This is where the magic happens. To get the menu to slide in, change Instant to Move In and make sure the direction is to the right. We can now concentrate on the Overlay's properties.

6. Use these values in the Overlay settings area:

    •   Ease Out: Speed 500 ms.

    •   Location: Top Left. You can do this by either selecting Top left in the pop-down menu or by clicking the middle icon. This setting determines the location of the Overlay.

- Close When Clicking Outside: Select. This is a rather handy setting. You want the user to make a selection in the menu. You never close the menu by clicking on it. This choice makes the Overlay, not the Menu, close the menu.

- Add Background: Selected. This will open the color and opacity choices for the Overlay.

- Color: Black (#000000).

- Opacity: 70%.

7. If your dialog box matches Figure 8-22, close the dialog box.

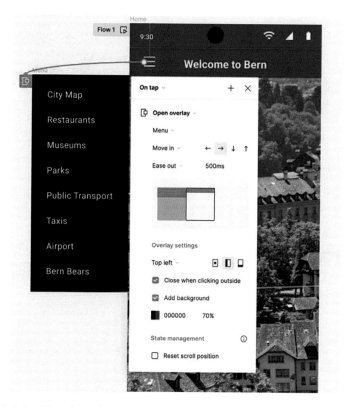

Figure 8-22. *The Overlay settings*

8. Test. The menu slides into the upper left corner and the screen turns dark. Click anywhere outside of the menu and the menu slides back and the screen returns to its start state.

Using a Blur to Obscure the Image

In the previous exercise, the Overlay was applied to the entire screen. Here's how to have the interaction affect just the image.

1. In Prototype mode, delete the previous interaction in the Prototype panel, by clicking the minus icon to the right of the interaction.

2. In the Layers panel, drag the Menu container into the Home frame. The menu will disappear because it is sitting on the pasteboard.

3. Duplicate the Home frame and name the duplicate frame SlideIn.

4. Select the Menu in the SlideIn frame and move it into position.

5. Click on the image, and in Design mode, add a Layer Blur effect with a Blur value of 20 or whatever value you feel works for you (Figure 8-23).

Figure 8-23. *Using a Layer blur to obscure the image*

6. In the Prototype mode, drag a wire from the Home frame hamburger icon to the SlideIn frame to open the Interactions dialog box. Use these settings:

   - Trigger: On tap

   - Action: Smart animate

   - Ease: Ease out

   - Duration: 500 ms

7. Select the City layer in the SlideIn frame and drag a wire back to the Home frame.

8. When the Interactions panel opens, change the
    Easing to Ease In. This is chosen because the start of
    the motion is visible.

9. Test.

Your Turn

We have been focusing on the fundamentals of microinteractions in this
chapter. Let's apply the microinteractions to a mobile app design for a
Bern, Switzerland, nature adventure tourism option. As discussed in
the chapter, keep in mind Dan Staffer's four parts of microinteractions
and Issara Willenskomer's principles of UX in motion. First, we will start
by creating the interactions for a sidebar menu. Next, we will create a
repeatable nature card component with a drop-down accordion text
description for the selected card. By the end of this exercise, your project
will resemble Figure 8-24.

Figure 8-24. *Microinteractions.fig previews, mobile app, sidebar
menu, and accordion nature card*

Create an Overlay Side Menu Interaction

1. Import and open the Microinteractions.fig file found in your chapter download. When the file opens (Figure 8-25), you will see three frames: components, Side menu, and a Swiss - Nature, Alps. We will start by linking the two frames together to create an overlay trigger and loop interaction.

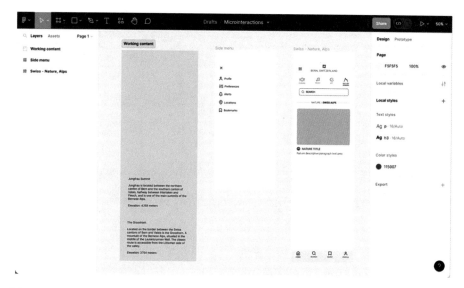

Figure 8-25. *Opened chapter file Microinteractions.fig*

2. In the Swiss - Nature, Alps frame, select the hamburger menu icon. Switch to the Prototype mode, and add an interaction to the Side menu frame with the following values (Figure 8-26):

   - Trigger: On tap.

   - Action: Open overlay, Side menu.

   - Move in, left arrow.

- Ease: Ease in, 250 ms.

- In the Overlay settings, choose Top left.

- Check the Option For: Close when clicking outside.

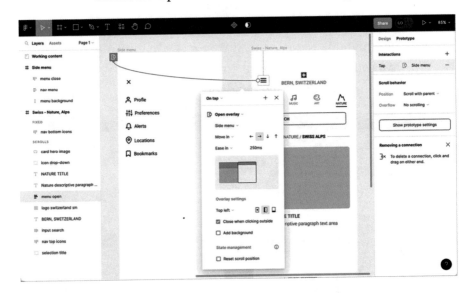

Figure 8-26. *Hamburger menu interaction settings*

3. In the Side menu frame, select the close icon "X", and add the following interaction:

    - Trigger: On tap

    - Close overlay

4. Test the Side menu interactions Alt-Control-Enter (Windows) or Option-Command-Return (Mac).

Style the Overlay Side Menu Interaction

Now that the overlay Side menu interaction is working, let's add some more design to the interaction. Switch to the Design mode.

1. Select the "menu background" layer and add a Stroke to the shape. Light Gray (# C6C6C6) with a 1 px width to define the edge of the menu.

2. Create a drop shadow effect with a rectangle filled with a linear gradient. Create a rectangle from the left side of the menu background layer to the left side of the Side menu frame. This new shape will match the size of the Side menu frame. Change the fill to a Medium Gray (#B6B6B6).

3. Change the fill to a linear gradient. Rotate the gradient from vertical to horizontal using the gradient top and bottom positioning dots and create a small gradient start and stop. Set the Blend mode to Multiply (Figure 8-27).

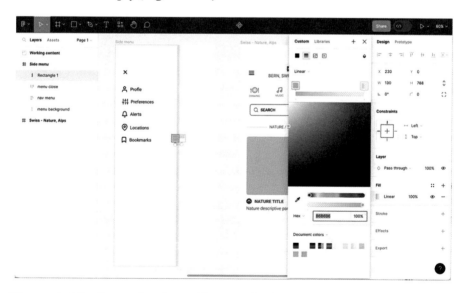

Figure 8-27. *Drop shadow effect applied to the Side menu*

4. Add a Linear gradient and Background blur to the Side menu frame fill. Select the Side menu frame and change the fill to a horizontal Linear gradient. Start the gradient at the gray vertical line #FFFFFF, 100%. Set stop at the left edge of the frame, #FFFFFF 0% (Figure 8-28).

5. Scroll down the Property panel, and in the Effects area, add a Background blur, 15%.

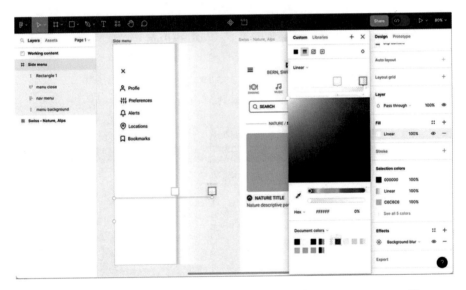

Figure 8-28. *Change the Side menu frame fill to a Linear gradient and add a Background blur*

6. Test the Side menu interactions (Option Command Enter/Alt Control Return).

Create a Card Template Area Using Auto Layout

The Swiss - Nature, Alps frame is the beginning of an accordion microinteraction card. Let's create a component of the current content and add a variant and the interactions between the variants. Once this is complete, we will add the content to an instance of the component.

1. Select the arrow icon and the title text, then create an auto layout from these elements (Shift A). In the Properties panel, change value for the Horizontal gap to 12. In the Layers panel, rename the auto layout "Card title".

2. Select "Card title" auto layout and the descriptive paragraph text below. Create an auto layout (Shift A). In the Properties panel, change value for the Vertical gap to 12. In the Layers panel, rename the auto layout "Card text".

3. Create a gray rectangle that groups the card hero image and Card Text. Add a corner radius of 10. Stroke weight 1 and a Medium gray Stroke (#979797).

4. Select the Card text Auto layout and the gray rectangle, card hero image, then create an auto layout (Shift A). In the Properties panel, change value for the Horizontal gap to 12 and the Horizontal and Vertical padding values to 6. Add a Corner radius value of 7. In the Layers panel, rename the Auto layout "Card" (Figure 8-29).

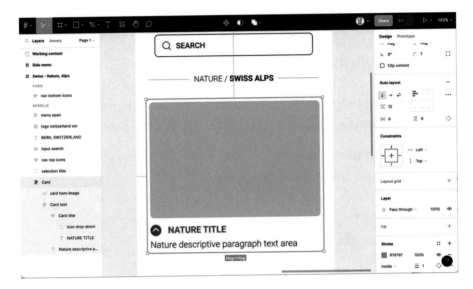

Figure 8-29. *Create a Card template using Auto layout*

Create the Card Component Variants

1. Move the Card from the "Swiss - Nature, Alps" frame to the dark gray "Working content" section to create a Component.

2. Select the Card in the "Working content" and create a Component by clicking the top-middle component icons, four diamonds.

3. Select the "NATURE TITLE" text Control (Windows) or Command (Mac). In the Properties panel, text area, create Text property by clicking the arrow/ diamond icon to the right of the text "NATURE TITLE". In the Create component property pop-up window, change the Name property to "Card title" and change the Value property from "NATURE TITLE" to TITLE.

4. Select the description text Control (Windows) or
    Command (Mac). In the Properties panel, text
    area, click the Text property icon to the right of the
    description text, and choose Create property....
    In the Create component property pop-up
    window, change the Name to "Card description"
    and the Value to "Description".

5. Select the Card component and create a Variant by
    clicking the Variant icon at the top in the middle of
    the toolbar, a diamond with a + icon.

6. In the Layers panel, change the layer name of
    "Variant2" to "State=Open". Then change the
    "Default" to "State=Closed".

7. In the Closed state, select the text "Description";
    in the Properties panel, Layer, click the eye icon to
    "hide" the layer.

8. In the Open state, select the Layer Group "icon
    drop-down" and rotate the icon 180 degrees
    (Figure 8-30).

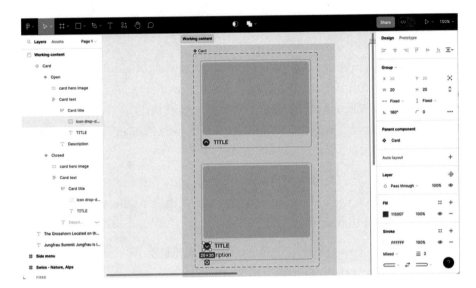

Figure 8-30. *Creating a template Component and Variant for the Closed and Open card states*

Apply an Accordion Microinteraction to the Card Component

1. Switch to the Prototype mode and select the Closed state. Add an interaction from the Closed state to the Open state with the following values (Figure 8-31):

   - Trigger: On tap

   - Action: Change to, state open

   - Animation: Smart animate

   - Ease: Custom: 0.5, 0, 0.5, 1

   - Timing: 300 ms

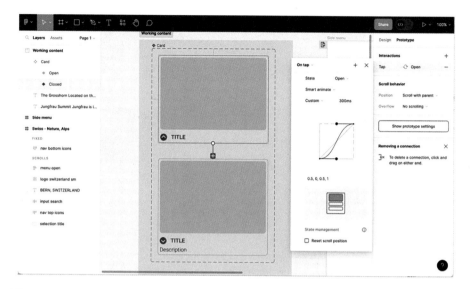

Figure 8-31. *Custom microinteraction between the Closed and Open card states*

2. Add an interaction from the Open state to the Closed state.

Add Content to the Card Instance

1. In the Design mode, select the "Swiss - Nature, Alps" frame. Click on the left-hand side Assets panel and drag an instance of the Card component into the frame below the text "NATURE / SWISS ALPS".

2. With the Card instance selected, change the State from Closed to Open in the Properties panel Card area. Select the gray rectangle, and in the Properties panel, Fill, change the Fill color to the supplied placed image "Jungfrau.jpg" (Figure 8-32).

Figure 8-32. *Replace the gray box in the Open state with the supplied "Jungfrau.jpg" image*

3. The Title and Description text for the Jungfrau card is found in the "Working content" selection. Copy the Title text "Jungfrau Summit". Select the card in the "Swiss - Nature, Alps", and in the Properties panel, Card, paste the text into the TITLE area and press Enter/Return.

4. Copy the Description text for the Jungfrau Summit. Select the card in the "Swiss - Nature, Alps" and paste the text into the Properties panel, Card, Description area, then press Enter/Return (Figure 8-33).

Figure 8-33. *Replace the text properties Title and Description with authentic text in the Open state*

5. With the Card selected in the Properties panel, change the Card State from Open to Closed.

6. Test. Click on the card to expand and contract the descriptive text.

Add a Second Card

1. In the Design mode, drag a Component instance from the Assets panel below the first card.

2. With the new Card instance selected, change the State from Closed to Open in the Properties panel Card area. Select the gray rectangle, and in the Properties panel, Fill, change the Fill color to the supplied placed image "Grosshorn.jpg".

413

3. Copy the Title text for the Grosshorn card from the "Working content" selection and paste it into the Properties panel, Card, TITLE area then press Enter/Return.

4. Copy the Description text for the Grosshorn and paste the text into the Properties panel, Card, Description area, then press Enter/Return.

5. To have both cards interact and move when either of the cards opens, select both cards and create an auto layout. In the Layers panel, rename the auto layout "Nature Alp Cards". Change the Vertical gap value in the Properties panel to 32 (Figure 8-34).

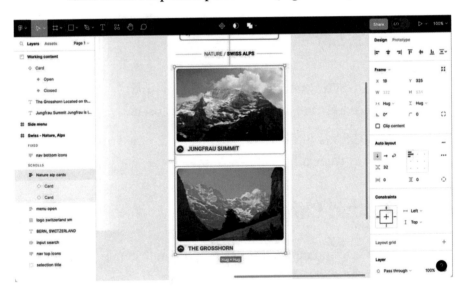

Figure 8-34. *Apply an Auto layout to both cards*

6. Test the interaction in the Preview. Click and expand both cards to see the descriptive text and interactions between both cards.

You Have Learned

This is an important chapter because you have discovered how to apply the fundamentals of microinteractions. Applying microinteractions can take a lot of time and testing for this portion of UX Design. Now, you should better understand why the full collaboration between the design and development teams is so important in this area.

The design-build-beta workflow (Figure 8-1) at the beginning of the chapter shows the loop of design, build, and beta to iterate to refine the process. Keep in mind both Dan Staffer's "The Four Parts of Microinteractions" as well as Issara Willenskomer's "The Principles of UX in Motion" to see and improve your own microinteraction skills. In this chapter, you have learned

- How to add microinteractions to elements on a screen

- Create a ripple interaction

- Apply UX motion design principles to create microinteraction

- Understand and apply the four parts of microinteractions

- Understand and apply the 12 principles of UX in motion

- Understand how to apply and control timing of interactions in microseconds

- Understand the differences between the easing options and create your own custom easing options

- How to apply Smart animations to control movement of elements over time

- Create components to apply a looping animation with scrolling text

- Apply an obscuration, blur, to create focus in an interaction

CHAPTER 9

Design System Fundamentals

"A design system is your single source of truth."

–Marcin Treder,
Former CEO, UXPin

Before there was the Design System, there were graphics standards. Had you worked for or with such companies as IBM, Apple, FedEx, or Citigroup prior to 1990, you would be handed a book outlining the company's graphic standards. That book told you where a logo was to be placed on everything from business cards to print ads. Included were typographic standards defining what font to use and when to use the various weights and sizes. In many cases, that typographic standard included a custom font. For example, prior to 2001, Apple used a customized version of Garamond and then gradually switched to today's Myriad Pro. IBM is affectionately known as "Big Blue" for a reason. IBM's corporate color is Pantone's PMS 2718 C, and the Hexadecimal version is #006699. The Citigroup red umbrella logo uses PMS 485 C, and the Hexadecimal version is #DB230B and its corporate font is Interstate, where the lowercase "t" has been modified to resemble an umbrella handle.

© Tom Green and Kevin Brandon 2024
T. Green and K. Brandon, *UX Design with Figma*, Design Thinking,
https://doi.org/10.1007/979-8-8688-0324-6_9

Design Systems have become the foundation of UX Design, but as you have seen, they aren't exactly new. As we are fond of saying about emerging technologies, "They all do the same thing. Just differently."

The "same thing" is an intense focus on keeping the user experience consistent. Look at anything from Apple without looking at the logo and you just know it is Apple talking to you. What's different is those books have been replaced with their digital equivalent: the Design System.

A Design System's purpose is to impose order on what could easily become chaos. Their whole reason for being is to provide a consistent experience from the first pixel to the last pixel from the Home screen to the last screen. They make it clear to the UX Design team what element goes where, what font to use and when, and what color to use and when. More often than not, the Design System resides in a Figma Library that is driven by a developer document residing on GitHub or a collection of components documented in Storybook.

Before we start, you need to understand a Design System is a collection of design elements logically organized to provide UX and UI Designers with the repeating elements that combine to create a user interface. This includes such things as user flows, interactions, buttons, modals, icons, cards, colors, and typography. They provide the team with that "single source of truth" when creating interfaces.

The Single Source of Truth

Without some sort of standardized workflow or toolkit in place, there is a real risk that the team's inefficiencies and inconsistencies between design and development will have a negative result on the product. This was standard practice in the early days of the Web. Designers, for example, would have radically different versions of buttons littered through their web pages that all did the same thing. Much of this was due to Microsoft and Netscape introducing proprietary features that really didn't work in other browsers forcing designers to create two versions of a site. When Internet Explorer 5 was released, designers suddenly had to know five different ways of writing JavaScript! The result was a group of web developers and designers banding together to create the Web Standards project, which was the genesis of today's W3C organization that introduced HTML5 and today's modular CSS3 (Figure 9-1), which has its roots in the W3C's Web Applications 1.0 specification. The Open Source Bootstrap, introduced in 2011, is a great example of how order is imposed from chaos (Figure 9-1). In many respects, it is a Design System.

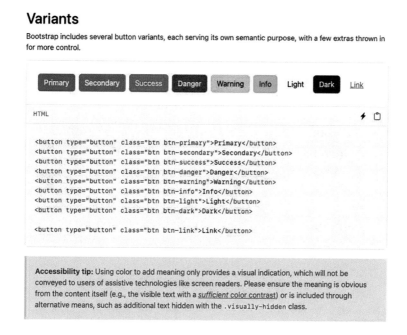

Figure 9-1. *Bootstrap's button standard with variants*

When it comes to UX Design, that button (Figure 9-2) and its variants have become Figma components residing in a Design System library. Instead of wondering which button to use, which color to use, which type style to use, and even which assets to use and when, all of this is clearly stated in the Library and the supporting documentation (Figure 9-2).

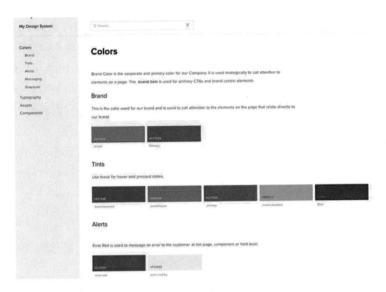

Figure 9-2. *Sample Design System documentation*

A unified Design System is now the single source of truth.

One final advantage to the creation and use of a Design System: return on investment. This includes the following:

- Reduced timelines from design to market. Having a component-based toolkit available to everyone involved accelerates releases without compromising quality.

- Cohesive, collaborative workflow. Use a Design System with approved assets and code base and designers and developers are no longer siloed.

- Less time and budget wasted. Designers and developers are no longer caught up performing repetitive tasks.

Where Do You Start?

There is a common misconception that you start with the fundamentals like colors, typography, components, design patterns, and so on. According to Dan Mall of SuperFriendly, that might just be a really bad idea. "Design systems should be a collection of processes," writes Dan in an article entitled "The Folly of Design System "Foundations"" (`https://superfriendly.com/design-systems/articles/folly-of-design-system-foundations/`). "The best ones," he continues, "focus more on what you can do and give you the tools to do it." He suggests you do not spend an inordinate amount of time aiming for perfection. Instead, he says, let the Design System develop as you go along.

This is where it gets interesting because if you are an enterprise organization with a lot of sites and apps, then you approach it one way. If you are new to the topic, then you likely will start another way.

For large or mature organizations, you are almost there. The first thing to do is to audit your current sites and apps looking for common patterns. Such things as type and color have most likely already been set, so why bother? For you, according to Dan Mall, a Design System is a system for creating interfaces that integrate with other organizational systems.

If you are new to the game, don't waste time picking out just the right shade of blue, just the right typeface, or worrying about the stroke thickness, size, and stroke color used with a card. Of course, you are going to need a color palette and typeface, but you need to build something, not waste time fretting about inconsequential details.

For those of you planning to put a Design System into place, here are some suggested steps to get started:

- Create an interface inventory of everything in the product.

- Document inconsistencies in the interface. The more inconsistencies you discover, the easier it will be to get buy-in from the stakeholders for the development of a Design System.

- Get buy-in from the team. This means both the development and design teams.

- Clearly present your design principles. These can be used as the basis for every new pattern you may add.

- Unify your visual design and document it. You may be surprised to learn the number of design patterns you will use will be rather small. Regardless, each must be clearly documented.

- Create your library.

These steps are vague because no two organizations or teams will have the same approach. What we can say is this is a deliberative process and will take time to put together and deploy across the organization or the team. Getting deep into each step of the process is well beyond the scope of this book. As such, this chapter is an overview of Design Systems in Figma and where you fit in the process.

Take Stock of What You Have

This process starts with your understanding that every exercise in this book contains a UX Design pattern. UX Design patterns are the familiar building blocks for building user interfaces. Designers use UX Design patterns as reusable components to solve common usability issues. In Figma, components are made up of the component and its variants (Figure 9-3).

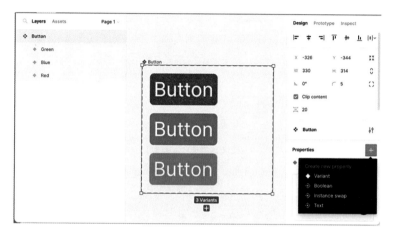

Figure 9-3. *A button component with its variables*

For example, a design pattern we see regularly is a button. A button contains states and will change as the state changes. Users use those changes as visual clues and instinctively know the purpose of a button is to let the user do something. You should also know there is a bit of confusion around UX patterns and UI patterns. The distinction between them is minor, with a lot of overlap, but there is a difference:

- UX Patterns: These are reusable patterns that aid user flow and navigation such as infinite scroll on a website or social media platform.

- UI Patterns: These are reusable patterns for visual and interaction design. Click a hamburger icon or a triple ellipsis icon, and a side menu or pop-down menu appears.

As you may have guessed, UI patterns tend to make up the bulk of a Design System. A Design System is composed of two basic parts: the common designs used and documentation.

A great resource for common design patterns is `https://ui-patterns.com/`. The patterns are grouped by their purpose and the problems they solve.

To start, you should create an inventory of all the different patterns, colors, text styles, and assets used in the project. Do this and inconsistencies in both the content and code will be exposed. If you are starting with a blank screen, then a good place to start is by creating a Pattern Library that could be based on the wireframes or medium-fidelity prototypes.

Though you can create your own, if you select the Design System Category on the Figma Community page, you have access to a number of "pre-rolled" Design Systems (Figure 9-4) for websites and mobile projects. We can't endorse any one of them other than to say they are fully customizable. With that said, there are two you really should have in your back pocket: iOS and Android.

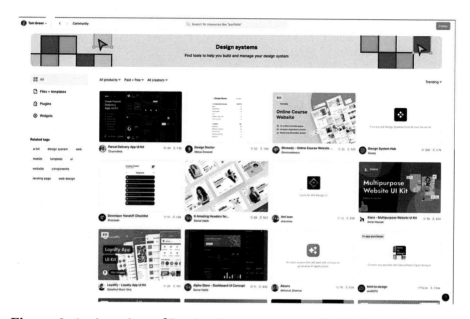

Figure 9-4. *A variety of Design Systems are available through the Figma Community site*

If you head to the Community site and enter iOS, you will see Apple has provided a Design Resources kit, which you can open directly in Figma (Figure 9-5). We also should add if you visit the Design Resources directly on the Apple website, you will be taken to the Figma Community. These resources, essentially, are the current iOS Design System and can be moved into a Team Library or used by the development team in a GitHub Repo.

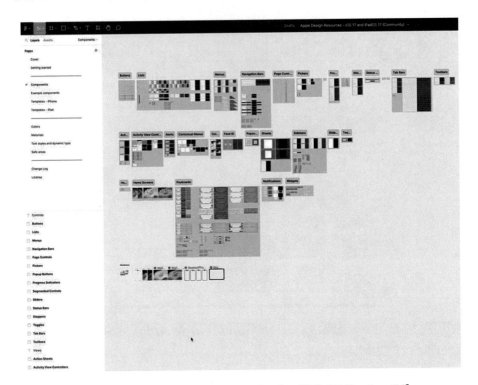

Figure 9-5. *The iOS 17 Components in the iOS 17 Design Library*

Google's Material Design is the other main Design System when it comes to mobile design. If you head over to Google's Material Design site, the design kit is available in the Resources section. Click it, and you are taken to the Community site where you can download the Material 3 Design kit as shown in Figure 9-6.

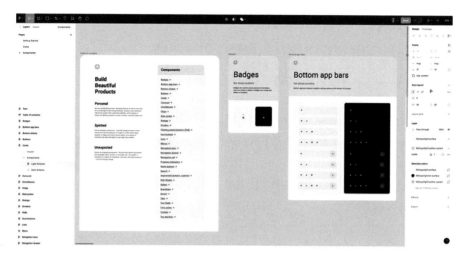

Figure 9-6. *The Material 3 Design kit showing the components*

You should also note the iOS and Android kits contain both light and dark versions of the components. As stated earlier, these Design kits can be added to a Team Library or used locally by dragging the components from the Assets panel onto the frame. Like regular components, they can be edited, and the change will ripple through all instances of the component where it is used.

The Design kits from Apple or Google are a great place to start, but designers may find them too restrictive or contain elements here and there in the kits that may be useful. With that in mind, let's look at the process of building a Design System.

Editing a component used in a Design System is extremely dangerous. It has implications not only within the design but also with the development team. All changes to a component or Design System should be done in conjunction with the development team.

The Pattern Inventory

When building a pattern inventory, everyone involved has to know that this library is not the Design System. It is a tool to be used by both the design and development teams to present, document, and share the patterns. As pointed out earlier in this chapter, this is a cohesive, collaborative process intended to remove the silos between design and development. Involving both design and development, you will have created a multidisciplinary library that adapts more readily to change and has a long shelf life.

Creating the inventory will take time, and the more comprehensive it is, the more data the team will have to make informed decisions. What you don't do is create them in Figma. Use screenshots or copy these patterns from other projects, and if a category is missing, add it and use screenshots from other sites to illustrate the category.

Figma allows you to create these inventories using FigJam or the Pages feature of Figma. In either case, these documents can then be shared with the team and stakeholders and used to identify inconsistencies and variations in the patterns. An example would be a button that has rounded corners. Then you discover the same button elsewhere that has square corners, a lighter tint of the first button's color, and uses a similar font.

As you collect these patterns, the development team should be checking the front-end code to ensure consistency throughout the code base. The development team commonly employs a modular approach to organize the elements of a Design System. If this is the case, then use that architecture to organize the pattern collection based on category. For example, the lowest level of that architecture may include elements such as buttons and cards and you may wish to name that category "element button" along with any links or tokens that may be associated with that category.

Tokens may be a new term for some of you. We will get deep into this subject later in this chapter.

If a modular system is not in place, then categorize the patterns in the inventory (Figure 9-7). In this case, generalities such as Buttons, Cards, Forms, and so on will make life easier for the team and stakeholders to identify inconsistencies.

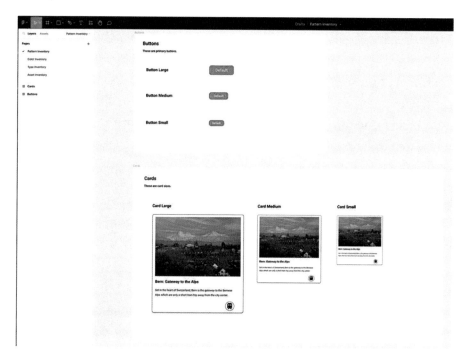

Figure 9-7. *The Pages feature of Figma can be used to hold the pattern inventory*

The creation of a Pattern Inventory is a phenomenal tool for shining a bright light on inconsistencies and for making the business case for the development of a Design System if one does not exist. For example, a Figma page containing a collection of tables will quickly show which ones are outdated and need to be redone or even discarded.

We aren't going to tell you how to decide which patterns work and which don't, that is up to you and your team. By the end of this decision-making process, a Pattern Library can be pulled together and become an integral part of a Design System.

We are going to conclude this section by clearly stating that no Pattern Library will fix bad design.

Patterns can be poorly designed, misused, or used together in ways that hinder the user experience. It is also easy to look at a Pattern Library as stifling creativity, leading to projects that are bland and homogenous. Maybe, but at its heart, the Pattern Library is a reflection of the Design System driving it. Conversely, if your policy is to allow creativity and experimentation, a well-constructed Pattern Library fosters experimentation and collaboration and creates a foundation for a common design language. Just keep in mind that until the Pattern Inventory transforms into a library, you have nothing more than a series of frames in Figma pages.

The Color Inventory

Building a color inventory is a time-consuming and painful process. We are 100% sure you will uncover redundancies. We know of one organization that uncovered over 100 variations of a single color and over 60 shades of gray. Some of this can be laid at the feet of designers who felt a color to be used wasn't "just right" and made the change. As one of the authors stated in the Apress book, *A Guide to UX Design and Development*: "If there is one source of chaos, color has to be it."

The process of inventorying color is the same as that used for creating a pattern inventory. The difference is you or the development team will need to comb through all of the code files, including CSS, and include the color variables. Put them together as color chips in a Figma or FigJam page and we are pretty sure you will have an "OMG" moment and, in conjunction with the developers, start making some pretty fundamental decisions. By the end, you will have landed on the basis for the color library and can start naming them.

When naming colors, decide upon a naming convention that is both consistent and meaningful. Here are a few examples of naming conventions:

- Abstract: Brand

- Actual name: Brand Blue

- Actual colors: #006CFF

- Numbers: Blue-1

- Function: Primary Blue

- Combination: #FF0943 Red (error or danger)

Once the color inventory is reduced to the essentials and a naming convention is established, the inventory (Figure 9-8) can become a library that also serves as documentation guidance to the design team.

Figure 9-8. *A color inventory, reduced to its essentials, can become a color library*

Color decisions are relatively easy. It is the naming that will be the basis for some pretty interesting conversations between the designers and developers. In this section, we are dealing with generalities. A much fuller discussion around naming is presented later in this chapter.

The Typography Inventory

Complex projects can quickly render typography unmanageable. The temptation to change font size or style is always present, especially with the ability to zoom in and out of a digital prototype. Make sure to view the prototype on a device at 100% zoom. If an inconsistent typographic scale is used across the project, the information architecture becomes convoluted and users will find it hard to understand or even read. An inconsistent typographic scale will also increase maintenance costs due to code fragmentation.

As in the previous sections, creating the typographic inventory can be both a time-consuming and frustrating process as you discover just how many typographic styles are used. One method of identifying the myriad of fonts is to go through the UI and check all the styles using a browser console (Command/Ctrl-Shift-I) or the developers can pore through the code base to identify the fonts used. The results could be added to a spreadsheet or other document. List fonts, weight, color, alignment, spacing, and category or description of the font. With that data in front of you, typographic issues will become evident, such as

- Most frequently used fonts

- Average font size

- Average line height

- Average paragraph spacing

- How many characters per line in body copy?

From there, you identify the typefaces that are the most popular and most readable and develop the specs from there. If you are developing a mobile project, both Apple and Google, in their Design Resources, will do this work for you. This does not mean these are "dictums from on high," meaning you aren't tied into using Google's Roboto or Apple's SF Pro.

Once the typographic inventory is reduced to the essentials and the fonts and styles agreed to, the inventory (Figure 9-9) can become a library that also serves as documentation guidance to the design and development teams.

There is a great plug-in that is designed to scoot through documents and list all of the font families and styles used in the document. Look for the Font Fascia plug-in on the Community site.

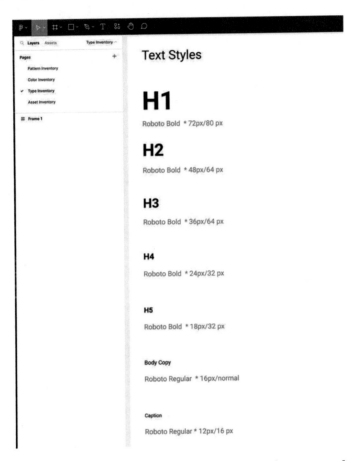

Figure 9-9.   *The typographic inventory is reduced to a standard and can be added to a library*

The Asset Inventory

In strict terms, an asset library would contain all the logos, icons, photos, and line art commonly used in an enterprise project. If this is a "one-off" project, you still need a library to ensure conformity. Again, especially for enterprise-level projects, you will need to inventory all the icons used and, when duplicates are found, remove them. Images should be in the .JPG or .PNG format. For websites, the WebP format for images is also gaining traction. Developed by Google, this format was created to make online images more efficient than .JPG when it comes to loading times. For mobile projects, images should also include their scaling factors.

Icons and line art should be in the .SVG format. If you are looking to standardize your icons, Google's collection is contained in the Design Kit or can be obtained through the Google Material Design Icons plug-in for Figma. You should also indicate size and color variations. If your project includes both Light and Dark modes, the icons should clearly state which mode applies.

Once the inventory has been completed and the decisions made, it would be a good idea to group them as shown in Figure 9-10. By grouping the assets and their variations, the design and development teams will have that "single source of truth."

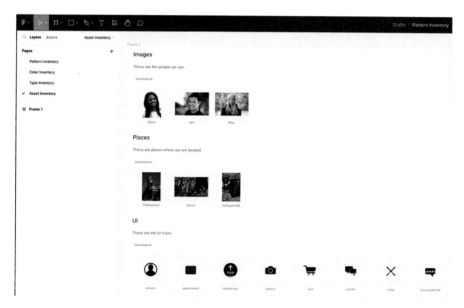

Figure 9-10. The Asset library ensures conformity

In this section, you may have noticed the final decisions are moved into a Library. You may have also noted we have included brief usage guidelines. It is extremely important that you fully document usage in the Library, which will be shared with both the developers and the designers. For the designers, they will have clear guidance around what goes where and when. Developers won't have to make assumptions when a project moves into the Development phase of the project. This Shared Library will form the basis for the Design System, which will be composed of Components, Type Styles, and Colors. Think of this Shared Library as the classic Graphics Standards manuals that tell you what you can and cannot do when designing your projects.

Figma Design Tokens

From a design point of view, there is a big issue when it comes to components. You may have set the style for components such as buttons that have a border, text, and a color. If your Design System has the individual style for each piece of that button, the issue becomes what if they only wanted some of the values to change or the decision is to add a dark theme or a different color to the Hover state in very specific instances. The bottom line is there is a lot of extra work in front of the design and development teams. This is where design tokens come into play. In this section, we will be focusing on color tokens because color is commonly where issues will arise.

To start, a design token is basically a naming method used to express design decisions between designers and developers. Think of them as being a method for managing design properties and values across a Design System. Tokens were originally invented by Salesforce as a way to enforce design consistency across all of their products. The reason they have caught on is due to their being able to be stored in a platform-agnostic manner. There are several advantages to the use of tokens over styles. They include the following:

- Developers can build faster because tokens can be referenced in their code base from the naming conventions for the token. Make a change in Figma and it can be easily changed in the code base.

- Miscommunication is reduced. Developers no longer have to make assumptions based on a design change.

- Scalability: Tokens give both designers and developers the flexibility to make changes or additions in the future.

In Figure 9-11, there is a simple button component; as you can see, a simple button is not that simple after all when you look at the properties contained within that button. Each one of those properties can be a design token.

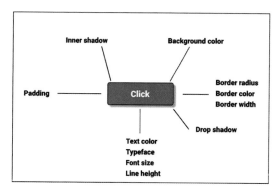

Figure 9-11. *A simple button component is composed of a number of possible design tokens*

When that button component is in a frame, the default and hover background colors are generically named Styles. The Default is #25B0EB, and the Hover value is #0852AA. Let's also assume that the default blue color is used for Text Links. Rather than going with the generic Blue, the name is changed to Blue-100, which is the "nickname" for the blue. Seeing as how it has two uses, there would be a ButtonBackground Style and a TextLink color style. This is where design tokens absolutely shine.

Let's assume the decision is made to change the Button Background color to a darker blue, such as #0B3B73. The button will change, but the Link color won't. The result is the development team ripping through the code, changing the color to something like Blue 400 for all the buttons but keeping the link color to Blue-100.

Remember what we said about naming. This is where naming design tokens makes life easier for both the designers and the developers. Instead of Blue 400, you could have the link color changed to PrimaryLink and the Button color changed to PrimaryButtonBG and this button color becomes #0B3B73 and only the instances of the button's color will change because the link to Blue-100 is removed and remapped to PrimaryButtonBG.

In many respects, the naming of tokens is also a method of organizing and structuring them. There are three common structures: Primitive, Semantic, and Component specific. Examples of how to apply token naming is shown in Figure 9-12, and communicates what (Primitive), how (Semantic), and the where (Component specific).

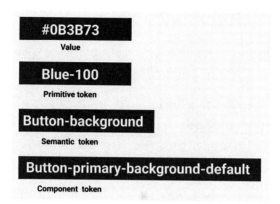

Figure 9-12. *Token names have a hierarchy*

Primitive tokens, also referred to as Global tokens, are the base group. In this case, #0B3B73 is now known as Blue-100, so we now know what color is attached to Blue-100. By naming it semantically – Button-background – we know how the color will be used. Naming it as a component token, we know Blue-100 will be the background color of a button and that background color will be applied to a button component's default state. This should also tell you a component token named Button-primary-background-hover can be applied to the Hover state of the component.

Now that you have a basic understanding, let's look at Design Token Variables next.

Tokens in Figma are evolving. At the moment, gradients and transparency can't be used in a token, but Figma has made assurances tokens will be expanded to include these properties and more.

Creating a Component Token

We have spent time examining tokens. Let's put what we have learned into practice and create a Component token.

1. Open the Token.fig file found in your chapter download. You will see two color chips, and in the Local styles area of the Properties panel, both color styles are identified by their Hexadecimal values.

2. Select the first generic style – #25B0EB – and click the Edit style button. The Edit color style dialog box opens (Figure 9-13).

3. Change the name to Button-primary-background-default. This will be the color of the Button component's default state.

4. Select the second style and change its name to Button-primary-background-hover.

Figure 9-13. *The Edit color style dialog box is where the Component style is named*

5. Select the Frame tool, create a frame that is 200 by 100 pixels, and set the corner radius value to 30.

6. With the Frame selected, click the Styles button (four dots) in the Fill area of the Properties panel.

7. When the Libraries panel opens (Figure 9-14), select the Button-primary-background-default color. It is applied to the frame.

Figure 9-14. *The Component token value is applied*

8. Convert the frame to a Component named Button and add a variable.

9. The color hasn't changed. To apply the Hover color, select the Style and click the broken chain link. This detaches the color style, and the Fill color panel appears.

10. Open the Color library and select the darker hover style. The variant now has the Hover color (Figure 9-15).

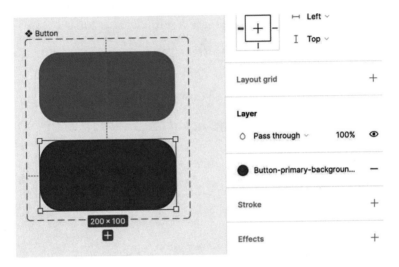

Figure 9-15. *The hover color has been applied to the Hover state of the Button component*

11. Switch to the Interactions panel, drag a wire to the variant, and add a While hovering action.

12. Create a new frame, open the Assets panel, and add an instance of the Button component to the frame. Test.

Figma Design Tokens and Variables

A relatively new feature in Figma is the ability to create variable tokens.

A variable is something that can take on single or multiple values. In Figma, variables store reusable values such as color values, text, and numbers that can be applied to all kinds of properties. Even better is that these variables can be contained in collections, which is a serious workflow boost when it comes to organizing tokens.

In this exercise, we are going to be creating color variables, naming them semantically instead of attaching them to components, and then applying them to elements in a page. Creating variable tokens is a lot different than creating the design tokens from the previous exercise. Let's get started.

1. Open the Variables.fig file found in your chapter download. When it opens, you will see a series of color chips in the Colors frame and a Card frame. Make sure nothing is selected, and if you look over to the Properties panel, you will see there is a Local variables section.

2. Click the Local variables section to open the Create Variables dialog box.

3. Click the Create variable button to open the pop-down (Figure 9-16), which asks you to choose the variable type. They are

   - Color, is used for fills

   - Number, is used for dimensions, corner radius, and Autolayout properties

   - String, is used for text

   - Boolean, which allows you to apply True/False logic for such things as toggle switches (there will be a Boolean exercise in the next chapter)

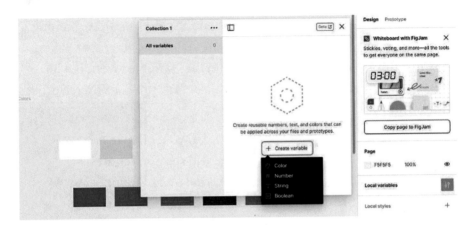

Figure 9-16. *There are four types of variables that can be created*

4. Double-click the color's name and enter 0. The color
   variable and its color have been established. If you
   click the ellipsis, the Edit color variable dialog box
   opens (Figure 9-17), and you can perform such tasks
   as describing its use.

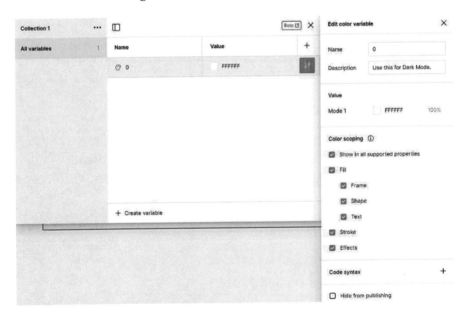

Figure 9-17. *Variables can be edited*

5. To add the rest of the colors, click the Create variable link, click the color chip, and click on the color to add. We are going to use these names. For the grays from left to right, name them 0, 50, 100, 200, 400, 800. For the colors, from left to right, name them ocean, watermelon, forest, royal, and tomato (Figure 9-18).

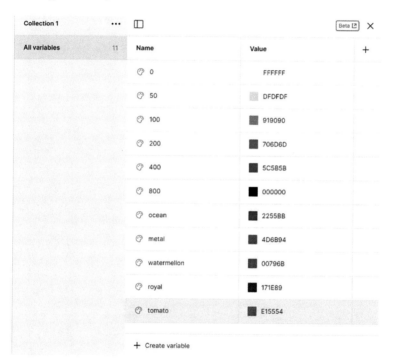

Figure 9-18. *The colors are added and named in the Variables dialog box*

The great thing about variables is they can use whatever name you wish. Thus, the silly names for the colors.

Organize the Variables

Having a list of gray variables with numbers and names is not exactly efficient. You can group them and rename the groups. Here's how:

1. With the Shift key held down, select the grays, right-click, and select New group with selection from the pop-down menu.

2. Double-click the group name and rename it color/grey.

3. Select the colors, group them, and name the group color/brand. You now have two groups, and as shown in Figure 9-19, they are separated.

Figure 9-19. *The colors are grouped and separated*

4. With the colors separated into specific groups, they can also be part of a collection. Select the Collection pop-down by clicking on the ellipsis. Select Rename Collection from the pop-down and change the name to Primitives.

5. In the next step, we convert the variables to tokens.

At the moment these variables really don't do much other than letting us know the color. Here's how to turn variables into semantic tokens that reflect what the color is and where it is to be used. We will be using the colors in the Primitive collection for only a couple of uses: Text, Surface, and Border. Here's how:

1. With the Dialog box open, select Create New Collection named Tokens and select Color as the variable.

2. Rename this color variable to conform to a semantic style by changing the name to text-primary.

3. Select Fill Color, and when the Color Picker opens, select the Libraries tab. Click on the 800 color chip.

4. Change the name from the Hex value to the name in the Primitives library as shown in Figure 9-20.

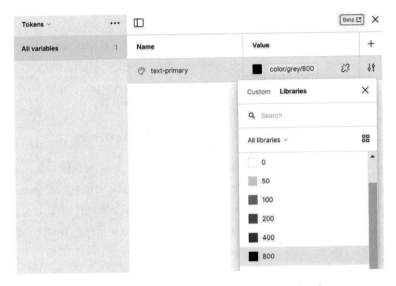

Figure 9-20. *The semantically named token is linked to a Primitive color*

5. Add another variable named text-invert and link it to 50 in the Primitives collection. This style is aimed at Dark Mode.

6. Add another variable named background-primary and link its color to the Ocean Primitive.

7. Add another variable named background-invert and link its color to the Royal Primitive.

8. Add two more variables for borders. Name them border-primary and border-invert. Change the border Primary color to 800 in the Primitives and the inverted color to 50 in the Primitives. We now have, as shown in Figure 9-21, six semantically named variable tokens.

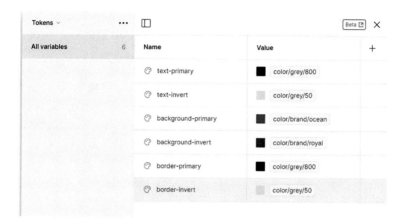

Figure 9-21. *Sematically named color tokens*

9. Create groups for the text, background, and
    border tokens.

Applying Variables

As you have seen, you can create tokens based on a series of color
chips without first creating design tokens. They can all be created using
variables. From there, the collection can be added to a Shared Library or
to the Design System. The important aspect of this approach is the naming
system for these variables, which must be consistent and is something that
has to be decided prior to their creation. We should also add that variables
can also be component tokens. For instance, the border-primary token can
also be component-border-primary. They are just names though it would
be a good idea to create a collection containing the component tokens.
With our tokens created, here's how to apply them:

1. Open the Card layer in the Layers panel. We are
    going to clean up this card using the tokens.

2. Select the Pill layer.

3. In the Fill area of the Properties, open the Library and select the background-primary token. The shape changes color.

4. Select the text in the button and apply the text-invert token.

5. Select the body text and apply the text-primary token. The card (Figure 9-22) springs to life.

Figure 9-22. *The tokens bring the card to life*

The text on the button doesn't seem quite correct. It is a little too gray. It should be white. Let's add a new text variable.

1. Select Local variables in the Properties panel, and when the variables open, select the text group.

2. Add a new color variable and link it to the white primitive 0.

3. Name this new variable text-reverse.

4. Close the panel, select the text in the button, and change the variable to text-reverse.

Though you just added a new token to the Design System, doing so is a huge mistake. The same goes for "tweaking" a token. A change you may think is inconsequential could have huge implications when it comes to development, especially with enterprises. Our advice is to discuss your proposal with the development team and any others involved.

You Have Learned

There was a lot covered in this chapter because when it comes to Design Systems, you can't make it up as you go along. It is a methodical and time-consuming process that, when implemented, turbocharges the design process and makes life easier for the developers as they incorporate the tokens and assets into their work. It will be the developers' task to rip the Figma prototype to shreds, and if both design and development are intimately involved in the development of a Design System, you will both be speaking the same language.

CHAPTER 10

Building Stuff

"The amount of fun you can have with Figma should be illegal."

–Tom Green

Throughout this book, we have been focusing on a series of techniques you would commonly employ as you build your prototypes. A lot of the exercises focused on a single concept showing how to apply it in general or in some instanced for a specific use. Thus, you are most likely wondering, "How do all of those techniques work together?"

This chapter brings them all together to illustrate how to Build Stuff. These are a collection of the common design patterns you may be required to build. We will not only show you how to build them efficiently but also present the projects in such a way as to give you the freedom to do it yourself. We will also expand on topics previously covered in the preceding chapters. They give you the opportunity to further explore components, variables, and a couple of new plug-ins that answer a common question: "How did they do that?"

Finally, the use of the word "Stuff" in the chapter title is deliberate. By regarding preloaders, carousels, and videos as nothing more than "Stuff," they remove the mystique around them. Once you learn how to build one for the first time, you know what to do when a subsequent project includes something like a "Revolving Carousel." If you have built one, then your reaction is, "Yeah, I know how to do that in Figma."

© Tom Green and Kevin Brandon 2024
T. Green and K. Brandon, *UX Design with Figma*, Design Thinking,
https://doi.org/10.1007/979-8-8688-0324-6_10

What stuff are we building? This chapter includes such stuff as

- Image carousels

- Onboarding sequences using LottieFiles

- Controlling video

- Playing with variable values

- Creating loader animations

- Expanding text input boxes

- Creating a slide show

Some of the projects are rather uncomplicated, while others expand on the knowledge you have learned so far. Let's get started.

One of our maxims is: "Test early and test often." It is common in today's UX environment to test components and designs on a regular basis. This means User Testing and running Accessibility plug-ins such as Stark or Adee to ensure accessibility standards are being achieved. Every project in this chapter should first be reviewed by the development team to give them an understanding of your intent and to understand what they may be required to develop. If the component or page is important enough, it should be User Tested, and the feedback from Development and User Testing will most likely result in "tweaks" to the component or page. There is no such thing as "The End" when it comes to UX Design. Even when the project is released into the wild, there will be regular updates and "tweaks" over the life of the project.

Building an Image Carousel

This design pattern is a great way of putting a lot of content in a small space. As is common, the user will drag content to the left or the right to reveal the next piece of content. In this exercise, we are going to start with a simple carousel using three images. The next one will create a common carousel where the images expand as they move into the viewport. The final example uses a circular, not horizontal, motion to move the images into the viewport. Let's start building a simple carousel. Here's how:

1. Open the SimpleCarousel.fig file found in your chapter download. The file contains three images and a Tablet frame. The images are going to be put into a Carousel.

2. Select the three images and add them to an Autolayout container. Add a 35-pixel gap between the images.

3. Change the Autolayout frame name from Frame to Container.

4. Open the Container, select the three images and give them a corner radius of 20 pixels (Figure 10-1).

Figure 10-1. *The images are placed into an auto layout container and the corners rounded*

455

5. Create a new Frame and change the width to 1000 pixels and the height to 800 pixels. Change the Fill color to #275CE7 (Blue). Name this frame "Carousel." Move the new frame behind the auto layout container. Select the Carousel and the Container and center them vertically and horizontally.

6. Select the Ellipse tool and draw a white circle that is 50 × 50. Create two copies. Reduce the opacity of the fills for the right and left dots to 70%. Add all dots to an auto layout container and name the container dots. These three dots let users know there are three images and that the center image is in the viewport (Figure 10-2). Center the three dots below the middle image.

Figure 10-2. Providing users with feedback

7. In the Layers panel, move the Container into the Carousel frame.

8. Create three copies of the Carousel frame and rename the copies to Carousel2 and Carousel3.

9. These three frames are not going to become a
    component. Instead, they are going to be part
    of a Component Set. So far, the components we
    have created are individual reusable elements.
    Component Sets are collections of related
    components with different variations or states.

10. Select the three frames and choose Create
    component set from the top Component icon pop-
    down menu (Figure 10-3). Name the component set
    Carousel.

11. In the Layers panel, twirl down Carousel2, select
    the Container, and using the Shift key, press the left
    arrow key until the third image is in the viewport.
    Select the Middle dot and change its transparency
    value to 70% and change the transparency value for
    the dot on the right to 100%.

12. In the Layers panel, twirl down Carousel3, select
    the Container and position the first image in
    the viewport. Set the second and the third dot
    transparency value to 70%; change the transparency
    value for the first dot to 100% (Figure 10-3).

Figure 10-3. *The component set is ready to have the
interactions added*

13. Switch to Prototype mode. Select the Container in
     the Carousel frame, and as shown in Figure 10-4,
     add the following interaction:

- Trigger: On Drag

- Change to: Carousel2

- Transition: Smart animate

- Ease: Ease out

- Duration: 300 ms

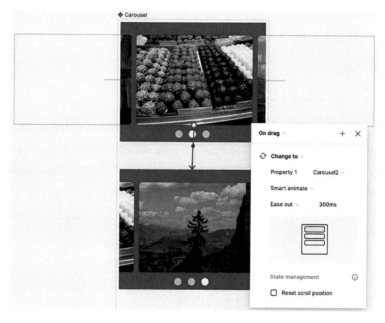

Figure 10-4. *Adding the Drag interaction*

14. With the Container in the Carousel frame still
    selected add another Drag interaction to the
    Carousel3 frame.

Pay attention to the Trigger and be sure it is a Drag trigger,
not On tap.

---

15. For Carousel2 and Carousel3, add Drag interactions back to Carousel. In the Prototype Interactions, note the order of the interactions, drag the interactions above or below, and rearrange the interactions if needed.

16. Open the Assets panel and drag the Carousel component into the Tablet frame.

17. Press Shift-Space bar to do a local test.

Create a Complex Carousel

In the previous exercise, you created a simple Carousel with multiple Drag triggers. In this exercise, we are going to get a bit more complex. When the user drags an image, the image grows while the others shrink. To get yourself started, open the ComplexCarousel.fig file.

1. When it opens, you will see the three images from the previous exercise are sitting in an auto layout container named Carousel with a Horizontal gap of 20. When you twirl down the Carousel container, you will see each image is in a frame. Let's get started.

2. Select the three frames in the container and set their Horizontal resizing Property from Fixed to Fill container. As the frames expand, the images expand to fill the width of the container (Figure 10-5).

Figure 10-5. *The frames in the container have their width changed to Fill container*

3. The Markets and Church images need to be resized. Select the Markets image and set its width value to 130 and change the Church width to 70. Reduce the Church text to 16 pixels and center the text.

4. Select the Carousel container and change its width to 490. We have our starting point.

5. Select the Carousel container and convert it to a component.

6. Add two variants.

7. Twirl down Variant2, select the three frames, and set their width to Fill container. Select the Church text and change its size to 24 pixels, then align the text below the altar.

8. Select the Church frame and set its width to 130.

9. Select the Alps frame and change its width to 70. Select the Alps text and change its size to 16 pixels; then center align the text in the frame.

461

10. Twirl down Variant3 and change the width of the
     frames to Fill container.

11. Change the Alps width to 130 and the markets width
     to 70. Change the markets text size to 16 pixels.
     Center it (Figure 10-6).

Figure 10-6. *The frames in the variants have all been resized*

The various states of the component have been set.
We can now add the interactivity. It will be the same
for each variant, as shown in Figure 10-7:

- Trigger: Drag

- Animation: Smart animate

- Ease: Gentle

- Duration:800 ms

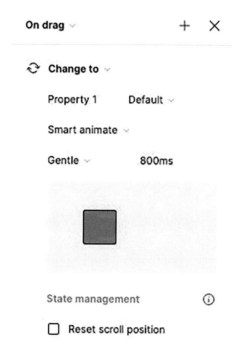

Figure 10-7. *Use these settings for all of the interactions*

12. Switch to Prototype mode and make the following connections:

- Select the Alps frame in the Default and connect it to Variant2.

- Select the Alps frame in Variant2 and connect it to Default.

- Select the Alps frame in Variant3 and connect it to Default.

- Select the Markets frame in the Default and connect it to Variant2.

- Select the Markets frame in Variable2 and connect it to Variant3.

- Select the Markets frame in Variable3 and connect it to Variant2.

- Select the Church frame in the Default and connect it to Variant3.

- Select the Church frame in Variant2 and connect it to Variant3.

- Select the Church frame in Variant3 and connect it to Default.

13. Create a new Frame with a width of 700 pixels and a height of 500 pixels. From the Assets panel, drag an instance of the component into the new frame.

14. Test by either pressing Shift-Spacebar or selecting Present to view in a browser.

Create a Spinning Carousel

At first glance, creating a spinning carousel appears to be a daunting task. The images will have to be placed on a circle, and each one will need to be precisely rotated and placed on the circle. This is where one of our maxims – Let the software do the work – comes into play.

Figma has no ability to accurately create path animations, hence the manual labor involved. But no longer! There is a Figma plug-in named To Path that will do the work for you. You will need to add this plug-in to Figma because we will be using it to create the spinning carousel. Let's get started.

1. Open the SpinCarousel.fig file found in your chapter download.

2. Create an ellipse that is 900 × 900 and place it in the Spinner frame. Don't worry about Fill color. Use whatever Fill is applied.

3. Move the ellipse to the bottom of the frame and be sure it is vertically and horizontally centered.

4. Add a new frame, named Carousel, that is 300 pixels wide by 400 pixels tall to the pasteboard.

5. Select the frame, and in the Fill options, add the City.jpg file from the images folder.

6. Select the Text tool and add the word Bern to the Carousel frame. We set it to Roboto Bold, 48 pixels, Center Alignment, white. Feel free to use your own font.

7. Select the circle and remove the Fill.

Using the To Path Plug-in

1. With the Shift key held down, select both the Circle and the Carousel frame.

2. Right-click on the pasteboard and select Plugins ➤ To Path. The To Path plug-in interface (Figure 10-8) opens, and you can enter spacing between objects, an Offset value on the path, and Alignment.

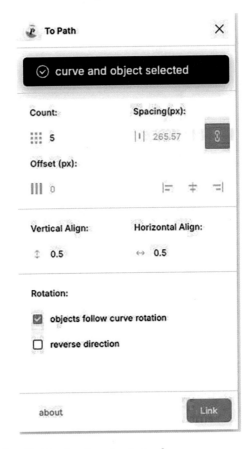

Figure 10-8. *The To Path plug-in interface*

3.   In the To Path interface, change the count to 6, and in the bottom right of the panel, click the Link button. The Carousel frame is placed along the path. In the Layers panel, all of the frames on the path have been grouped, and the circle is in the group (Figure 10-9). You can delete the Carousel frame on the pasteboard.

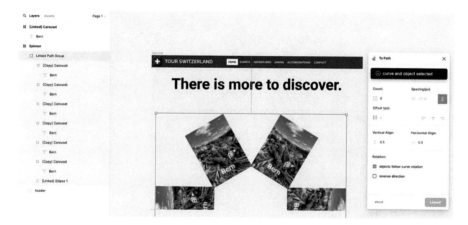

Figure 10-9. *Six copies of the Carousel frame are placed on the ellipse*

Rotating the Carousel

1.   Select the Linked Path group layer and rotate it 30 degrees to have one of the images appear in the start position.

2.   Rename the selected frame to Bern.

3.   Select each of the remaining frames and replace their fills with an image from the images folder. Change the text and rename the layer (Figure 10-10).

Figure 10-10. *The images have been added, the text changed, and the Layers renamed*

4. Using the Text tool, add the word Discover. Set it in Roboto Bold, 32. Select the text frame and create an auto layout container; set the Horizontal padding to 30 pixels and the Vertical padding to 15 pixels. Add a Fill of blue (#007BE6) to the container with a corner radius of 40 pixels. Change the text to a white Fill (#FFFFFF).

5. Name the auto layout container Button and move it in the middle of the image carousel (Figure 10-11). We will use this button to rotate the Carousel.

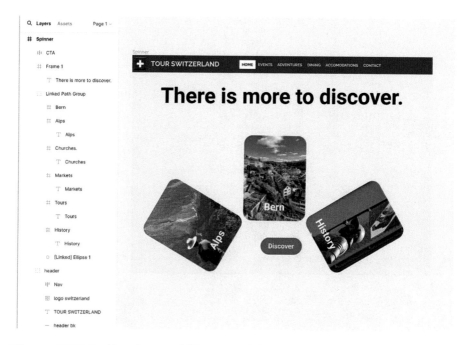

Figure 10-11. *Ready to add interactivity*

6. Select the Button and Linked Path Layer groups and convert them to a component named Spin.

7. Move the component onto the pasteboard and create a Variant.

8. Inside Variant2, rotate the Path Group 90 degrees to show the image on the right.

9. Switch to Prototype mode, select the Button in the default, and drag a wire to the Variant.

10. Set the Trigger to On click, the animation to Smart animate, the ease to Ease In and Out, and change the duration to 2000 ms. That is two seconds.

11. Select the Button in Variant2. Add a wire from the Variant to the default and use the previous Interaction settings.

12. Open the Assets panel and drag an instance to the Spinner frame (Figure 10-12).

13. Test.

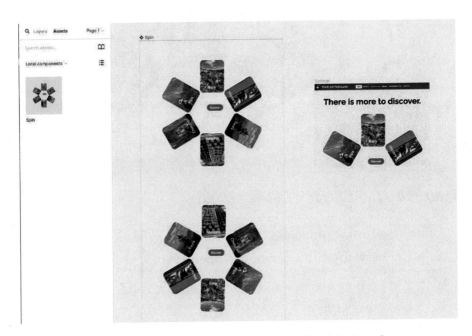

Figure 10-12. *The Component is created and added to the Spinner frame*

Create Video Controls

Video has become ubiquitous and, when it comes to users, is a major irritant. There is nothing worse than a video playing with no way to turn it off, kill the sound, or pause it. Before we start, there are a couple of important video rules:

- Video must be in the .MP4 or .WebM standards.

- Video size can be no more than 100 MB.

- Video is treated much like images. It is a shape fill.

- Video playback is not supported in the Figma mobile app, which is primarily used for testing your Figma files.

- Video can only be added to paid Professional teams, Organization teams, or Education teams.

In this exercise, we are going to create a project that places video in a web page, and we are going to also create a mobile version. Let's get started.

You may not be familiar with the webm standard. WebM is a royalty-free open source format designed to work smoothly with the HTML5 video standard. If you are using webm video, you need to be aware that Apple's Safari browser doesn't support this format along with older browsers such as Internet Explorer and others. If you are creating a web video, the video track needs to be encoded using the VP8 or VP9 compressors, and the audio track must be encoded using the Vorbis or Opus compressors.

---

1. Open the Video.fig file from your chapter download. You will see a Rectangle in the Video frame and the video and audio control components are on the pasteboard and in the Assets panel.

2. Select the rectangle and add a video fill. Use the CableCar.mp4 video file from your chapter download.

3. Preview the video and you will notice both the video and the audio are not playing.

4. Let's fix that.

5. Select the video in the Video frame and switch to Prototype mode. Three video properties (Figure 10-13) are in the Video area:

   - Autoplay: This is the default and should be deselected. In cases where the video is playing in the background with no sound, then autoplay is acceptable.

   - Loop: The video will restart playing when the video ends. Deselect it. If it is a short video, 10 to 15 seconds, then feel free to loop the video.

   - Audio: Audio is turned on by default. Deselect it if you are going to add controls to the video.

Figure 10-13. *The Video properties are found in Prototype mode*

6. At this point, the video is nothing more than a static image because it won't play. Add an interaction and add a Click event. From the interactions pop-down, select Play/Pause video, as shown in Figure 10-14. If you have deselected audio, select it. When a video has Autoplay turned off, adding a Play/Pause interaction will start the video, and the audio will play. Test the video. When you click on it, the video plays, and when you click on it again, it pauses.

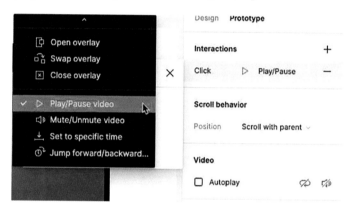

Figure 10-14. *Controlling video is done by using interactions*

We are not huge fans of this technique because the user has no idea there is a video and they need to click the video to play it and pause it. If you do use this technique, do your users a favor and add something telling them what to do.

Let's use the video component buttons to control the video.

1. Select the video Rectangle in the Layers panel and rename it "Cable".

2. From the Assets panel, drag two instances of the VidPlay component to the Video frame.

Tip   You can't use the Alignment options in the Properties panel to align to the center. Instead, select both components, hold down the Shift key, and select the Horizontal Alignment button in the Properties panel. The icon changes to indicate they are a "group" and will align them both to the Video frame.

3.   Select the Play component on the right. It needs to be changed to the AudioOn component. The selected component appears in the Properties panel. Select the pop-down and select the AudioOn component and the component switches to display the AudioOn icon (Figure 10-15).

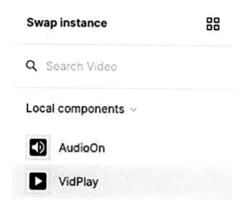

Figure 10-15. *Use the Component pop-down to swap components*

4. To play the video, select the Play component instance
   you just placed and add an interaction in the Prototype
   mode. When the panel opens, add a Click event and
   select Play/Pause Video. To connect the button to the
   video, select the None category in the Interactions
   panel and select Cable (Figure 10-16).

5.   Test. The button acts as a Play and Pause button. If you reopen the Interaction, you will see the Play/Pause has changed to toggle.

Figure 10-16. *You can link to events such as the video right in the Interactions panel*

Create Interactive Video Controls

Let's now add some user feedback to the video. We are going to learn a few things about working with components and layers. We are going to rename a bunch of layers without a lot of typing and double-clicking. What we are going to do with the Play button is to change the background color and swap the icons without creating separate frames for each button. Here's how:

1.   Open the ControlVideo page in the Layers panel. You will see the video and four icons under the Controls frame.

2.   Select the four icons and press Command/Ctrl-R. The Rename layers dialog box opens.

3.   Click once in the Rename to text input and enter "icons/".

4.   Click the Current name button and you will see they have been renamed (Figure 10-17).

5. Click the blue Rename button. If you check out the Layers, they have all had "icon/" added to their name.

6. With the icons selected, select Create multiple components from the Create component pop-down. If you check the Assets panel, you will see they are an Icons area. You will see why in a minute.

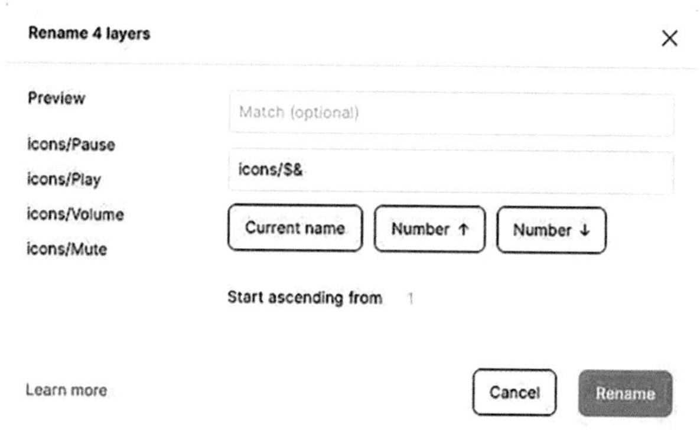

Figure 10-17. Rename layers with a single click

Now that they have all been renamed, let's create a single button component for all of the controls.

7. Duplicate the Play icon and move it above the Controls frame. Convert it to a component named Button and add a Variant.

8. With the Button component selected, in the Properties panel, Current variant, change the Property 1 value to State.

9. Click the Edit property button and change Variant2 to Hover (Figure 10-18).

10. Select the Hover variant and change its Fill color from black to #C7C7C7 (Light Gray).

11. Switch to Prototype mode and add an Interaction, While hovering, trigger between the default and the Hover variant.

12. Add an instance of the Button component to the Controls frame. Switch to Design mode and test. The button changes color.

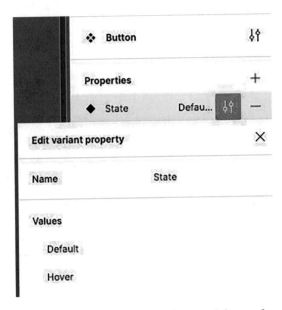

Figure 10-18. *Variant names can be changed from the Properties panel*

Swap Component Icons

Rather than creating a bunch of components, we can use one component by changing the icon in each button. Here's how:

1. In the Design mode, select the Button component and click the + icon in the Properties panel to open the Create new property dialog box and select Instance swap.

2. Enter "Icons" as the name.

3. Open the Value pop-down and navigate to the Icons (ControlVideo ➤ Icons) and select the Play component. Click the blue Create property button and you will see an instance of the Icons in the Component Properties (Figure 10-19).

Figure 10-19. *We will use the Icons components to swap with the Play component in the frame*

4. On the Controls frame, duplicate the instance of the Play button and drag it to the right. This will be used to swap the icon and create the Pause button.

5. Select the duplicated play button. In the Properties panel, click on Button to open the Swap instance panel. Click Icons and select the Pause icon to switch the icon from Play to Pause. Repeat this to

create the Volume and Mute buttons. As shown in Figure 10-20, we now have the proper buttons in place.

Figure 10-20. *The proper icons are in place by swapping instances of the Button component*

Adding Interactivity to the Buttons

1. Switch to Prototype mode.

2. Select the Play button and drag a wire to the video.

3. Add an On click event and select Play only instead of Toggle. Repeat this step for the Pause button, but select Pause only.

4. To control the audio track, you need to first turn it on in the Properties panel. Select the video, and in the Video properties, click the Sound button.

5. Select the Volume button and add an On click event. Open the Play/Pause pop-down and select Mute/ UnMute Video. Open the Toggle pop-down and select Unmute only.

6. Select the Mute button, add Mute/Unmute, and select Mute only from the Toggle pop-down.

7. Test.

Though this may seem to be a rather complicated example, discovering how to turn icons into components and then swapping them into a parent instance adds a great productivity boost to your design efforts.

Create a Progress Bar

Progress bars are a common UX Design pattern. They can show the loading progress of audio, images, video, or whatever else you decide needs some sort of progress indicator. Their purpose is to let the user know how much time an element has left while the video, for example, plays. In this example, we are going to create a progress bar for an Instagram reel. Let's get started:

1. Open the Progress page in the Video.fig file found in your chapter download. It is an Instagram story featuring a video of the Zytglogge in Bern (Figure 10-21). The most important information you need to know about this video is it has a duration of ten seconds. We have already set it up to Autoplay with no looping. When it plays, you can see and hear the King tolling the hours.

Figure 10-21. *We start with a video inside an Instagram Story frame*

2. Select the Rectangle tool and draw out a rectangle on the pasteboard. Set the width to 1080 px and the height to 20 pixels. Fill the rectangle with #D9D9D9 (Gray).

For Instagram, the height is usually 4 pixels. We are using 20 pixels for you to see the process.

---

3. Duplicate the rectangle to have one copy over the other. Select the top rectangle and name it "Top." Name the bottom rectangle "Base" and set its opacity to 20%.

4. Select both rectangles and convert them to a component named "Progress."

5. Select the component and add a Variant. Name the Variant "Fill" in the Variant properties.

6. Twirl down the Default component, select the Top layer, and set its width to 0.001 px. The reason for such a small number is you don't want to see any part of the progress showing at the Start. That small number makes it practically invisible (Figure 10-22).

Figure 10-22. *The Top layer of the default Variant has its width changed to 0.001 px*

7. Switch to Prototype mode and drag a wire from the Default to the Fill variant. Use these settings as shown in Figure 10-23:

    -   Trigger: After delay

    -   Duration: 1 ms

    -   Smart animate

    -   Ease: Ease in and out

    -   Duration: 10,000 ms

Figure 10-23. *Adding a delay with Smart animate*

8. Drag an instance of the progress component to the
   Instagram frame and test.

Smart animate has a hard limit of 10,000 ms, which translates to ten
seconds. This explains why the video has a duration of ten seconds.
Keep in mind this is a prototype. If your video has a duration of more
than ten seconds, the developer will handle increasing the duration of
the indicator.

Create a Shopping Cart with Local Variables, Conditions, and Expressions

The ability to work with variables in Figma will not only please your developer but also make your workflow more efficient. In this exercise, we are going to create a shopping cart where users can select a variety of experiences. When they do select a tour, they can also enter how many people will be attending and the amount payable will change along with how many items are in the cart. This is all done using the various types of variables: the strings, numbers, and Booleans available when you create a local variable. Here's how:

1. Open the Cart.fig file found in your chapter download.

2. Click once on the pasteboard, and in the Properties panel, select Local variables. When it opens, click Create New Variable, String, and name the Collection in the top left "Tours".

3. Add a string variable. Change its name to "TourName" and enter the Value "Day Trip to Brienz".

4. Add a Number variable. Change the name to "Price" and change the value to 12.

5. Add another Number variable. Change the name to ItemCount and leave the value at 0. Close the Variables dialog box.

   With the variables established (Figure 10-24), we can turn our attention to replacing the cards in the Tours frame with the Tour component.

Figure 10-24. *Creating the local String, Number, and Boolean variables*

6. Select the Tour component and duplicate it. Drag the duplicate out onto the pasteboard. Cut the Tour instance Ctrl (Windows) or Command (Mac) + X, and it is added to the Clipboard.

7. Select the four cards in the Tours frame; right-click and select Paste to replace from the pop-down menu. You now have four instances of the Tour component instead of four separate cards (Figure 10-25).

Figure 10-25. *Four instances of the Tour component have replaced the cards*

Adding Variable Modes

We have four cards that offer various tours. In order to present those tours, we are going to have to create three more variable sets.

1. Click in the canvas and open the Local variables panel. Click the icon in the upper left corner to open the Variable sidebar. Each column is a Variable mode.

2. Double-click the Value title and change it to Brienz. Changing the name makes it easier to work with the components once the variables are established.

3. Click the + sign to add a new variable mode. Change the Mode name to Rafting. Change the text to Aare River Rafting and the price to 45.

4. Add another Mode +, named Walking. Change the text to Bern Walking Tour and the price to 15.

5. Add another Mode +, named Bistro. Change the text to Bistro Visits and the price to 20 (Figure 10-26).

6. In the top left of the panel, find Collections 1 and click the triple dot icon to the right; select Rename collection to change the name to Tours. Then close the panel.

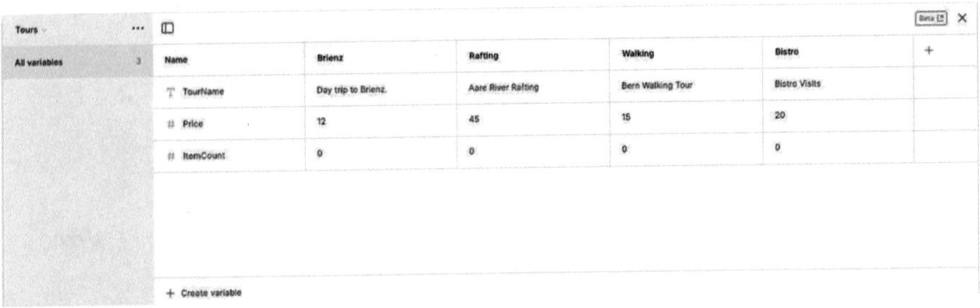

Tours ⌄ •••		Name	Brienz	Rafting	Walking	Bistro	+
All variables	3						
		T TourName	Day trip to Brienz	Aare River Rafting	Bern Walking Tour	Bistro Visits	
		# Price	12	45	15	20	
		# ItemCount	0	0	0	0	
		+ Create variable					

Figure 10-26. *The Local variables are created*

Linking Local Variables with Component Instances

With the variables established, we can now link them to the remaining cards. Seeing as how this is done for each card and the technique is the same, we'll only change the Brienz card. Here's how:

1. In the Tour component, select the text "Day Trip to Brienz", hold the Command/Control key, and click the text.

2. In the Text properties, there is an Apply variable, polygon icon. Click it and select the Tour Name variable to link both items (Figure 10-27).

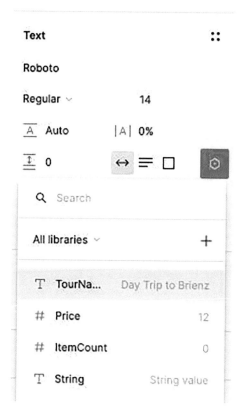

Figure 10-27. *Applying a text string variable to a text block*

3. Select the price text in the component and link it to the Price variable.

4. In the Travel frame, select the second Tour instance in the top right. In the Properties Layer panel, click the Change variable mode, double polygon icon. Select the Tours variable collection and select Rafting. The text and the price change. Repeat this for the other two components.

Warning   You may not see the Change Variable mode button in the Layer. The Figma Community has identified this as a bug. If this is the case for you, click the ellipsis and select Detach instance.

To finish our cards, all we need to do is to swap out the images with the one that applies.

5. Double-click the image inside the Rafting card. You will see it is an instance of the Train component on the pasteboard.

6. Click the Train pop-down to open the Swap Instance dialog box.

7. Select River and the image changes. Repeat this for the other two cards (Figure 10-28).

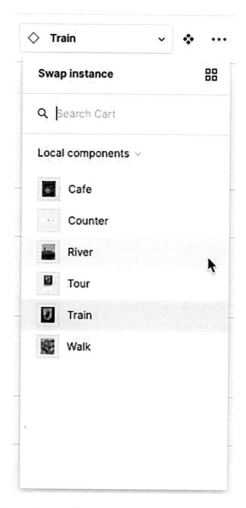

Figure 10-28. *Identifying the image components that will be swapped*

Using Expressions in the Prototype

To this point, we have designed the project using variables. The time has arrived to make it work. The plan is to put the plus and minus signs to work. For example, the user orders two day trips, one rafting experience, a walking tour, and a bistro visit. That is five tours totaling $104. Those values should be passed to the Cart frame. If an item is subtracted, the values in the Cart frame will instantly adjust. As well, the user can see how many items are in their cart at the top of the Travel frame.

1. To start, we need to create a new Variable collection for the Cart frame by clicking anywhere on the pasteboard, and in the Properties panel, select Local variables. Open the Local variables panel, and from the triple dot icon, select Create collection and name it "Cart".

2. Click the Create variable, Number variable, and rename Number to TourCount.

3. Create another Number variable and name it Total.

4. Select the 0 in the shopping cart and assign the TourCount variable to it. By doing this, the number will increase every time a plus sign is clicked. What we don't do is make the plus sign functional in each tour. Instead, we will make it functional in the Counter component on the pasteboard.

Creating an Expression

It is obvious that for each click of the plus sign, the 0 in the Counter component increases by one and when the minus sign is clicked, it decreases by one. This process is not done by creating a new variable. It occurs through an On tap trigger. Here's how:

1. Switch to Prototype mode and select the + sign in the Counter component.

2. Open the Interactions and select On Tap.

3. Open the None pop-down and select Set Variable.
    The variable list will appear; select ItemCount
    in the Tours collection. The ItemCount variable
    appears, and we are now being prompted to write
    an expression.

4. Click the "Write expression" text and a new
    dialog box appears. There is no complicated
    math required. Select from the Tours collection
    ItemCount.

5. The variable appears, and as shown in Figure 10-29,
    you are prompted to pick a math function. Click
    Addition.

6. Enter 1 after the red plus sign. We have created an
    expression that adds 1 each time the plus sign is
    clicked.

7. What we now need to do is to pass that increasing
    value to the 0 in the Component.

8. Switch back to Design mode, select the 0 in the
    Counter component, and attach the ItemCount
    variable to it.

9. Test. Clicking the plus sign on any of the cards
    changes the value by 1.

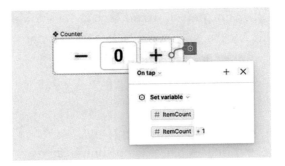

Figure 10-29. *Attaching an expression to an interaction*

Create a Conditional Expression

The subtract button needs to be handled a bit differently. If we were to wire it up but use a subtraction expression, the odds are pretty good eventually; you will be moving into negative numbers. This means we have to set up the interaction in such a way that 0 is as far as the user can go.

1. In the Counter component, select the minus sign, add an On tap interaction, add the ItemCount variable, and select Subtraction as the expression.

2. Change the Expression to ItemCount-1. Test. What we now need to do is to make sure the subtraction value does not become a negative number.

3. Return to the Prototype mode and open the minus sign, On tap interaction.

4. Click the + sign and select Conditional. The condition will be if the ItemCount value is equal to 0, then nothing happens.

5. In the if area, select the ItemCount variable and the
    "Greater than or equal to" expression. Enter 0 after
    the Expression (Figure 10-30).

Figure 10-30. *Creating a Conditional Expression*

If you test the component, it still shows negative
numbers. Let's fix that.

6. Open the interaction under the Conditional. There
    is still an issue, and it lies with the Conditional. It is
    currently set ItemCount>=0. That means if you click
    the subtract button, it will show -1 and go no further.
    This is because Figma is looking at the 0 and saying,
    "The value is 0 so I can go back."

7. Click inside the Conditional and delete the
    equal sign.

8. Select the gray arrow icon to the left of the Variable
    and drag the variable into the if area below the
    Conditional as shown in Figure 10-31. If you follow
    the conditional logic, it basically says if the value of
    ItemCount is greater than 0, then reduce the value
    by 1. You don't need to add an Else statement. Test.

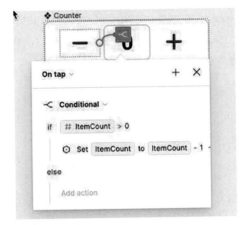

Figure 10-31. *Nesting the Variable inside the Conditional statement completes the logic*

Adding Variables to the Shopping Cart

As you tested the Travel frame, you may have noticed the 0 in the shopping cart didn't change. The reason is the value in the Counter component isn't being passed to it. Here's how:

1. In the Counter component, open the plus button interaction and collapse the variable.

2. Click the plus button and select Set variable. This time, you are going to use the TourCount variable.

3. Add the ItemCount variable. We need to make this more specific. Click on the ItemCount and select Brienz from the pop-down window. Select addition. Add another ItemCount variable and attach it to the Rafting card and add a plus sign. Repeat this two more times. When you create the last one, don't add addition or a plus sign. If you follow the logic,

the number shown in the shopping cart is the sum of the ItemCount variable for each of the cards (Figure 10-32).

Figure 10-32. *The TourCount variable is the sum of each ItemCount in each card*

4. Select the subtract button in the Counter component and repeat the previous steps.

5. Test. The number in the shopping cart increases or decreases as you add or subtract items.

Calculating Multiples Using Variables

Our final task is to tie the number of items in the shopping cart and the final total to the Order Summary in the Cart frame. Though calculating the final bill may seem to be complicated, it isn't. It is basic math: multiply the number of items by the price and send that result to the Cart frame. Before we start, select the Cart icon on the Travel frame and drag a wire to the Cart frame. Do the same thing with the Back button on the Cart frame.

Our first task is to link the total number of items in the shopping cart in the Travel frame. Here's how:

1. In the Cart frame, select the number 12 in the Tours.

2. Change the Variable in the Text Properties to TourCount.

3. Test.

Next, we need to create a total price for all of the orders. This may seem to be complicated, but essentially, we are going to be multiplying the Price number in the Tours variable collection by the number of items ordered. The result of this calculation will then be passed as the value for the Total variable in the Cart variable collection. In many ways, the process is much the same as when we created the Item count values for each of the cards. Here's how:

1. Select the number 12 in the Cart frame, and in the Text properties, change the variable to Total.

2. Select the + icon in the Counter component. Switch to Prototype mode and open the variables for the + icon.

3. Click the Add action button in the Interactions panel and select Set variable in the pop-down menu.

4. When the Variables open, select Total in the Cart collection.

5. In the Expression area, select #ItemCount -
    Multiplication - #Price - Addition. Repeat these
    three more times, representing one for each tour.
    Don't select Addition for the last one.

6. Click the first #ItemCount variable to see
    the available modes; select Brienze; now the
    #ItemCount should look like this: #ItemCount:
    Brienze. Add one mode to each #ItemCount.

7. Click the first #Price variable to see the modes;
    select Brienze so that the #Price should look like
    #Price: Brienze. Add one mode to each #Price.

    As in the Addition variable, repeat the previous step
    three more times as shown in Figure 10-33.

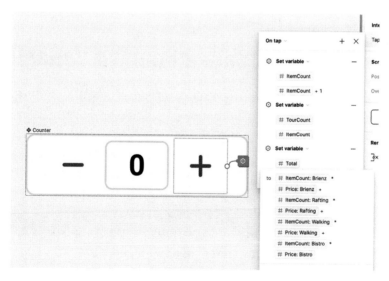

Figure 10-33. *Creating the variable calculation for the Total price*

8. Select the minus sign in the Counter component and repeat the last step, only this time using subtraction instead of addition.

9. Test.

We won't deny this has been a rather complex example. It was, but you learned how to create Variable collections and create and use Addition, Subtraction, and Multiplication Expressions and Conditionals to calculate the values for the number of items ordered. You also discovered how to not only add or remove items but also how to add a total number of items to both the Cart icon on the Travel frame and the Tours value in the Cart frame. You also learned how to use Variable expressions to show the user how much those items cost in the Cart frame.

Give yourself a pat on the back because you have discovered the power behind the use of variables in Figma.

Bonus Round: Create a Boolean Variable

The one Variable property we haven't covered is Boolean. A Boolean is rather easy to understand. It has either one of two properties: it is either True or False. They are like lightbulbs, they are either On or Off. Here's how it works:

1. Open the Boolean.fig file found in the chapter download. As you can see in Figure 10-34, there is an alert telling the user something went wrong. The plan is to close this alert using a Boolean variable.

Figure 10-34. *We start with an alert*

2. Click once on Local variables. When the dialog box opens, click the Create variable button and select Boolean from the pop-down list.

3. When the Collection opens, change the name from Boolean to Alert and change the value from False to True by clicking False. Doing this will keep the Alert visible (Figure 10-35).

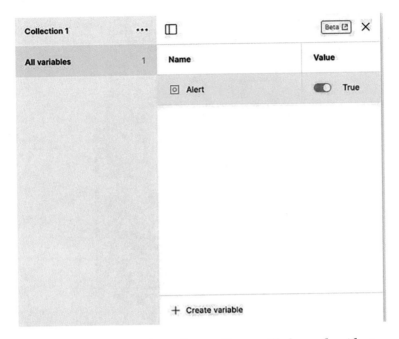

Figure 10-35. *Changing the value to True will show the Alert*

4. To tie the Variable to the Alert instance, select the
    Instance, and in the Properties panel, right-click on
    the visibility icon in the Layer and select Alert. You
    will see the Alert instance is now tied to the Layer
    (Figure 10-36).

Figure 10-36. *The Alert variable is now tied to the instance*

5. Switch to Prototype mode and select the X in the Alert.

6. Select an On click trigger and set the variable as the Action.

7. Select the Alert variable and select False as the expression as shown in Figure 10-37. Test.

Figure 10-37. *The Alert variable is changed from True to False*

Animations Using LottieFiles

With the demise of Flash, animation in the mobile space became a lot more difficult to implement. The great advantage of Flash was its ability to create animation using vectors, which are nothing more than code. In 2015, an engineer named Hernan Torrisi created an After Effects plug-in named Bodymovin. This plug-in exported After Effects animations as JSON files, which are a text-based representation of JavaScript files.

Two years later, the wizards at Airbnb created iOS and Android libraries of these animations and named them Lottie after the German pioneer of silhouette animatiosn, Charlotte Lotte Reiniger. At the same time, they launched those libraries as LottieFiles, which was a platform for sharing and testing Lottie animations.

What makes JSON so appealing is the animations are code based, which makes them smaller, faster, and more scalable than animations created in After Effects and other applications. They can also do a lot of things GIFs or PNGs can do, chief of which, they can be easily edited by anyone. As you may have guessed, being code based, your developers can easily implement them during development. In this exercise, we are going to create a preloader. The first will be to import an animation using the LottieFiles plug-in, and the second exercise will create a LottieAnimation from a Figma artboard using the Aninix plug-in.

Before we start, you will need to install the LottieFiles and Aninix plug-ins from the Figma Community site. You will also need to create accounts with both companies in order to give the plug-ins access to your Figma account.

---

1. Open the Lottie.fig file found in your chapter download. There are two frames: LottieLoader and AninixLoader.

2. Select the LottieLoader files and open the LottieFiles plug-in. Select the Discover tab and you can click through a collection of Free animations by clicking the Next button.

3. Select an animation; we have chosen the preloader
    shown in Figure 10-38, and you can view a preview.
    You also have a few choices:

    •   Click the Play button and the Loop button to stop
        the animation, which lets you scrub through the
        animation.

    •   You are also told how many animation "frames" are
        in the animation.

    •   You can turn off Transparency by clicking the
        Transparency icon.

    •   The color chip lets you change the
        Background color.

    •   Click the Customize button and you can change the
        animation's color palette or apply your own.

    •   Choose either the .SVG or .GIF format.
        Before choosing a format, consult with the
        development team.

Lottie SVG animations will only display a single frame and won't play
when previewed.

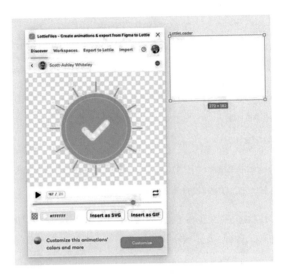

Figure 10-38. *The LottieFiles plug-in interface*

4.   Click the Insert as GIF button. The dialog box
      (Figure 10-39) that opens lets you choose the
      size and whether to turn off Transparency. Select
      Small in order to have the animation fit into the
      LottieLoader frame.

Figure 10-39. *Choosing the GIF size and managing Transparency*

5. Click the Insert GIF button, move the file into position inside the LottieLoader frame, and test.

Using Aninix to Create a Lottie Animation Using Figma

In this exercise, we are going to put the three colored circles in the AninixLoader frame into motion using the Aninix plug-in, turn it into a Lottie animation, and drop that Lottie animation into Figma. Just keep in mind that Aninix allows you to create only two projects if you are using a free account.

Here's how to create an Aninix animation:

1. Right-click on the AninixLoader frame and open the Aninix plug-in. Select Editor.

2. When the dialog box shown in Figure 10-40 opens, you will see the frame has been selected. Click the blue Create a new project button to open the Aninix editor.

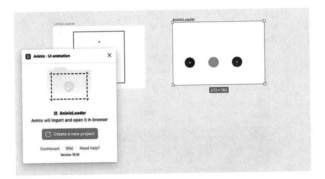

Figure 10-40. *The first step is to sync the selected frame with Aninix*

When the Editor (Figure 10-41) opens in the browser, those of you who use After Effects will find this is a familiar place. Of course, there are differences. At the bottom is a timeline placing the Figma layers on the timeline. Over on the right are general properties for Background color, FPS, and Duration. Change the Duration to two seconds.

Yes, two seconds is an eternity. We are using this value for demonstration purposes only. The best practice for duration would be one second. Feel free to change the duration to one second.

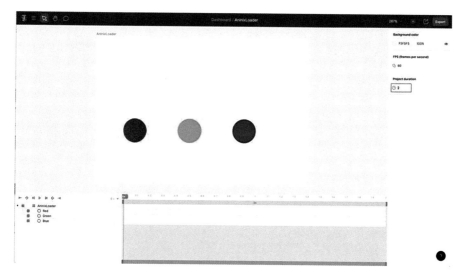

Figure 10-41. *The Aninix interface*

3. With the Shift key held down, select the three layers
    in the timeline. The interface will change to show
    you the properties. The diamond icon on the right
    side of the properties is how you add keyframes.

    We are going to add three Position keyframes for
    each layer at the 0, 1-second, and 2-second marks.

4. With the Playhead at the 0 mark, click the Keyframe
    icon for X and Y. This will be the start of the
    animation. Do the same thing at the 1-second and
    2-second marks. The timeline will change to show
    you blue diamonds (Figure 10-42) for each of the
    keyframes, and each layer tells you that Position
    keyframes have been added.

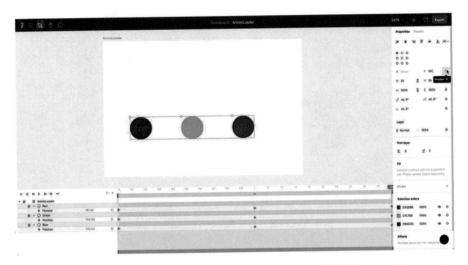

Figure 10-42. *Position keyframes have been added for each layer in the timeline*

The plan for this animation is to have the red and the blue circle change position and for the green circle to move upward.

5. Select the middle keyframe for the red circle and change its X position to 176.

6. Select the middle keyframe for the blue circle and change its X position to 36. This essentially swaps their locations.

7. Select the green circle and change its Y position to 42. You have just created the keyframes (Figure 10-43) for the animation.

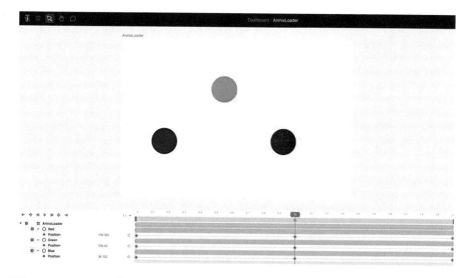

Figure 10-43. *The positions of the circle have been changed at the one-second point on the timeline*

8. To preview this animation, click the Play button on the timeline. The circles change position as the animation loops.

9. To add easing, select a position layer. The easing properties (Figure 10-44) open. Select Ease in-out from the pop-down menu.

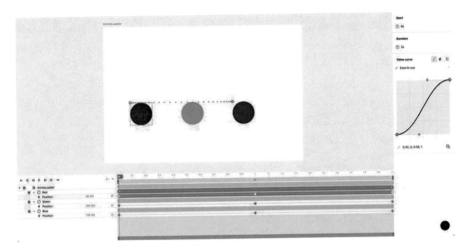

Figure 10-44. *Easing is applied to each layer in the timeline*

Those dots you see over the circle show frame-by-frame animation.
Each dot represents a frame

Converting an Aninix Animation to a Lottie File

With the preloader animation working as expected, the animation needs to
be converted to a Lottie file. Here's how:

1. Click the blue export button. The pop-down defaults
    to a .mp4 video. Select mp4 to open a pop-down
    and select .json (normal) in the Lottie section
    (Figure 10-45).

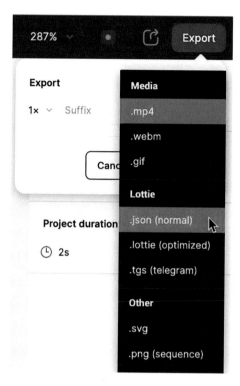

Figure 10-45. *The file will be exported as a Lottie file using the .JSON (normal) choice*

The .json (normal) option will keep your developer happy. Choose optimized and the .JSON file is minimized. Normal hands the developer the .JSON code in a line-by-line format.

---

2.   When asked, save the Lottie file to your Chapter 10 download folder.

3.   In the browser, log into your Lottie account and click the Go to Dashboard button. When it opens, click the upload animations button. When the Upload

dialog box opens, click the Browse button and navigate to your Chapter 10 folder containing the .JSON file and select it. The animation will open and start playing.

4. Close the browser and return to your Figma file.

5. Open the LottieFiles plug-in and click the Workspaces link to access your LottieFiles account.

6. Locate the animation and select Insert as GIF.

7. Test.

When it comes to handing off the Figma file to your developer, be sure to include the .json file in the handoff.

Add Diversity with the Humaaans for Figma Plug-in

We are going to wrap up this chapter by calling your attention to the Humaaans plug-in for Figma.

Diversity and inclusion are policies that should be set before the project gets underway. The reason is we have no idea who our users are or where they are located. By embracing diversity and inclusion, you will be appealing to potential users who "look just like me." Finding diverse and inclusive line art for onboarding sequences or other uses can be an issue. This is where Humaaans from Pablo Stanley can help.

This royalty-free collection of bits and pieces of Inclusive line art opens up a significant number of creative opportunities. This collection is available as a plug-in for Figma, or if you open www.humaaans.com, a collection of line art images and templates are available.

1. To start, install the Humaaans for Figma plug-in and open the Diversity.fig file found in your chapter download.

2. Open the Humaaans for Figma plug-in. If you scroll through the choices (Figure 10-46), you can see there is quite an extensive collection of people and bits and pieces.

Figure 10-46. *The Humaaans for Figma interface*

3. Select the gentleman in a wheelchair. As you can see, by simply clicking on an image, it is instantly added as a frame. Move the frame into the Humaaans frame.

4. The great thing about these images is they are editable vector images. If you select the image and look at the Properties panel, you see three colors in the Selection colors area. Below the three colors, click See all 11 colors, and all the colors in the image appear.

5. Open up the humaaans/siting-3 layer and all of the bits and pieces that are contained in the image. If you select the Coat-front layer and open the Fill color in the Properties panel, all of the colors used in the illustration are there (Figure 10-47).

Figure 10-47.

6. Let's now build a character. Add a frame to the pasteboard that is 300 by 600 and name the frame Woman. This frame will hold our character.

7. Open Humaaans and scroll down to add a body.

8. Drag the symbol out of the frame and add it to the woman's frame. Rename the symbol Body. Add legs and a head and you have created your own illustration (Figure 10-48).

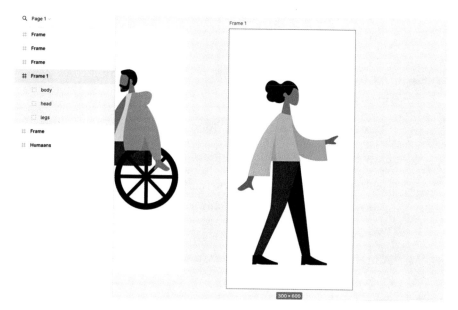

Figure 10-48.

So there you have it. You can now easily create images of people reflecting the diversity of your potential users.

You Have Learned

This has been a rather large and complex chapter. The reason is to fill in many of the knowledge gaps not covered in the previous chapters. For example, the shopping cart exercise is a deep dive into Figma's variable types that focuses on creating Variables and employing them in your Figma projects. Also, each project is a Design Pattern that can be added to a Design System. You have also learned that as you create these projects, they should be created collaboratively with the developers.

In this chapter, you have learned

- How to build a basic image carousel

- How to create component variants and animate them

- Use the To Path Figma plug-in to animate elements on a path

- Create a custom interactive video controller

- How to create a loading progress indicator

- Use Figma's variables feature, including Conditionals and Expressions to create a shopping cart using only two components

- A method of moving variable values between Figma pages and components

- Discovered how a Boolean variable works

- How to add Lottie animations to a Figma frame

- How to create a Lottie animation using the content in a Figma frame

- The importance of using and creating line art that promotes inclusion and diversity

CHAPTER 11

Developer Handoff

"Everything changes, and nothing stands still."

—Heraclitus, Greek philosopher

Developer handoff is the final step in the UX Design process. Though the developer has been involved in all aspects of the process, this is the point where the UX Designer steps aside and the developer takes over. As you have gone through this book, you have created mobiles and web pages. What we haven't stressed is it is not uncommon for the designer to prototype an interaction and then work with the developer to refine that interaction. When everyone is satisfied, the prototype of that interaction or page is then handed off for development. Rarely, if ever, is a Figma prototype handed to a developer with a cheery "Here you go."

As a UX designer, you need to understand that a Figma prototype is both a deliverable and is disposable. As a deliverable, your Figma prototype demonstrates your intent. When it is handed off for development, that prototype becomes a disposable document as the development team writes the code that brings the project's intent to life. Thus, all of the hours and weeks you have poured into creating the Figma prototype are essentially ripped up and tossed on the floor as the prototype is regarded by the development team as nothing more than reference material.

© Tom Green and Kevin Brandon 2024
T. Green and K. Brandon, *UX Design with Figma*, Design Thinking,
https://doi.org/10.1007/979-8-8688-0324-6_11

Regarding the prototype as nothing more than reference material is essentially the purpose of the new Dev Mode in Figma. The developer can flip that switch in your prototype and introspect the underlying code behind every element and interaction found in a Figma frame. This doesn't mean the developers will simply copy and paste the code. They never do. What it means is they can look at the code and decide not to use it or to rewrite it to make it more efficient. You also need to understand if a Design System is involved in the project, the code for the tokens and styles for that Design System are already in place and sitting in a GitHub repository or some other location.

Finally, developer handoff doesn't necessarily occur when the project gets a final sign off. Handoff is a continuing process. It starts when the relationship between the design and development teams is established. Do this and design is not separated from implementation. This is why Figma is constantly stressing that Figma's heart and soul is "collaboration" and "sharing." This fosters a continuing dialog between development and design right at the start of the UX process, which involves designing and iterating together. The reason is simple: visual and interaction design details and issues will reveal themselves over the course of the design process.

We are going to start this discussion around the development handoff with the process that will reveal those issues: User Testing.

Handoff Starts with User Testing

As we have mentioned several times, the design of a prototype is only one step in the process of launching a successful website, mobile app, or a touch screen interface. User Testing is where all the design ideas and research come into play.

You are not the user. The user is key to the product – that is who you are designing the product. What you need to understand is if something is hard to use, people won't use it as often. This is why, throughout this book, we have stated the main goal of User Testing is to understand the users' behavior. Testing identifies problems and opportunities as they use the product, with a focus on functionality and ease of use. You will need to work with users who have not been part of the design, development, or management teams in order to observe their interactions and improve the user's experience before launching the project to the public. User Testing makes sure that the user and their goals are at the center of the product design. Here are some ideas to keep in mind:

- Before inviting users to test the product, make sure that you have a clear direction of what you want to be tested. Identify key tasks the user needs to complete for the success of the project and the user.

- Choose a facilitator who will be able to help explain the purpose of the project and the tasks they would like the users to achieve through the process – for example, find a specific item, find a specific piece of information, complete the purchase of a product, etc.

- Create a consent form for each user to allow their results to be shared with the production team. Video their interactions and reactions.

- Have the facilitator observe and ask questions during each session, without guiding their answers; the feedback recorded here will help give more understanding to any problem from the user's perspective and, in turn, give the production team a deeper understanding of problems as they consider potential solutions.

- Defining the experience of the user while completing the requested product tasks offers insights into the product and is considered part of qualitative testing. Completing tasks within a set time and a level of success is often considered part of quantitative testing.

- A User Testing group can start with as few as five people. Basic User Testing can be done cheaply and within a short period of time – two or three days.

Once the User Testing has been completed, the facilitators report and present their findings back to the design and development teams. Make sure that time has been set aside for the teams to review the results, with the goal of better understanding issues and opportunities that may have come up during the testing. Good solutions to problems happen by discussion and taking the time to understand what the problems are; bailing water from a sinking boat and not fixing the hole in the boat doesn't fix the main issue.

One of the worst mistakes you can make when it comes to User Testing is to involve acquaintances and family in the process. They will tell you what they want to hear, not what you need to hear. The same goes for the members of the design and development teams. They are too close to the project. Use them to critique, not to test.

Device Preview Using the Figma Mobile App

If a mobile device is required for testing the project, for example, a mobile app or a mobile website, then using the Figma mobile app is perfect for the task.

Figma has created a free mobile app that can be downloaded from the Google Play Store for Android users or the App Store for iPhone and iPad users; be sure to check the technical specifications for the app as they can change when the app is updated.

The Figma app does not allow you to create designs on a mobile device, instead it allows you to open saved mobile Figma files, view the prototype, and test the interactions. It also allows for comments that will be saved in the Figma file and can be viewed on the app and in the original Figma files.

Download the Figma app for the mobile OS that you are using and sign into the app with your Figma username and password. When the app opens, your recent Figma files are displayed, and you can search for specific Figma design files to find a specific project (Figure 11-1).

Figure 11-1. *Figma mobile app screens – Recents and Search*

When you open the Figma app, the bottom navigation allows you to view your recent files, search your drafts and team files, be notified of activity in your files, and mirror a Figma file. Clicking the Mirror icon allows you to display, "mirror," the exact Figma frame selected in your browser or desktop version of the Design file, directly on your mobile screen. It will display interactions from the draft file on the mobile device.

Figma saves your Draft/Design files into the cloud, which means you can select a recently edited file or search for a specific Figma file to open in the mobile app. Device testing is ideal for User Testing. An opened file displays an alert showing how to add a comment on the file. Comments created on the mobile app will be saved and displayed in the in-browser or desktop version of the Figma design file (Figure 11-2).

Figure 11-2. *Figma mobile app adds a comment; view the comment in the in-browser or desktop app*

Using the mobile app gives a feeling that the app is real and is perfect for testing your project user goals and interactions on an actual device. Test a project on the mobile app to see if there are any missing links or awkward interactions that should be corrected. By working on larger screens to create mobile projects, we risk misjudging how larger or small text appears within a mobile device. Review heading text size and colors, subheadings, paragraph text, buttons, and icons. This helps to reveal any bias applied from the desktop design that has filtered its way to the mobile device. Test mobile projects on both an iOS and an Android device, as there may be differences.

When you are testing a Figma file on a mobile device, you are able to set flows to define the start of the project. Flows are added to a frame in the Prototype mode. For example, select a frame in a Figma file that you want to be the start of the user journey – the beginning of a launch screen. Switch to the Prototype mode in the top right of the desktop Figma. In the Properties panel, find the flow starting point and click the + icon to the right to add a flow to the frame. Multiple flows can be defined in a Figma design file to define the start of key areas in a project. "Flow 1" is the default title for the first flow. Change that title to add a descriptive title to the flow (Figure 11-3). This helps add clarity to the document when you are collaborating with other designers and a development team.

The value of using the mobile app is the design is presented in context. Figma frames don't provide that context. All they do is show intent.

Figure 11-3. *Add a descriptive flow, and description, to a frame to define the start of a mobile app*

When a flow has been added to a frame, you may notice an edit icon to the right of the flow title. Clicking that icon will allow you to add a description of the flow as well, giving further information on the flow to other designers, collaborators, and developers who have access, including text, bulleted or numbered lists, and links.

Now, when the Figma file with the defined flow is opened in the Figma mobile app, the app knows exactly which frame to start with.

If a flow has been added to a frame by accident, flows can be removed. Select the frame, and in the Prototype mode Properties panel, click the - icon to the right of the flow starting point.

The Figma mobile has a hidden menu that allows you to select a different flow if there has been more than one flow created, exit the prototype, restart, view file, turn commenting on, turn off hotspot hints, and share (Figure 11-4). To access this menu, press and hold two fingers on the mobile screen until the menu displays.

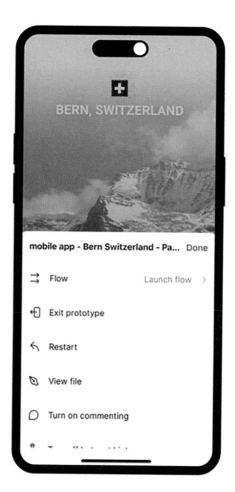

Figure 11-4. *Hidden menu in the Figma mobile app*

During a User Test with the mobile app, it may be a good idea to turn off the hotspots so that a user is not guided to links created in the Figma file that are not intuitive. You may choose to leave commenting off as well and save user comments to be recorded by the facilitator to allow for discussion and a deeper understanding of hindrances in completing a specific task.

Using the Figma Presentation Mode for Sign-Off

Before using the Figma Presentation mode, let's set up the prototype settings to make sure that the project is being displayed in the device we have designed the project for.

1. With the Design file open, and no frames or items selected, click to the Prototype mode.

2. In the Properties panel, click the button Show prototype settings. Now you have the option to choose a device from the drop-down menu. Figma offers choices from common mobile phones, tablets, and laptops, along with smartwatches, even a Macintosh 128k (Figure 11-5). The device you select here will be the device that the project is displayed in for the presentation.

Figure 11-5. Prototype mode; choose a device for the Presentation mode – Android Large

3. Start the Presentation mode by clicking the Play icon in the top-right corner of the Figma desktop app or in-browser version. When the Presentation mode starts, a new window or tab is opened, and the content of the selected frame is displayed. If a frame is not selected the default flow 1 frame will be displayed (Figure 11-6).

Figure 11-6. *The Figma Presentation mode interface – Android Large*

The top-left navigation bar includes a Figma icon that takes you back to the Figma Dashboard; next is an icon to hide or show the flow options within the prototype project. The comment icon allows you to add comments to any screen in the Presentation mode. Clicking on the title displays the option to open the file in the Editor mode.

4. Click the blue Share button to share the presentation in a View only or Editing mode.

5. The Options drop-down menu is an important menu for the presentation. The first option can be particularly important when the presentation starts by scaling the project to fit to screen, which is good for seeing the entire project on the screen. This can cause issues where elements may display too small, a website design, or too large, a smartwatch design. Choose the option for actual size (100%) to view the project at the actual size that your users will view the project at.

6. Another option that we find works well for presentations is the Hide Figma UI option; when you do this, all the icons and text are hidden from the screen. The quick keys to hide or show the Figma UI are Ctrl (Windows) or Command (Mac) + \. The other options can be turned on or off as needed for the presentation audience.

7. The last double arrow icon on the right, when clicked, expands the presentation to full screen, filling the monitor with the presentation and hiding all other open applications.

8. A recommended presentation setting would be to view the project at 100%, in the Full screen mode with the Figma UI turned off (Figure 11-7).

Figure 11-7. *Presentation mode, viewed at actual size (100%), full screen with the Figma UI turned off*

The user can navigate through the presentation using the linked buttons, icons, text, and images. The user can also navigate through the prototype frame by frame using the left and right arrow keys or, if the Figma UI is displaced, using the left and right arrow icons below the frame.

With the Presentation mode allowing for commenting, shared presentations offer the ability for quick feedback and changes that can be made to the Design file and refreshed to see the updated results.

Getting a final sign-off on a project means that the project at its current state has been accepted by the key stakeholders. All deliverables in the project have been completed. Files have been prepared, exported, saved, and organized. Documentation has been completed or currently exists and is followed, and there are no outstanding issues or activities before the handoff to the developers.

Consider creating a Figma presentation where the deliverables and content have been displayed and accounted for. The shared presentation means that the key stakeholders are not required to be in the same place at the same time. Stakeholders may be remote and view the presentation in their time zones or a mixture of in-office and remote audience where they can meet to discuss, review, and clarify any issues with the product and give their approval before moving into the next step.

Share the presentation in a View only format with the key stakeholders to allow them to comment on any elements they see that may have been missed or need to be corrected or areas that need to be expanded on before the handoff.

Commenting allows for interaction between all involved; anyone can add a comment and position the comment icon to the exact location where the comment is focused on.

When a comment has been added, it can be replied to once or multiple times to gain insight into the issue. Comments also act as a communication piece from the designers to the key stakeholders. As a designer, feel free to add your own comments and ask for clarity on a specific area or issue. Comment threads can be deleted if they have been added by mistake. Comments can be marked as resolved, which is different than deleting a comment; resolved comments are no longer displayed as clickable icons in the project; however, they can still be viewed from the Properties panel in case there is a need to review the resolved comments. Resolved comments are displayed in the Properties panel with a green check mark to show the difference between existing comments.

What Is a Handoff?

Congratulations! The design stage has been approved and it is now time to pass the designs to the developers. Designers may be tempted to think that their job is now complete and it's time to send or share the Figma file – it's not that simple. The handoff is a key step in the process of completing the final project.

We have mentioned many times in this book that UI/UX involves collaboration and coordination between the teams and key stakeholders of the project. If this is the first time you are talking with the developer, there will be a lot to share and comment on.

Handoff meetings will help the developers save time and be able to ask questions as well as give their own insight into specific development issues that may be present to meet the project deadline. Hopefully, you will also end with the developers being excited to work on a well-thought-out project by having them see themselves as part of the project and not the end of the project.

Before meeting with the developer, walk through the project as though you were the user to make sure that there aren't any lingering issues in the user journey. Take time to organize the frames to match the user flow and add clear descriptive titles to each of the Figma frames. You may want to add clear flow paths between elements or frames; there are plug-ins that can be found in the Community to help quickly add flow paths, such as Autoflow, Flowy, etc.

Share design documents with the developers so that they can be aware of guidelines that have been set and need to be followed throughout the project – required fonts, font properties for headings, subheads, paragraph text, buttons, credits, icons, etc. Include the required brand colors used in the project and the color values in RGB and hexadecimal. Note specific styles of icons and images used in the project, along with any other unique design features, to help keep consistency in the project. Note if there are any deviances from the design guidelines to help answer these questions ahead of time.

If there are text-heavy pages in the project, consider creating external documents to allow for the text to be easily shared and copied during the development process.

Set up a meeting with the developer and share the Figma file link using the "Can view" permissions to avoid any potential issues with the ability to edit the approved file. In the meeting, go through each user journey to show how the user will work through the process. Allow the developers to add comments in the Figma file (Figure 11-8) to document questions they may have that need to be looked at further. Listen to the developer's questions to hear where there may be confusion and more clarity is needed. Developers will also have insight on how to help move the project forward in areas that can save time for them.

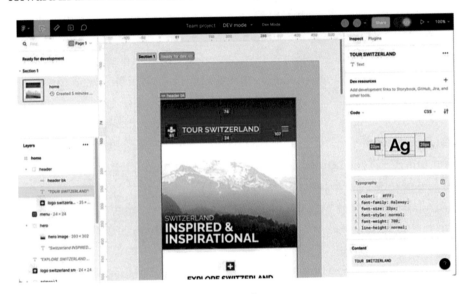

Figure 11-8. *Shared Figma Dev Mode screen*

Show how elements with interactions have been created; show how the states, the triggers, the easing, the timing, etc., have been created. If there are any animations or multi-frame animations, show these to the developers as well so that they can see what your intentions for interactions and microinteractions and how they have been applied.

Note if there are any missing assets that need to be provided to the developers, such as missing fonts, videos, Lottie files, images or icons, etc. Create a way to allow communication with each other during the development process to remove questions quickly.

Set up check-in times where the developer and designers can meet to discuss and review the progress from the developer in an effort to catch any issues that may have arisen. Remember that this can be a messy process where there are iterations here to accommodate for any technical issues not addressed in the design and User Testing phases (Figure 11-9). Consider creating a prerelease signoff form for both the designers and developers before launching the project. There has been a lot of time and effort into creating the project so do not forget to celebrate with the teams when the project is released.

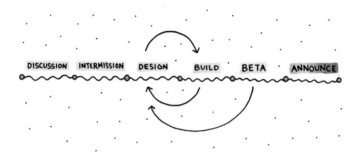

Figure 11-9. *The Intercom process is a collaborative effort between the design and development teams*

Preparing Assets for Handoff

As mentioned earlier, you will need to prepare assets to hand off to the developers, and these fall into two categories: assets that can be exported from Figma and external assets that need to be shared.

Let's start with preparing assets inside Figma to share with developers; make sure that you are in the Design mode to be able to prepare images and graphics for export.

1. With the Figma file opened, select an image that you would like to have the developer download by either selecting the image in a frame or selecting the image from the Layers panel. A quick way to select an image that has been placed inside a frame or group or auto layout is to hold the Command key on macOS or Control key on Windows and then click the image.

2. At the bottom of the right-hand Properties panel, click the plus icon to add the export feature to this image. Once the Export option has been added to the image, you will need to define the properties of the exported element (Figure 11-10). The first option will be the retina display option; by default, 1x is displayed – we will talk more about the raster image x factor in the next section. Next, a suffix may be added to the end of the file export to add more definition to the image, for example, draft or final. The file format can also be selected with a choice from .PNG, .JPG, .SVG, or .PDF. For images, generally, .JPG is selected for compression or .PNG is selected if the image has a transparent background. There is even an option for a color profile selection. Twirl down the Preview option and you can see exactly what the exported image will look like.

Figure 11-10. *Define the Export options for a raster image from Figma*

There is an issue when exporting images that have a Layer blend mode applied; by default, the Export option will be to export the original placed image and it will ignore the blend mode, which can cause frustrations and make you consider recreating the image as a grayscale image in a photo editing application. In this example (Figure 11-11), the image has a second fill placed below the photograph as a solid black color. The photograph is displayed as a grayscale image because the layer has an applied "Luminosity" blend mode. If the option for ignoring the overlapping layers is left checked, the image will export as the original color image. You can change this by unchecking the Export option to "ignore overlapping layers," and the image will export as the designer intended.

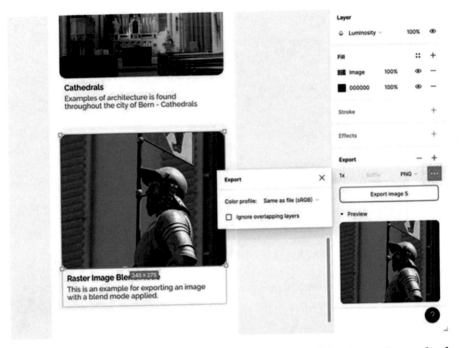

Figure 11-11. *Exporting an image with a Layer blend mode applied;
uncheck the "Ignore overlapping layers" option*

3. Icons and graphics like logos or symbols that
    have been created using the Pen tool or placed as
    vector graphics should be selected and exported
    as .SVG files and not .PNG or .JPG, unless there is
    a requirement from the developer to use a raster
    file format. SVG files do not have the option for an
    exported resolution option, 1x, 2x, etc., as .SVG files
    can be scaled in code and they maintain their image
    quality no matter what size is defined (Figure 11-12).

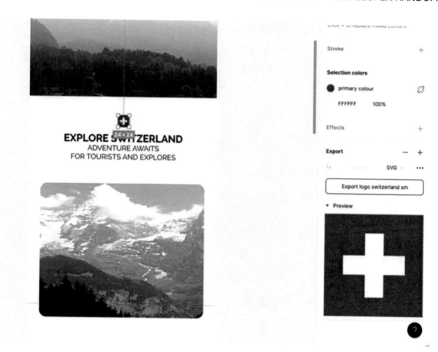

Figure 11-12. *Define the Export options for a vector graphic from Figma*

Is there a faster way to export multiple images or graphics?
Yes, make sure that the images will be exported using the same properties and avoid selecting a raster image and a vector graphic at the same time. After you select your first image in the frame, select another image using the Shift key. If you are selecting multiple image layers in the Layers panel, use the Ctrl (Windows) or Command (Mac) to select multiple, individual layers. Notice that the Export button changes from "Export Image" to "Export X Layers" (Figure 11-13).

Figure 11-13. *Define the Export options for multiple image layers selected in Figma*

4. If you have included video files in your project, you will need to share these videos using another method, as Figma does not currently allow for the export of videos from a Design file.

5. Make sure that all fonts have been collected and are shared legally with your developers as well. You will have documented all the fonts used along with the type styles that have been defined in the Figma file. It is a good practice to check and make sure that no additional fonts have been added to the design before handing over the project. A good plug-in to display fonts used in the project is Font Fascia; running this plug-in will display fonts used on the current page or uncheck this option to view fonts

used in the Design file; not only does it display the
fonts used, it also displays the text where the fonts
have been applied (Figure 11-14).

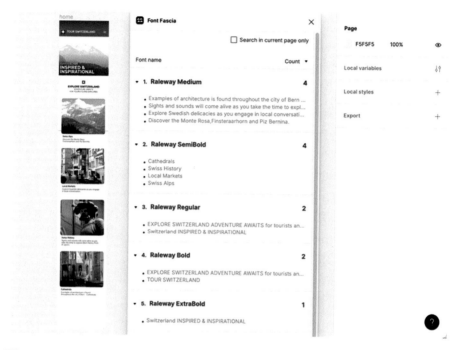

Figure 11-14. *Running the Font Fascia plug-in to display all fonts
used in the Design file*

Frames or sections can be selected and exported as JPG, PNG, or
PDF files if they need to be shared as a whole design file as opposed
to individual assets.

The X Factor of Raster Images

You may be asked to export images at a higher resolution for retina display or high-density screens. Most mobile devices have a retina display screen; laptops and external monitors have been adopting the same technology. Retina displays offer a higher pixel density where your eyes cannot easily see pixels that make up the image on the screen. When images are exported at a 1x resolution, the images may start to display pixels and appear as a lower-quality resolution on a screen.

As an example, Apple has been using retina displays in their iPhones since the iPhone 4 was released in 2010. Higher-density displays are important on devices that we look at from a close distance; again it multiplies the pixels in a square inch and appears as though there are no pixels on the device. This is similar to the printed page or when Postscript language was developed for laser printers, replacing the output of dot matrix printers with the quality of sharp curves and edges of a Postscript printer. You can clearly see the difference a retina display offers when you are looking at text on a screen.

Exporting raster images from Figma offers the default of 1x density, which equates to a pixel resolution of 72 pixels per inch. Images exported at 2x density will have a pixel resolution of 144 pixels per inch, and those exported at 3x density will have a resolution of 216 pixels per inch. Currently, Figma allows for raster images to be exported in the following densities: 0.5x, 0.75x, 1x, 2x, 3x, and 4x as well as a specified width or height.

Normally, when you are asked to export images at a higher pixel density, you will be required to export the images at a few different pixel densities for the developer to serve up the correct image based on the device display. Figma makes these options easy to apply to exported images by adding multiple Export options from the selected image or images. With an image selected at the bottom of the Properties panel, in the Export section, click the plus icon once for the default 1x density, and click the plus icon again to add a second option, 2x. Add as many density options as are required for the project (Figure 11-15).

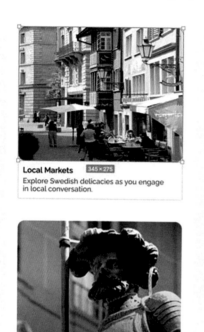

Figure 11-15. *Export multiple density options at once for a raster image*

When an image is exported with multiple densities applied, Figma will save a ZIP file containing separate images, one for each density. Notice that the images will all have a suffix denoting the density to make it easier for you and the developer to identify and choose the required resolution (Figure 11-16).

Figure 11-16. *Multiple raster images exported at different densities*

Code Introspection

Exporting design files as code is not a feature that Figma currently offers. Figma started as a design-only digital tool; however, Figma has stated that developers account for a third of their weekly active users. This means that the audience for Figma is shifting Figma from a design-only tool into a tool that is used by designers, collaborators, and developers (`www.figma.com/blog/everything-you-need-to-know-about-dev-mode/`).

A shared file with the option of "View only" will allow users to inspect elements in the shared file: Width, Content, Typography, Colors, and Effects (Figure 11-17). The shared files will also allow access to Export mode, where raster images or vector graphics can be exported in their respective file formats. This is a good start to expanding beyond the Design mode and works with all free Figma Starter accounts.

Figure 11-17. *Shared Figma file Properties view*

To get the most out of a shared Figma file, as a developer, you will want to access the Dev Mode. This allows you access to see more coding properties to help you translate design into code. Copy and paste the code into your code editor, as well as export the required assets straight from the browser.

Files that need to be viewed in the Dev Mode need to be moved into a paid plan or a Team; the free Figma Starter account does not offer access to the Dev Mode. To upgrade to a paid account, select your default Teams (free) and click the bottom blue text "upgrade to a paid plan" and this will link you to the paid options (Figure 11-18).

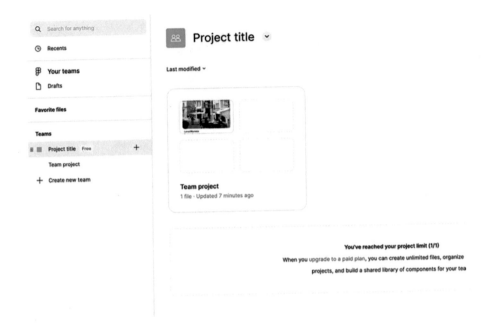

Figure 11-18. *Upgrade to a paid account from the default free Figma Team*

There are two levels of paid accounts currently with Figma: Professional or Organization; choose the option that works best for you (Figure 11-19). If you are a current student or teacher and have a Figma Education account, you can have access to a paid Teams account for free when you upgrade from the Starter account. Below the blue button "Upgrade to Professional," there is a note that this is free for students and educators; verify that you are a current student or educator for this account (www.figma.com/education/).

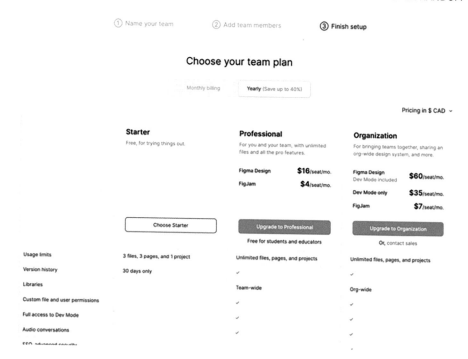

Figure 11-19. *Upgrade to a paid account from the free Figma Starter account*

Now that you have upgraded to a paid account, you can move draft files from the Figma Dashboard into a Teams account. Simply right-click on the draft to be moved and select the "Move file…" option; next select the Team and project you want the draft to be placed into. Open the Team draft file. In the top black bar, to the right of the blue Share button, click the </> toggle switch; the document buttons turn green, and the top tools change (Figure 11-20).

You will also notice that the top toolbar has changed from the Design mode to the Dev Mode. The first tool is the Selection tool to select elements in the design and view their properties. The second tool has a ruler icon and is a measurement tool. This tool gives the ability to drag the mouse cursor across an element, creating a starting and an end point. This will now display a red dimension line on the canvas. The red dimension

547

line can be selected and repositioned outside the element. The next document icon is an Annotate tool; select an area and you can add notes about the area, along with selecting a property of width, height, corner radius, fill, or font attributes.

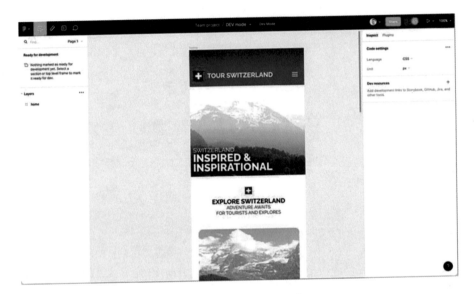

Figure 11-20. *Toggle to the Figma Dev Mode*

In the right-hand Properties panel, there are options to select an Inspect or Plugins mode. In the Inspect mode, you can set the Code settings Language option; choose between CSS, iOS, and Android; the default measurement unit can be selected as well, either PX or REM. The development resources allow you to add other tools such as GitHub, Jira, Storyboard, etc.

Selecting elements in the prototype will immediately display values and properties of the element, for instance, spacing, dimensions, type properties, font family, style, size, weight, height, hexadecimal values, etc. With a text selected, the Code section displays the spacing values and code snippets that can be copied and pasted into a code editor.

The Content area offers the option to copy the actual text and paste it into the code as well to avoid any text/errors as they are translated from design to code. All colors in the selection will be displayed as hexadecimal values as well in the Selection colors area (Figure 11-21).

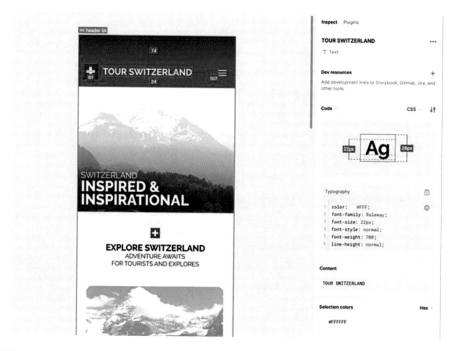

Figure 11-21. *Dev Mode selected item properties are displayed*

Selected raster images or vector graphics can also be exported with access to the same options for file format and image density, 2x, 3x, etc. In the example of the hero image behind the Inspired text, there is a gradient applied to the image; the gradient CSS code is also available to be copied, along with the CSS width, height, and flex-shrink values.

By selecting components with animations applied as a tap or hover effect, the Inspect properties displays the CSS code for animation-timing-function and animation-duration that can also be copied into a code editor. While Figma still does not export fully functioning coded websites or apps from the Dev Mode, you can start to see that these features will help connect the designer and developer and speed the potential time from design to code.

Another feature of the Dev Mode is that you can view changes to a frame that have been made in the Design mode and compare date-stamped versions of the document to see what changes have been made to the file. This is another tool that improves the handoff communication between the developer and designer as the Dev Mode can show exactly what changes have been made between the time of discussing a change and when a change has been made to the file.

Extensions have also been incorporated into the Dev Mode, like VS Code. In the Properties panel at the top, above the Dev resources section, you will see the title of the selected item, and to the right three dots ...,select these dots and you now have the option to "open in VS Code." This launches the VS Code app and displays the file and code options inside the app. If the Figma plug-in is not installed in VS Code, the option to install it will pop up. It also allows you to scroll around inside the Figma file display area and select other areas to see the code properties presented. To zoom in and out of areas of the Figma, remember to use the Figma shortcuts like Shift + (zoom in) or Shift - minus (zoom out).

Figure 11-22. *Figma file Dev Mode opened in VS Code*

When you return to Figma, you may still be in the Dev Mode; if you need to change back to the Design mode and continue designing the project or make required edits to the Design file, click the top green </> toggle icon.

The Design/Build Iteration Cycle

At the beginning of the chapter, we quoted the Greek philosopher Heraclitus: "Everything changes, and nothing stands still." This is true for the design/build iteration cycle. Often projects can be thought of as completed and on to the next.

Be prepared to make changes to the project based on many different inputs, input from client requirements, changes in technology, developer insights, and User Testing, to name a few. Learn to be in this fluid mode for the project no matter which part of the process you are part in; keep a focus on the project goals, knowing what the goals are helps in guiding discussions surrounding the project.

Remember that the goal is to create a product that your users will find not only functional but that they will actually want to use.

As your project is released into the wild either as website, corporate intranet, mobile app, or interactive screen for a vehicle or appliance or an interface to a device – this is where the rubber hits the road, and you will start to hear from users globally. Hopefully, with success stories where the project has been a help in completing their tasks much easier, as well as complaints where there are issues that need to be addressed.

Listening to user feedback is crucial in creating a good relationship with your user base, as well as maintaining a successful project. Collect feedback. Review the issues with the design and development teams and all key stakeholders to see what the problems are and how they might be solved. Often, there is a gap between what the user says and how they engage with the product; understanding specifics can identify where the issues may be generated.

Participate by responding to comments from users, making them know that their voice is important and that they are being heard. Responding to complaints with solutions is another way to show active listening to the user base. Users may also offer insights into new directions for the project as well and help you expand services. This also has the potential to open doors for opportunities with the app that you may not have thought of before. As you build your community, you are also building trust in the product. Don't forget to respond to compliments as well – you will need the encouragement.

It can be a compliment when no one notices the hours a designer spent on refining one aspect of the project because it just feels natural that the interface would work this way or when a developer finds a unique use of code – if things work well, people may just not notice because you have met their expectations – make sure to celebrate these successes as well.

As the project matures, you will need to revisit the design, the documentation, and the back-end development and complete User Testing again as the project updates. Make sure that you are offering support and meeting the goals of the users. This is by no means an easy process to undertake, but the value that is created from this process to the company and the users can be the difference between an app that is downloaded and used vs. downloaded, tried, and then deleted.

You Have Learned

In this chapter, you have

- Understood where User Testing fits in developer handoff

- Learned how to use Device Preview using the Figma mobile app

- Discovered a method for using the Figma Presentation mode for sign-off

- Learned what is meant by developer handoff

- Learned the importance of preparing assets for handoff

- Discovered the X Factor for raster images has everything to do with OS

- Learned how a developer will use the new Dev Mode for Code Introspection

Conclusion

You have reached the end of this book on UI/UX Design using Figma with a focus on applying the core UX/UI Design concepts to the Figma application to create portions of a mobile app and website design. We hope that, with all of this knowledge, you feel confident to tackle design problems within a UI/UX framework. Knowing how to do something is important. Knowing why you are doing it will help you craft successful solutions that focus on the user and their needs – after all, where would we be without clients and users?

As we have stressed throughout this book, Figma is nothing more than a prototyping application that brings your design intent to the forefront. When the hundreds of screens or pages are handed over to the development team, they are ripped apart and either become reference material for the developer or left on the cutting room floor. We don't say this to marginalize Figma. Instead, as you have moved through this book, you have discovered Figma is an industry standard powerhouse with tools that are deep, indulgent, and integral to the UX Design process.

Never forget that UX Design is both a mission and a process. The mission is to create an app or website that gives the users a positive experience. Figma supports the process that attains that mission.

When you reach the end of the UX Design process, take some time to reflect upon the pain, joy, exhilaration, and simple satisfaction of having created something users will actually use. Most of all, you have discovered just how much fun it is to work in a team composed of designers, developers, and other specialists focused on the UX Mission to create something that is both new and unique.

We agree and, as we say at the end of each book we write

The amount of fun you can have with Figma should be illegal. If you agree, we'll see you in jail.

Index

© Tom Green and Kevin Brandon 2024
T. Green and K. Brandon, *UX Design with Figma*, Design Thinking,
https://doi.org/10.1007/979-8-8688-0324-6

F, G

H

I, J, K

Printed in the United States
by Baker & Taylor Publisher Services